Advance Praise for *Realism and Democracy*

"Elliott Abrams has done the country another important service. This outstanding book reminds us that the enduring power of America is that, at our best, we see our interests as our values, and our values as our interests. Now more than ever, Americans and their leaders need to understand that support for human rights has been, and should remain, a key pillar of U.S. foreign policy. This book could not be more timely or more significant."

– Senator John McCain

"Elliott Abrams gives us a brilliant review of the fight for freedom, showing with clarity what works and what does not. But even more, he highlights the possibilities for progress that may be gained from a determined, long-term strategy advocating democracy and human rights."

– The Honorable George P. Shultz

"A powerful and persuasive argument that realism as well as American ideals should lead us to support the struggle for freedom."

– Joseph Lieberman, former US Senator from Connecticut,
Senior Counsel, Kasowitz, Benson, and Torres

"Since the 1980s, no US official has done more to advance the cause of democracy and human rights than Elliott Abrams. Here bringing his vast experience to bear on American policy in the Middle East, he makes a powerful, pragmatic case for promoting democratic reform in Egypt and other Arab autocracies. Sure to be controversial in the best sense – his arguments cannot be ignored."

– Robert Kagan, Senior Fellow, Brookings Institute,
author of *The World America Made*

"Drawing on his experience as a maker and an observer of American foreign policy over many decades and presidential administrations, Elliott Abrams offers a powerful and timely case for why the United States should continue working to advance democracy, human rights, and universal values in the Middle East – not just for instrumental reasons, but also as ends in and of themselves."

– Senator Marco Rubio

"America's greatest asset in world politics is its association with freedom. Elliott Abrams brings unique experience as an American official who understood the power of freedom – and realized that an American strategy to advance democracy advances American interests. Here he explains how men like Scoop Jackson, George Shultz, and Ronald Reagan worked to support liberty and democracy – and how to build on their legacy today, including in the Arab world. Every official in the State Department should be required to read this book."

– Natan Sharansky, Chairman of the Jewish Agency, human rights activist and former political prisoner in the Soviet Union

REALISM AND DEMOCRACY

America is turning away from support for democrats in Arab countries in favor of "pragmatic" deals with tyrants to defeat violent Islamist extremism. For too many policy makers, Arab democracy is seen as a dangerous luxury. In *Realism and Democracy*, Elliott Abrams marshals four decades of experience as an American official and leading Middle East expert to show that deals with tyrants will not work. Islamism is an idea that can only be defeated by a better idea: democracy. Through a careful analysis of America's record of democracy promotion in the region and beyond, from the Cold War to the Obama years, Abrams proves that repression helps Islamists beat democrats, while political openings offer moderates and liberals a chance. This book makes a powerful argument for an American foreign policy that combines practical politics and idealism and refuses to abandon those struggling for democracy and human rights in the Arab world.

Elliott Abrams is Senior Fellow for Middle Eastern Studies at the Council on Foreign Relations. He served as Assistant Secretary of State for Human Rights under Ronald Reagan and as a Deputy National Security Adviser in the administration of George W. Bush, where he handled Middle East policy for the White House. His previous book, *Tested by Zion*, is the definitive account of the Bush administration and the Israeli-Palestinian conflict and won the Bronze Prize in 2013 from the Washington Institute for Near East Policy as outstanding book of the year on the Middle East. Abrams is a member of the board of the U.S. National Endowment for Democracy.

REALISM AND DEMOCRACY

American Foreign Policy after the Arab Spring

Elliott Abrams

A Council on Foreign Relations Book

CAMBRIDGE
UNIVERSITY PRESS

CAMBRIDGE
UNIVERSITY PRESS

One Liberty Plaza, 20th Floor, New York, NY 10006, USA

Cambridge University Press is part of the University of Cambridge.

It furthers the University's mission by disseminating knowledge in the pursuit of education, learning, and research at the highest international levels of excellence.

www.cambridge.org
Information on this title: www.cambridge.org/9781108415620
DOI: 10.1017/9781108234894

© Elliott Abrams 2017

First published 2017

Printed in The United States of America by Sheridan Books, Inc.

A catalogue record for this publication is available from the British Library.

Library of Congress Cataloging-in-Publication Data
Names: Abrams, Elliott, author.
Title: Realism and democracy : American foreign policy after the Arab Spring / Elliott Abrams.
Description: New York, N.Y. : Cambridge University Press, 2017. |
Includes bibliographical references and index.
Identifiers: LCCN 2017020173 | ISBN 9781108415620 (hardback)
Subjects: LCSH: Arab countries – Foreign relations – United States. |
United States – Foreign relations – Arab countries. | Arab Spring, 2010– |
Arab countries – Politics and government – 21st century. | BISAC:
POLITICAL SCIENCE / Government / International.
Classification: LCC DS63.2.U5 A357   2017 | DDC 327.73056 – dc23
LC record available at https://lccn.loc.gov/2017020173

ISBN 978-1-108-41562-0 Hardback

The Council on Foreign Relations (CFR) is an independent, nonpartisan membership organization, think tank, and publisher dedicated to being a resource for its members, government officials, business executives, journalists, educators and students, civic and religious leaders, and other interested citizens in order to help them better understand the world and the foreign policy choices facing the United States and other countries. Founded in 1921, CFR carries out its mission by maintaining a diverse membership, with special programs to promote interest and develop expertise in the next generation of foreign policy leaders; convening meetings at its headquarters in New York and in Washington, DC, and other cities where senior government officials, members of Congress, global leaders, and prominent thinkers come together with CFR members to discuss and debate major international issues; supporting a Studies Program that fosters independent research, enabling CFR scholars to produce articles, reports, and books and hold roundtables that analyze foreign policy issues and make concrete policy recommendations; publishing *Foreign Affairs*, the preeminent journal on international affairs and U.S. foreign policy; sponsoring Independent Task Forces that produce reports with both findings and policy prescriptions on the most important foreign policy topics; and providing up-to-date information and analysis about world events and American foreign policy on its website, www.cfr.org.

The Council on Foreign Relations takes no institutional positions on policy issues and has no affiliation with the U.S. government. All views expressed in its publications and on its website are the sole responsibility of the author or authors.

To
Raphael, Maya, Samson, Levi, Lily, Shiloh,
and those to come

The creation of a free society, as the history of existing democracies in the world makes clear, is no easy matter. The experience of the Turkish republic over the last half century and of some other Muslim countries more recently has demonstrated two things: first, that it is indeed very difficult to create a democracy in such a society, and second, that although difficult, it is not impossible.

The study of Islamic history and of the vast and rich Islamic political literature encourages the belief that it may well be possible to develop democratic institutions – not necessarily in our Western definition of that much misused term, but in one deriving from their own history and culture and ensuring, in their way, limited government under law, consultation and openness, in a civilized and humane society. . . .

[T]he forces of tyranny and terror are still very strong and the outcome is far from certain. . . . The war against terror and the quest for freedom are inextricably linked, and neither can succeed without the other. The struggle is no longer limited to one or two countries, as some Westerners still manage to believe. It has acquired first a regional then a global dimension, with profound consequences for all of us.

If freedom fails and terror triumphs, the peoples of Islam will be the first and greatest victims. They will not be alone, and many others will suffer with them.

Bernard Lewis, "Democracy and the Enemies of Freedom," *Wall Street Journal*, December 22, 2003. Available at www.wsj.com/articles/ SB107205654377356100

Contents

Preface

For Arab lands, the first decades of the twenty-first century were the best of times – and the worst of times.

Those old Dickensian lines are a good summary of the "Arab Spring" and its grim aftermath. On December 17, 2010, a Tunisian street vendor named Mohamed Bouazizi set himself on fire and spurred a revolt in Tunisia that brought down the twenty-four-year dictatorship of Zine El Abedine Ben Ali less than a month later. Ben Ali fled into exile in Saudi Arabia. The uprisings spread – to Egypt, Libya, Syria, and Yemen. In Egypt, where President Hosni Mubarak had ruled since his predecessor's assassination in 1981, the uprising led to his resignation on February 11, 2011, less than two months after Bouazizi's self-immolation. In April 2011, Mubarak was arrested and ordered to stand trial. In Yemen, a rebellion began in December 2010 that resulted in the resignation and departure from the country of its president, Ali Abdullah Saleh, in 2011. The fighting soon included a sectarian bid for power by the Houthis and significant foreign military intervention to defeat them. The Libyan dictator, Muammar Qadhafi, faced small protests and tried to put them down with force, but they soon spread into an armed uprising that became a civil war. NATO forces intervened in March 2011, and the capital, Tripoli, fell to rebel forces in August. Qadhafi was killed in the fighting in October 2011. In Syria, President Assad also faced demonstrations, and like Qadhafi, tried to put them down with force. The result has been a bloody conflict, with nearly 500,000 dead, half the population driven from their homes, and millions of refugees in neighboring countries.

The "Arab Spring" also affected the Arab monarchies. After demonstrations began on February 20, 2011, King Mohamed VI of Morocco introduced constitutional amendments that he claimed would move the country toward a constitutional monarchy. They were adopted in a national referendum held on July 1, 2011. The late King Abdullah of Saudi Arabia announced a vast spending program of $130 billion designed to dampen the desire for political reforms. In Bahrain, demonstrations beginning in February 2011 were immediately repressed, and in the following month forces from Saudi Arabia, the United Arab Emirates, and other Arab countries intervened to support the monarchy.

When the Arab Spring (henceforth without quotation marks) began, it gave rise to high hopes. Perhaps this would be the end of "Arab exceptionalism," by which was meant the apparent immunity of Arab states from the expansion of democracy that had been so widespread since the 1970s. In that decade and in the 1980s democracy had spread throughout Latin America, with elected governments replacing military regimes and leaving Communist Cuba a rare exception. In Asia, the military regime in South Korea, the Marcos dictatorship in the Philippines, and one-party rule in Taiwan were replaced by democratic governments. The fall of the Soviet Union opened the way to democracy in many countries in the former Soviet space, though obviously not all, and eleven newly free countries entered the EU.

Now, it seemed, the Arabs would join in. "This is the new, democratic Arab world," Fareed Zakaria wrote in *Time Magazine*.[1] CNN commentators spoke of "the burgeoning democracy movement across the Middle East" that would lead al-Qaeda "to irrelevance."[2] In the *New Statesman* in London, the French academic Olivier Roy opined, "The protest movement is both democratic and nationalist and . . . will install governments with greater legitimacy."[3] In the *New York Times*, the former United Nations Under-Secretary-General Jean-Marie Guéhenno wrote, "The Arab revolutions are beginning to destroy the cliché of an Arab world incapable of democratic transformation."[4]

Optimism was widespread, but since 2011 the global trend in the direction of democracy has appeared, after all, to halt at the frontiers of the Arab world. Even after the Arab Spring, no Arab state has achieved democracy (if indeed it was an accepted goal) with the exception of Tunisia. The fall of their regimes led to years of disorder and violence in Yemen, Syria, and Libya, and in Egypt an elderly general was replaced by a middle-aged general who followed the same playbook in repressing and constricting political life – but took it even further.

So disillusion has set in. Daniel Byman of Georgetown University wrote as early as December 2011 that "it is too soon to say that the Arab Spring is gone, never to resurface. But the Arab Winter has clearly arrived" and will bring with it "chaos, stagnation, and misrule."[5] By January 2015, Tarek Masoud of Harvard could write an article in the *Journal of Democracy* titled "Has the Door Closed on Arab Democracy?" and there conclude that the widespread optimism had been "stunningly unwarranted."[6]

The effects of this disillusion and pessimism involve far more than incorrect predictions about the likelihood or timetable for democracy to spread in the Arab world. They also involve American policy toward the region. If democracy is several generations distant, or is indeed impossible and perhaps even undesirable in many places, why should the United States actively support it – and thereby complicate our relations with existing governments that are often valuable allies? Why sacrifice important current relationships for hopeless dreams or, at best, theoretical notions about political change? Even if the goals are good ones, why assume that the United States is positioned to do anything useful and that we really know how to promote progress toward democracy in the Arab world? And why assume that the goal of democracy is sensible in the Arab case, where free elections may bring to power Islamist groups whose values are so different from ours and whose members do not appear to be democrats at all?

Those questions are the subject of this book, whose topic is American foreign policy in the Arab world. I believe that support for Arab democracy should remain an American foreign policy goal. "Arab exceptionalism" surely exists in the sense that there is such a thing as Arab culture and politics, but I will argue that while it presents many tough obstacles to democratization, it does not destroy the possibility of progress. Moreover, the alternative – which is American support for varying forms of dictatorship in which the population is deprived of any real role in the political life of their own country – is inherently unstable. I will also discuss ways in which American support for democracy can be more effective.

The pace of change after the self-immolation of Mohamed Bouazizi left the impression that democracy might come quickly, just as the fall of apparently permanent regimes had come so quickly. But it is one thing to dynamite a political structure and another thing to build a new and stable edifice in its place. The failure to achieve or sustain democracy in parts of the former Soviet space teaches this lesson, as do stories like those of Bolivia, Venezuela, Ecuador, and Nicaragua. President George W. Bush used to call the expansion of democracy and the elimination of tyranny "the work of generations," and in this he was surely correct.

The debate over American support for democracy is often cast in terms of how best to fight terrorism and violent extremism. That will be a long war, and it is argued that surely it is more important for us to win that fight first – and protect ourselves – than it is to seek greater respect for human rights. But repression and tyranny are not a cure for terrorism and violent extremism; they are a contributor to it. Regimes that prevent peaceful political debate and activity strengthen extremist forces and weaken moderate ones. Islamist extremism must be combatted with force – but not only with force. Islamists have ideas, and not only their guns but their ideas as well must be defeated. That cannot be accomplished by illegitimate regimes whose only claim to power is brute force.

It is true that a great part of the struggle against Islamist extremism, and perhaps the central part, is a religious debate among Muslims about the meaning of Islam in the twenty-first century. In that debate the U.S. government cannot play a large role. Statements from U.S. presidents that "Islam is a religion of peace" will never have any impact, nor should they: who is an American politician to define the true meaning of any religion, much less one he or she does not practice? Persuading Muslims to embrace an Islam that insists on respect for human rights and political democracy and rejects extremism and violence is critical – but only Muslims can enter that debate with other Muslims and hope to win it.

In the Arab world, the American role in that war of ideas is different; it is about politics rather than religion. The issue facing American policy makers is not how rapid but sustainable change can be achieved in Arab nations; that prospect is very unlikely and in any event is not susceptible to American control. The question facing the United States is whether to abandon support for democracy, and therefore for democratic activists, in Arab countries or perhaps to abandon it in any sense except the delivery of lip service. Must we, should we, choose sides in a struggle that will be long and complicated and cause us trouble with rulers who might otherwise be useful allies? My own answer is yes, for practical as well as moral reasons.

The notion that the United States should actively work to expand the frontiers of democracy across the globe is not self-evident, nor has it always characterized American foreign policy. When I became politically conscious and active in the late 1960s and early 1970s, at the height of the Cold War, support for human rights and democracy was a controversial subject – pressed in various ways by the Soviet Jewry movement and groups such as Freedom House, and resisted strongly by the Nixon administration on *realpolitik* grounds. Working for the late Senators Henry M. Jackson and Daniel P. Moynihan, and then in the Reagan and George W. Bush administrations, I had a ringside seat to many of these debates and then climbed into the ring myself.

So this book begins with the story of how modern American human rights policy developed – as I saw it and joined the fray. And then we turn to the Arab Spring and the current debate over the proper role of democracy in American policy in the Middle East.

Acknowledgments

Since leaving the government in 2009 I have been a senior fellow for Middle Eastern Studies at the Council on Foreign Relations (CFR), the perfect place for writing this book or any other. I thank the Council's President Richard Haass and Director of Studies James Lindsay for their advice and support during all my time at CFR and during the writing of this book.

While I was drafting the manuscript and reviewing written materials, Ari Heistein and then Zachary Shapiro were my research assistants at the Council, and they deserve my thanks for their valuable help and unfailing good cheer.

My thinking about the issues discussed in this book has benefited greatly from the work of many others – scholars, current and former officials, and friends – in Washington and the Middle East. Worthy of special mention are those working at the National Endowment for Democracy, on whose board I serve; fellow members of the Egypt Working Group in Washington; and my colleagues at the Council on Foreign Relations.

Rebecca Nagle of the Wylie Agency then took the manuscript and arranged for it to be published, and I greatly appreciate her diligence and support. Of course, none of this would be possible without the donors to my program and more broadly to Middle East Studies at the Council. I am grateful for the generosity of Paul E. Singer, Roger Hertog, James Tisch, Tina and Steven Price, Walter Stern, Norman Benzaquen, Martin J. Gross, the Lisa and Michael Leffell Foundation, the Lynde and Harry Bradley Foundation, and the Achelis and Bodman Foundation.

Forty Years of Human Rights Policy

T HE DEBATE OVER HUMAN RIGHTS AND AMERICAN FOREIGN policy reflects the American rise to world power.

President Reagan used to call America a "shining city on a hill," taking the phrase – initially from the Sermon on the Mount – that had been used in 1630 by John Winthrop, the Puritan governor of Massachusetts Bay Colony. The new colony – and later the new nation – was to be a model watched by the entire world. Its power would be that of example.

This is one approach to American influence, and the only approach possible for a struggling young colony in the seventeenth and eighteenth centuries and then for the new republic. But as American power grew in the nineteenth and especially the twentieth centuries, so did American ambitions – and American responsibilities. There are some examples from the post–Civil War period of direct efforts to change the behavior of foreign governments toward their citizens, but it was World War I and its aftermath that provided the opportunity, temptation, and justification to interfere in the internal arrangements of foreign lands. Wilson's Fourteen Points were both an assertion of war aims and an explanation to the American people of why we were entering the war in Europe. The answer was that we would make the world a better place, and thereby increase our own prosperity and security. Wilson told Congress in January 1918:

> What we demand in this war, therefore, is nothing peculiar to ourselves. It is that the world be made fit and safe to live in; and particularly that it be made safe for every peace-loving nation which, like our own, wishes to live its own life, determine its own institutions, be assured of justice and fair dealing by the other peoples of the world as against force and

selfish aggression. All the peoples of the world are in effect partners in this interest, and for our own part we see very clearly that unless justice be done to others it will not be done to us. The programme of the world's peace, therefore, is our programme.[1]

But Wilsonian idealism did not guide American policy for most of the twentieth century. The bloody costs of World War I itself, the defeat of the League of Nations treaty in the Senate, the rise of fascism in Europe and Japan, World War II, and then the Cold War with the Soviet Union led foreign policy in different directions: to the desire for isolation from the world's seemingly intractable problems or to pragmatic "power politics" approaches where we took our friends and allies as we found them. We dealt only with sovereign governments, and how they treated their own people was for the most part not our business. We didn't have to like it, but the world was a dangerous place. Wilson had said, "Unless justice be done to others it will not be done to us," but we could protect ourselves. The more common attitude was summed up in the remark Franklin Roosevelt is alleged to have made in 1939 about the Nicaraguan dictator Anastasio Somoza: "Somoza may be a son of a bitch, but he's our son of a bitch."

But there were at least two major problems with this approach, and they became increasingly visible during the Cold War. First, it was not very practical: if we sided with dictators who engaged in vast repression, we might turn the population against us – thereby benefiting the other side, namely the Soviet-backed leftist or Communist groups. This was the insight that led President Kennedy into the "Alliance for Progress," an economic aid program for Latin America seeking "a hemisphere where all men can hope for a suitable standard of living," but also including the expansion of freedom as an objective. As Kennedy put it in March 1961 when introducing his program, "To achieve this goal political freedom must accompany material progress."[2] A year later Kennedy spelled out the political or Cold War rationale for the Alliance for Progress in one sentence: "Those who make peaceful revolution impossible will make violent revolution inevitable."[3]

So pragmatism and the rivalry with the Soviets required attention to the internal political situation of other lands, lest the repression and injustice lead to support for the Communists. But there was a second problem with an approach that suggested indifference to political freedom around the world, and that was ideological. The United States presented the Cold War not as a typical struggle between empires, of the sort the world had seen for millennia. Instead, we viewed it as, and argued that it was, a struggle between good and evil – between freedom and slavery, between individual rights and one-party dictatorships, between a nation "under God" and "godless Communism." The theologian Reinhold Niebuhr (who might be termed, at the risk of oversimplification, a "Cold War liberal" or "liberal anti-Communist") put it this way: "we are embattled with a foe who embodies all the evils of a demonic religion." Communism was "an organized evil which spreads terror and cruelty throughout the world."[4]

Fair enough, but how could we explain the evils of Communism and Soviet power if we were supporting evil regimes ourselves – and seemed indifferent to their crimes? How could we protest the lack of freedom of speech or press or assembly, or of free elections, in the Soviet empire if in our own areas of influence we tolerated the same repression?

And here, in a sense, is where I came into this American debate on human rights policy and the role of promoting democracy. I was a "Cold War liberal" in college and law school (I entered Harvard College in 1965, and graduated from Harvard Law School in 1973), which put me in sympathy with what had long been the prevailing winds in the Democratic Party. But the times they were a-changing, as Bob Dylan sang it in 1964.

I teach now at Georgetown University's School of Foreign Service, to students who were on average born between 1995 and 2000. The Cold War is a historical phenomenon to them, more or less like the War of 1812, and the Soviet Empire seems an ancient concept, another historical fact to be studied, just like the Spanish Empire. Because they know the outcome – the Soviet collapse in 1991 – it is hard to convey to them the struggle as many Americans saw it in the 1970s.

The United States seemed to be losing that struggle. The "nonaligned movement" and the "third world" countries seemed to be in closer alignment with the Soviet Union than with us. In the United Nations, we were constantly defeated. There were various ways the political and civil

liberties cherished by the United States were deprecated, beyond simply lying about the condition of freedom in the Soviet Empire and in
very many third world nations. Most common was the assertion that all
nations were after all imperfect, and everything was relative: the United
States emphasized freedom of the press, for example, but other nations
stressed social and economic "freedoms" like the right to housing or to
medical care. The fact that this was a lie (because in those countries the
material conditions were usually awful) did not seem to undermine the
ideological argument.

Why did the third world nations, which had attained independence
with brave assertions that they would now build more just societies, orient
themselves toward the USSR and not the United States?

Daniel P. Moynihan (who was then a Harvard professor and whom I
later served as chief of staff when he was a U.S. senator from New York)
explained the phenomenon in a brilliant article in *Commentary* magazine
in March 1975 titled "The United States in Opposition." There were two
reasons:

> First, the developing countries and the Communist countries had an easy
> common interest in portraying their own progress, justifying the effective
> suppression of dissent, and in the process deprecating and indicting the
> seeming progress of Western societies.... The developing nations could
> ally with the totalitarians in depicting social reality in this way, in part
> because so many, having edged toward authoritarian regimes, faced the
> same problems the Communists would have encountered with a liberal
> analysis of civil liberties. Secondly, the developing nations had an inter-
> est in deprecating the economic achievements of capitalism, since almost
> none of their own managed economies was doing well.[5]

American defeats in the United Nations and of the rise of a third
world ideology that deprecated freedom – and the United States – and
was aligned with the Soviets were also in part reflections of the Soviet
gains and American defeats on the ground. In Vietnam as the 1970s
began, the United States was proving unable to achieve its goals despite
sending more and more troops. Conversely the grim certainty of Soviet
power was affirmed in 1968 when 200,000 Soviet and other Warsaw Pact
troops put down the "Prague Spring" and the effort at liberalization in

Czechoslovakia. The global, including American, reaction to that invasion was weak to nonexistent, and the Russians had proved they would use their power to protect their interests. In Africa, 15,000 Cuban combat troops were sent to Ethiopia to advance Soviet goals there; 25,000 Cuban troops were dispatched to Angola in 1975 to ensure that on its independence the Marxist UNITA party would take power and keep it. The sense that Soviet power was rising and American power diminishing peaked in the dismal year of 1979, when the Soviet Union invaded Afghanistan, the Marxist Sandinista movement took power in Nicaragua and the Marxist FMLN group appeared on its way to power in El Salvador (both with Cuban help), the New Jewel movement seized power in Grenada and immediately established close relations with Cuba, and the shah of Iran, an important American ally, fell.

Meanwhile, many American scholars spoke and wrote about the achievements of the Soviets, their allies, and their system. In the leading economics textbook of the day, Paul Samuelson wrote that it was "a vulgar mistake to think that most people in Eastern Europe are miserable" – this, just a few years after that 1968 revolution in Czechoslovakia had been crushed – and predicted that Soviet GNP would surpass that of the United States around 2010. Not only were the Soviets gaining militarily, but the future seemed to be theirs economically as well.

Throughout the 1970s, the reaction of presidents from both the Republican and Democratic Parties was to accommodate to these new conditions – not to fight them. And strikingly, the ways in which presidents from each party did so were precursors to the debates over American human rights policy in the 1980s and since – including in the Obama years and during the "Arab Spring."

As a college student in 1968 and as a Democrat comfortably at home with the Cold War tradition of Truman, Kennedy, and Johnson, I supported Hubert Humphrey for the party's presidential nomination. Indeed I attended the raucous 1968 Democratic Convention in Chicago, where I did some minor staff work for the civil rights leader Bayard Rustin – who was working to nominate Humphrey.

But the Democratic Party split after 1968, primarily over Vietnam, and began to move steadily to the left. Its 1972 nominee, George McGovern, was not simply opposed to the Vietnam War. He had a broader critique of U.S. foreign policy and indeed of American society. He wanted less American involvement overseas and said in his acceptance speech that it was "time to turn away from excessive preoccupation overseas to the rebuilding of our own nation" because "the greatest contribution America can now make to our fellow mortals is to heal our own great but very deeply troubled land." His argument that "this is the time for this land to become again a witness to the world for what is just and noble in human affairs" suggested passivity: a witness is not an actor. At best we were to be the "city on a hill," providing a model but eschewing intervention in the affairs of others. American power and intervention were likely to make the world a worse and not a better place. In this speech he repeated the phrase, "Come home, America," six times.[6]

In 1972, as a law student, I supported Sen. Henry M. "Scoop" Jackson of Washington State for the Democratic nomination and campaigned for him for a couple of weeks in the Massachusetts and Florida primaries. Indeed I was on the Democratic ballot as a delegate pledged to Jackson in the Massachusetts primary that year (which Jackson did not win).

Jackson was fast becoming the leader of a wing of the Democratic Party whose views of American power and American foreign policy were very different from those of George McGovern and what had become the mainstream of the Democratic Party and that is what attracted me – and many others who were fairly called Cold War liberals. Moynihan was one of those, and his prescription in that *Commentary* article was not "come home, America," nor was he apologetic about the country. What Moynihan recommended was that we fight: "the United States goes into opposition." That meant that we would attack our critics, and start defending ourselves and our ideas, on both factual and ideological grounds. Moynihan wrote, "In Washington, three decades of habit and incentive have created patterns of appeasement so profound as to seem wholly normal." This must end. "It is past time we ceased to apologize for an imperfect democracy. Find its equal."

This was a fight I wanted to join. In 1975 I left the practice of law after only eighteen months and moved to Washington to work on Scoop Jackson's Senate staff. Jackson was a Cold Warrior who wished to push back against Soviet gains and harness all elements of American power to do so. He had no doubt about the virtues of American democracy and the evils of Soviet power and of Communism as an ideology. But Jackson believed the purpose of American policy was not simply achieving national security in the narrow sense, nor was it the victory of American over Soviet power: instead, it was the triumph of freedom over its enemies. Jackson's parents were immigrants from Norway, and that nation's experiences with Nazi occupation during World War II influenced his views enormously. So did his visit to Buchenwald in 1945 as a young congressman, which not only confirmed his view that tyranny must be fought but also deepened his sympathy for Jewish causes, including the State of Israel.

Jackson was a liberal Democrat on domestic issues, but this in a way deepened his support for freedom globally – and his commitment to the need to defend it. In 1948 – long before George McGovern was saying "come home, America," he said,

> You cannot talk about a better United States if the country can be destroyed. Look at what happened to Norway. Norway had a thousand years of political freedom. The Norwegians had clean air, clean water, clean land, a great environment. They had one of the highest standards of living in the world. They had one of the first national health programs, dating back to the turn of the century. What good did it do them when the hobnail boot took over in the spring of 1940?[7]

In the 1970s Jackson's views of human rights, of Jews, and of the Soviets came together in what became known as the "Jackson Amendment." During that decade, a human rights movement led and personified by Andrei Sakharov and a related but separate movement for the right of Soviet Jews to practice their faith, learn Hebrew, and emigrate from Russia, personified by Anatoly Sharansky, grew into major factors in international politics and U.S.–Soviet relations. The Soviet Jewry struggle was an almost perfect case study of the differences between the *realpolitik* approach and the more ambitious or more humanistic view, and Jackson's staunch leadership was precisely why I supported him and came to Washington to work for him.

As the 1970s began, the Soviet Jewry movement and the advancement of détente proceeded simultaneously. Negotiations with the Soviets over strategic arms limitations and economic relations moved forward in 1971, and Nixon visited the Soviet leader Leonid Brezhnev in May 1972 – the first US president ever to visit Moscow. There they signed seven agreements on various economic and military issues, and that summer Congress approved a three-year agreement on grain sales and the SALT I (strategic arms limitation) treaty. That agreement in essence froze the number of ICBMs where they stood, while the ABM or antiballistic missile treaty signed at the same time limited both nations to only two ABM systems. "Peaceful coexistence" was the catchphrase for the relationship. In October 1972 an important trade agreement with Russia was signed that promised MFN or most-favored-nation treatment and trade credits, and in April 1973 Nixon sent up to Congress the Trade Reform Act including that provision. Brezhnev returned Nixon's visit in June 1973, and a few more agreements were signed. Brezhnev and Nixon scheduled a meeting for June 1974, and talks continued on another SALT agreement and additional commercial deals.

Meanwhile the Helsinki Conference was held in July and August 1974 to complete negotiations that had been underway for two years and approve the "Final Act" of the Conference on Security and Cooperation in Europe. This was one of the high points of détente, and the goal of the Helsinki Accords was to improve East-West relations and lower tensions. The agreement was widely viewed as a victory for the USSR, because its provisions on respect for existing borders and the equality of all states suggested that the United States was finally, formally, and permanently accepting Soviet control of Eastern and Central Europe and the status of the satellite countries there. It seemed obvious that lines such as "the participating States will respect the equal rights of peoples and their right to self-determination" were meant by the Soviet leadership to be dead letters.

The Final Act contained a human rights section, which became known as Basket Three. It mentioned "the freer and wider dissemination of information of all kinds" and "human interaction" – the ability to travel for family visits or to reunite families, for example. Such things were promised in the UN Charter and in the Soviet constitution, so few expected that much would come of Basket Three in reality; certainly President Ford and Secretary of State Henry Kissinger had no intention of allowing it to get in the way of détente with the Soviets. The kind of ideological warfare recommended by Moynihan had little appeal for them.

But the Soviet human rights movement and the Soviet Jewry movement, both of them small and weak in the 1960s, grew powerful enough to clash with and in many ways defeat the Nixon/Kissinger détente policy and the *realpolitik* approach on which it was based. In 1970 Andrei Sakharov, father of the Soviet hydrogen bomb and one of the USSR's most distinguished citizens, co-founded the Committee on Human Rights in the Soviet Union. In that same year Aleksandr Solzhenitsyn received the Nobel Prize for Literature. It was becoming increasingly clear that there was resistance to the Soviet state and to the tightening of controls on society after the Khrushchev era.

Simultaneously the Soviet Jewry movement began to grow, initially to oppose Soviet anti-Semitism. Activism by Soviet Jews was spurred by Israel's victory in the 1967 war and a deepening pride and identification as Jews – as well as a demand by thousands of Jews for the right to study Hebrew and to emigrate to Israel. In 1970 the Soviet regime put on trial for treason sixteen Jewish activists who had tried to seize a plane and land it abroad, and the trial received a great deal of international attention. In 1972 the Soviet government reacted to the demand for the right to emigrate by imposing an "emigration tax" or "diploma tax," demanding that those with a higher education "repay" the state for its cost. The tax was equal to about ten years' salary and made emigration nearly impossible for those with higher education. This provoked widespread condemnation in the United States – including open letters from 21 Nobel laureates and 6,000 American scientists condemning the tax. The government of Israel, which until 1972 had not given much public support to the Soviet Jewry movement, began to speak out in its support. In the United States, there was not only massive support from the Jewish population but, increasingly over the years, also from the leadership of the major Jewish organizations. The courage of Soviet Jewish activists, now known as "refuseniks" – who faced not only anti-Semitism and the loss of jobs but also prosecution and long prison terms – elicited deep admiration throughout the American Jewish community.

Jackson, Moynihan, and other Cold War liberals – who soon were described with the epithet "neoconservatives" – urged that the United States should give at least powerful moral support to both the Soviet human rights movement and the Soviet Jewry movement. And in 1972 Jackson began to devise a plan that would place all these human rights concerns directly in the path of détente.

The Jackson Amendment was deceptively simple. Part of the Trade Act of 1974, in its final form it said that permanent normal trade relations with a nonmarket economy country, including most-favored-nation (MFN) tariff status and U.S. government trade credits or guarantees, would be denied if the country denied freedom of emigration to its citizens. Specifically, the Jackson Amendment said normal trade relations would be denied if the country "(1) denies its citizens the right or opportunity to emigrate; (2) imposes more than a nominal tax on emigration or on the visas or other documents required for emigration, for any purpose or cause whatsoever; or (3) imposes more than a nominal tax, levy, fine, fee, or other charge on any citizen as a consequence of the desire of such citizen to emigrate to the country of his choice." The Soviet Union recognized no right to travel or to emigrate and had imposed a steep emigration tax.

This was "linkage" – the idea that the United States would not only speak up for internal changes and human rights improvements in another country but would also tie other aspects of American foreign policy and bilateral relations to them. And here, linkage was being applied not to a poor or weak American aid recipient or to some American client state in the third world, but to the Soviet Union – a superpower. Sharansky has explained how critical was Jackson's role:

> Well I've asked, "Who are the people responsible for the demise of the Soviet Union?" And of course I believe that our movement played a very important role. But if you are speaking about specific names, I will speak about Andrei Sakharov, about Senator Jackson, and about President Reagan. The contribution of Senator Jackson was in the fact that he was the first who made the direct linkage between freedom of emigration and very important economic interest of the Soviet Union. And he did so against all the political thought in the United States of America and in the free world.

> Many of those people were saying, "It is our interest to have more trade with the Soviet Union, and when there is more trade there is less war." And we, Soviet Jews, knew that our only hope to be released was that the interests of the Soviet Union, economic and otherwise, would be so closely linked to our fate that the Soviet Union would have no choice.
>
> Sen. Jackson was the first to understand the power of this linkage.[8]

Creating this linkage was Jackson's goal, but Jackson and his supporters were not in charge of U.S. foreign policy: Richard Nixon and Henry Kissinger were. They not only did not believe in Jackson's linkage but actually seemed to believe in a form of "reverse linkage": the need to avoid any moves in the human rights context that might upset the Soviets and damage détente. On March 1, 1973 Israeli prime minister Golda Meir visited Nixon and raised the plight of Soviet Jewry in what was apparently a warm visit. But as the "Nixon tapes" later revealed, Nixon and Kissinger rejected her request that they push the Soviets to allow Jews to emigrate. "The emigration of Jews from the Soviet Union is not an objective of American foreign policy," Kissinger said as he and Nixon reviewed the meeting with Meir, and Nixon replied, "I know. We can't blow up the world because of it."[9]

A month later in April 1973, Nixon met with fifteen prominent Jewish leaders and argued that détente meant world peace and that the American Jewish community could not allow parochial interests, even humanitarian ones, to get in the way. Kissinger spoke repeatedly with Jewish leaders that spring. As one historian of the Soviet Jewry movement explained, "Over and over again, Kissinger made it clear that détente transcended human rights issues; that the most pressing danger to mankind was nuclear confrontation; that, therefore, all energies must be used to eliminate the possibility of confrontation.... He insisted that any one human rights issue...must not be allowed to jeopardize the striving for détente."[10] With this much direct pressure from Nixon and Kissinger, a number of Jewish leaders began to waver on supporting Jackson and the Jackson Amendment, but the grassroots in the Jewish community were solidly behind Jackson. And when more than 100 Soviet Jewish activists sent a letter to American Jewish leaders telling them not to abandon the Jackson Amendment, even the weakest Jewish leaders moved back toward resisting administration blandishments.

The two human rights movements in the USSR, the more general one and the struggle of Soviet Jewry, moved in parallel tracks and reinforced each other. The debate between the Nixon administration and Jackson continued into 1974, and it did not change when Ford succeeded Nixon in August of that year. The new administration battled with Jackson and the Jewish community, and had considerable support in business circles. Both sides fought hard for votes in Congress. And then in September 1974, Sakharov intervened in the debate with a remarkable open letter calling on Congress to support the Jackson Amendment:

> For decades the Soviet Union has been developing under conditions of an intolerable isolation, bringing with it the ugliest consequences. Even a partial preservation of those conditions would be highly perilous for all mankind, for international confidence and detente.
>
> In view of the foregoing, I am appealing to the Congress of the United States to give its support to the Jackson Amendment.... The Jackson Amendment is made even more significant by the fact that the world is only just entering on a new course of detente and it is therefore essential that the proper direction be followed [from] the outset. This is a fundamental issue, extending far beyond the question of emigration.... The amendment does not represent interference in the internal affairs of socialist countries, but simply a defense of international law, without which there can be no mutual trust.
>
> Adoption of the amendment therefore cannot be a threat to Soviet-American relations. All the more, it would not imperil international detente.... The abandonment of a policy of principle would be a betrayal of the thousands of Jews and non-Jews who want to emigrate, of the hundreds in camps and mental hospitals, of the victims of the Berlin Wall.
>
> Such a denial would lead to stronger repressions on ideological grounds. It would be tantamount to total capitulation of democratic principles in face of blackmail, deceit and violence. The consequences of such a capitulation for international confidence, detente and the entire future of mankind are difficult to predict.

I express the hope that the Congress of the United States, reflecting the will and the traditional love of freedom of the American people, will realize its historical responsibility before mankind and will find the strength to rise above temporary partisan considerations of commercialism and prestige.

I hope that the Congress will support the Jackson Amendment.[11]

Here Sakharov made Jackson's argument about détente with the prestige that only a Soviet Nobel laureate and human rights hero could provide. Supporting human rights, he was urging, is the road to real détente.

Jackson won the political struggle, in that the Trade Act of 1974 included his amendment and President Ford signed it into law in January 1975. Debate continues on whether the amendment itself led to more emigration, but it can safely be said that emigration increased whenever the Soviets wanted anything from the United States, from increased trade to approval of the SALT I and SALT II treaties. One student of strategic affairs who reviewed that record concluded that "the bottom line seems to be that when the Soviets deeply want arms control agreements they will make human rights gestures to smooth the way for them."[12] What was so striking to us in the Jackson camp was that the Soviets practiced human rights linkage more or less as Jackson urged that the United States should – including on the most delicate strategic arms issues. But in the Nixon/Ford/Kissinger camp, "linkage" was always rejected. A perfect example is the refusal of President Ford in 1975 (on Kissinger's advice) to meet with Aleksandr Solzhenitsyn. Why did he refuse?

On February 13, 1974, Solzhenitsyn was expelled from the Soviet Union and sent to Germany. In a February 21, 1974, cabinet meeting, Nixon discussed Solzhenitsyn and how the United States should react to his expulsion. The answer was to keep our eyes on the ball: détente, meaning state-to-state relations with the Soviets and negotiations over world politics. "Détente is the only chance for a live-and-let-live world in the years ahead," Nixon said; "we are trying to avert a disastrous nuclear conflict. The continuation of détente will determine whether there is a chance for a peaceful resolution of problems in the Middle East and Europe." Nixon added, "Not that the Soviet Union is good – the point is, what can we do about it?"[13] At a cabinet meeting held a few weeks later,

Kissinger said of the Soviets that "we can't frustrate them at every turn," and Nixon replied, "Of course their system is oppressive. The question is what do we do about it? I previously supported the Cold War approach. But it didn't work.... The Soviet Union is not going to change its system because we won't give them MFN."[14]

So the contrast between the Nixon/Ford/Kissinger approach and that of Jackson was stark. Those of us in the "neocon" camp refused to subordinate human rights concerns to what those administrations saw as far more important and "serious" matters like trade and détente. As I put it when writing about these subjects in the 1990s, "The Nixon–Kissinger policy diminished the sense of American exceptionalism, and in its place offered a vision of America henceforth indistinguishable from any other nation in its search for security."[15] We did not see America that way. Nor did we see human rights concerns as a narrow humanitarian effort to get some people out of prison or allow them (in the Soviet case) to emigrate to Israel. That was certainly an important and attractive element of our approach. But we were far more ambitious: we saw these concerns as a lever to force systemic change in tyrannical regimes, even one as powerful as the Soviet Union.

As Sharansky said decades later, "Sakharov believed that the struggle of Soviet Jews for freedom of immigration was a very important step towards freedom in Russia in general.... Sakharov agreed that it was important to change the regime. But he was saying, 'the moment there will be freedom of immigration, everything will change. Because one of the main tools of keeping people in fear is that Soviet Union is like a big prison, and people daren't even think about leaving it. The result is that they depend fully on the authorities. The moment Jews will help us to open the gates, all of life will change.' And he was right."[16]

So we believed that these "human rights" matters were matters of national security, not just charitable efforts to help unfortunate victims of repression. We did not believe that a real and permanent peace could be achieved with as vicious a regime as the Soviets, so we were willing to use the diplomatic and economic – and sometimes the military – power of the United States to push for internal changes in foreign regimes.

This was the theory behind "linkage." Sharansky spelled it out, speaking fifteen years later in 1987:

Jackson understood that you cannot deal with the Soviet Union by ignoring the issue of human rights. You cannot ignore the nature of the Soviet Union. You have to understand that if you want serious, real agreements based on trust, lasting agreements, you must demand from the Soviet Union that they change their behavior. We see the idea of linkage so clearly in Helsinki Act – there must be parallel progress in the first, second, and third baskets – in arms negotiations, economic cooperation, and in human rights. This idea could not have been so powerfully expressed in the Helsinki Agreement had there not been all those discussions for many years before the Jackson Amendment, about the legitimacy and nonlegitimacy of linkage.[17]

This is a critical issue not only in human rights policy but also in foreign policy more generally, then and now: should the focus be on people or on governments? What should foreign policy be *about* and what should be its fundamental concerns: states or their citizens? The Soviet citizens whose rights were being crushed by the state and Party were in a sense as much inconveniences for practitioners of détente, whose only concern was state-to-state relations, as for their own rulers.

This is not only a matter of historical analysis: we recently saw this contrast played out with remarkable fidelity in President Obama's Iran nuclear deal, which led him not only to downplay Iranian human rights violations, and to remain silent when popular protests broke out in Iran against the stealing of the election in June 2009, but also to subordinate U.S. human rights concerns in the region to that nuclear deal. During Obama's last five years in office, he watched as Syria became a charnel house. Obama's own one-time special adviser for Syria wrote in 2016 that "more than half of Syria's pre-war population now falls into one of the following categories: dead; dying; disabled; tortured; terrorized; traumatized; sick; hungry; homeless . . . . The administration of Barack Obama, if it stays on its present course, will make it through noon, January 20, 2017, without having defended a single Syrian civilian from the Assad–Russia–Iran onslaught."[18]

Similarly, at the outset of the Obama administration the new Secretary of State, Hillary Clinton, visited China and made it clear that human rights concerns were peripheral. Asked if the United States would continue to press China on issues such as Tibet, Taiwan, and human rights, she told reporters accompanying her that "successive administrations and Chinese governments have been poised back and forth on these issues, and we have to continue to press them. But our pressing on those issues can't interfere with the global economic crisis, the global climate change crisis, and the security crisis."[19] In a speech on January 6, 2010, after a year in office, Secretary Clinton said, "Development must become an equal pillar of our foreign policy, alongside defense and diplomacy."[20] The fourth "D," democracy, was simply absent.

Obama and his advisers took these positions not because they were immoral, any more than were Nixon, Ford, and Kissinger. They took them because they had their eyes on state-to-state relations, almost exclusively. Like Nixon, Ford, and Kissinger, Obama felt he had bigger fish to fry: as Nixon had put it in 1974, the goal was "peaceful resolution of problems in the Middle East." This approach also led Obama to support one repressive government after another in Egypt, from Mubarak to Morsi to Sisi, without much regard to their internal policies, as I will discuss in detail later in this volume.

Sharansky had always taken an opposite view: "it is the absence of democracy that represents the real threat to peace."[21] This is perhaps a better way of explaining this critical contrast between what I am calling the Jackson, Sharansky (and later, Reagan) view and that of *realpolitik* practitioners like Nixon, Kissinger, and Obama: their goal was peace with states, with existing governments, and in seeking that goal it was sometimes inevitable that individual rights were forgotten or postponed – or betrayed, depending on one's judgment.

That was one key difference in approach, and it remains central to human rights matters today. A second was, and is, as I suggested earlier, that proponents of a strong human rights and democracy policy are simply more ambitious and more optimistic. Practitioners of *realpolitik* believe in a narrow or pessimistic view of what American support for human rights and democracy can achieve. They believe illegitimate states are very strong, while Sharansky and Jackson believed they were in many ways very weak. As Sharansky has explained, "We saw the Soviet Union as a rotten, weak society, liable to fall apart quickly, if only the West stopped supporting it. The first step in the Soviet Union's demise would be the

West's enunciation of the true nature of the [Soviet] state. When Ronald Reagan, the leader of the free world, called a spade a spade and defined the roots of the struggle, the Soviet Union was doomed. And that's what happened. The same thing applies today."[22]

Sharansky attributes the weakness of such regimes in part to what he calls "double think." In any dictatorship, he says, there are a few true believers and a few dissenters who are ready to oppose the regime publicly and bear the punishment for doing so. The great majority of citizens know full well that regime propaganda consists of lies, and understand what's going on in the society, but they remain silent. Thus people living in dictatorships become double thinkers, he says: they say and write what the regime wants, but in their own minds they know it's all nonsense. That makes the regime far more fragile than it looks: it rules by force and force alone, without the consent of the governed, and can topple at a moment's notice. This was true of the Soviets, a great global empire, and was true of the apparently indestructible Middle Eastern dictatorships like that of Ben Ali in Tunisia and Mubarak in Egypt.

The more ambitious goal is systemic change and the beginning of a transition to democracy. As I used to say in the 1980s about more traditional human rights goals like getting an individual dissident out of prison, they can jail them faster than we can get them out. Working on individual cases was an extremely valuable element of human rights policy, to be sure. These individuals deserved our best efforts because they were struggling and suffering for the rights we trumpeted and said we believed in, and American actions on their behalf were in addition tests of our commitment and of our influence. Moreover, their fate had a real impact on the struggle for freedom because it affected the morale and the leadership of the human rights movement. But freeing individual dissidents was not enough; in addition to such human rights "casework," those of us in the Jackson-Sharansky camp argued that our goal should be the promotion of democracy.

Jackson's view that the Nixon/Ford/Kissinger policy was indifferent to human rights was widely shared in the Democratic Party, even if by the late 1970s his Cold War stance was not. During the Nixon–Ford years and even the Carter years, firm Democratic control of Congress meant that the growing concern about human rights policy could be translated into legislation. An article by Sandra Vogelgesang (who had served on the State Department Policy Planning Staff) in *Foreign Affairs* in 1978 suggested that

> Jimmy Carter did not discover human rights.... What Carter did discover was an issue in cyclical upswing. Disenchantment with U.S. experience in Vietnam ... had helped, together with the civil rights movement of the 1960s, to set the stage for emphasis on international human rights in the 1970s. Landmark congressional hearings, launched by Representative Donald Fraser in 1973, and increasingly explicit legislation countered alleged indifference to human rights on the part of the Republican White House and Secretary of State Henry Kissinger.[23]

Her article referred especially to Section 502b of the International Security Assistance and Arms Export Control Act of 1976, and to Section 116 of the Foreign Assistance Act of 1961 (as amended by Section 111 of the International Development and Food Assistance Act of 1977). Section 502b established this principle: "It is the policy of the United States, in accordance with its international obligations as set forth in the Charter of the United Nations and in keeping with the constitutional heritage and traditions of the United States, to promote and encourage increased respect for human rights and fundamental freedoms for all without distinction as to race, sex, language, or religion. To this end, a principal goal of the foreign policy of the United States is to promote the increased observance of internationally recognized human rights by all countries." Accordingly, the section stated, "No security assistance may be provided to any country the government of which engages in a consistent pattern of gross violations of internationally recognized human rights," except under certain specific circumstances. Section 502b also called for annual human rights reports to be compiled for every country receiving security assistance.

The 1977 amendments to the Foreign Assistance Act expanded the reporting requirement to every country receiving "development assistance" or what is usually called "foreign aid" as well. More importantly, it linked human rights to foreign aid: "No assistance may be provided ... to the government of any country which engages in a consistent pattern of gross violations of internationally recognized human rights, including torture or cruel, inhuman or degrading treatment or punishment, prolonged detention without charges, or other flagrant denial of the right to life, liberty, and the security of person, unless such assistance will directly benefit the needy people in such country." And of course, to these provisions we must add the Jackson Amendment itself, tying most-favored-nation treatment and trade credits to the right to emigrate in nonmarket economy countries. So by the late 1970s, both trade and economic and military assistance were tied to human rights.

Moreover, in these same years there grew up a much larger and stronger human rights movement in the United States. As Vogelgesang noted in *Foreign Affairs*, "The 'human rights lobby' on Capitol Hill and in New York has grown since the early 1970s from a relative handful with no voice to over 50 organizations exercising major influence through congressional testimony, background information for U.S. legislation and U.N. deliberations, pressure on multinational firms, and operation of a communication 'internet.'"[24] So Democratic disillusionment with the Nixon/Ford policies, the growing human rights movement, and Democratic activism in Congress on human rights matters formed the backdrop to Carter's embrace of the issue.

That embrace, now seen as a central aspect of Carter's presidency and indeed his life, came as a surprise. Daniel P. Moynihan once commented, "Human rights as an issue in foreign policy was by no means central to Jimmy Carter's campaign for the Presidency. It was raised in the Democratic platform drafting committee, and at the Democratic Convention, but in each instance the Carter representatives were at best neutral, giving the impression of not having heard very much of the matter before and not having any particular views."[25]

In 1980 William F. Buckley wrote, "Nobody knows exactly what impelled Jimmy Carter to seize on human rights as the touchstone of U.S. foreign policy."[26] As Buckley wrote then, there were press reports that it was only in preparation for the debates with President Ford that Carter first heard of the Helsinki Accords' "Basket Three" concerning human rights, and this subject had not previously been an apparent concern of his (nor had he been an early opponent of the Vietnam War).[27] But human rights soon became a central theme of Carter policy, at least rhetorically. In his inaugural address Carter said, "Our commitment to human rights must be absolute," explaining that "because we are free, we can never be indifferent to the fate of freedom elsewhere. Our moral sense dictates a clear-cut preference for those societies which share with us an abiding respect for individual human rights."[28]

Carter maintained this focus, rhetorically and institutionally. In one of his first major speeches, at Notre Dame's commencement in May 1977, Carter again spoke about foreign policy and human rights:

> I have a quiet confidence in our own political system. Because we know that democracy works, we can reject the arguments of those rulers who deny human rights to their people .... [W]e are now free of that inordinate fear of communism which once led us to embrace any dictator who joined us in that fear. I'm glad that that's being changed.
>
> For too many years, we've been willing to adopt the flawed and erroneous principles and tactics of our adversaries, sometimes abandoning our own values for theirs. We've fought fire with fire, never thinking that fire is better quenched with water ....
>
> [W]e have reaffirmed America's commitment to human rights as a fundamental tenet of our foreign policy.... [W]e can already see dramatic, worldwide advances in the protection of the individual from the arbitrary power of the state. For us to ignore this trend would be to lose influence and moral authority in the world. To lead it will be to regain the moral stature that we once had.[29]

By the end of 1977 he upgraded the position of Coordinator for Human Rights in the State Department, then held by Patricia Derian, to Assistant Secretary and established a Bureau of Human Rights and Humanitarian Affairs. In February 1978, after months of interagency study during his first year in office, Carter issued Presidential Directive 30 on Human Rights. Its first line stated, "It shall be a major objective of U.S. foreign policy to promote the observance of human rights throughout the world." This would affect not only our foreign economic aid and security assistance, as Congress had already insisted, but also our policy in international financial institutions like the World Bank where we would use our "voice and vote . . . to influence the Banks' actions."[30]

It would be a mistake to think that Carter policy was absolutist and that human rights considerations consistently crowded out such matters as security or commerce. The shah of Iran or the generals who ran South Korea, for example, were important allies, and "in both cases security dominated U.S. actions; the human rights issues, when they were raised, were raised in private."[31] In the case of the shah, Carter's rhetoric was quite incredible. Carter visited Iran for New Year's weekend at the end of his first year in office and had this to say while there:

> Iran, because of the great leadership of the Shah, is an island of stability in one of the more troubled areas of the world. This is a great tribute to you, Your Majesty, and to your leadership and to the respect and the admiration and love which your people give to you .... The cause of human rights is one that also is shared deeply by our people and by the leaders of our two nations.[32]

Even considerations of *realpolitik* could not justify those words. Similarly with respect to the brutal "dirty war" the military regime in Argentina engaged in against domestic opponents, "the U.S. stance became even more forgiving as the U.S. government sought to enlist Argentine support for the U.S. grain embargo following the Soviet invasion of Afghanistan."[33] The role of human rights was a matter of continuing debate within the administration, as documents declassified decades later showed. Memos released in 2016 "reveal a near-constant internal tension between U.S. eagerness to push human rights as Carter's signature foreign policy issue, and concerns that cutting off aid and trade with Argentina's ruling military junta could be counterproductive and might push it toward a closer relationship with the Soviet Union."[34] This kind of internal debate is inescapable, because the United States has many and varied interests and – as I would say repeatedly in defending Reagan administration policy in the 1980s – a government is not an NGO. Human rights NGOs should advocate for human rights, period, and leave it to others to try to take into account competing or conflicting interests. Governments do not have that luxury. Balancing interests as the Carter administration did should not be cause for criticism.

But the point here is that Carter did indeed engage in such balancing of interests, and whether he did it well or poorly he was right to do it.

When Ronald Reagan did the same thing a few years later, the criticism was much fiercer than that which Carter had suffered. It was a double standard, we in the Reagan administration felt, and an effort to impose completely unrealistic standards on the government.

Those of us in the Jackson or neocon camp were in fact extremely critical of Carter's human rights policy. Why?

For one thing we saw what Carter was doing as essentially casework, a form of foreign aid to individuals caught up in repressive systems. The line that "they can jail them faster than we can get them out" applied here: advocacy for individual cases, or pressure to get dictators to lighten up somewhat, was necessary but not sufficient. The cure was democracy: systemic change away from dictatorship to open political systems that would protect human rights. To put it another way, it could not be the best answer for the United States to be responsible, through endless rhetorical and diplomatic interventions, to protect human rights in country after country, year after year.

A far better approach would give greater priority to democracy promotion, putting people in those countries in a position to protect their own rights through free speech, freedom of the press, free elections, and so on. So we criticized the Carter emphasis on "human rights" rather than on democracy. And we saw it as insufficiently ambitious. Why not push for real democracy when that was possible? Why not at least advocate for protection of all civil and political rights? Why not make it clear that a decision by a dictator to allow some people to emigrate, or to free some journalists and human rights advocates from jail, was hardly cause for celebration, when the vicious system of repression remained entirely in place? As Sharansky explained, those repressive regimes could well be far more fragile than they appeared, and American support for transitions to democracy could help make them even more fragile.

The casework system that we attributed to Carter also meant that the focus was on regimes, rather than on their oppressed populations. It meant a never-ending series of conversations, bargains, concessions, compromises, and deals with those dictators, rather than vocal support for those struggling peacefully for a different system. And while those negotiations with dictators continued, other interests of the United States would almost certainly take precedence from time to time: in the Carter administration Argentina and the grain embargo on the Soviets, for example, or decades later President Obama's refusal to give rhetorical backing to the "Green Revolution" in Iran because he was negotiating with the regime over its nuclear weapons program. This was inevitable, unless the tyranny itself gave way to a democratic system.

We also deeply disagreed with Carter's adoption of Soviet definitions of human rights. As I mentioned earlier, the Soviets and the "non-aligned" nations pushed for a definition that included "economic and social rights," such as jobs and health care and housing. They argued that while we emphasized certain rights, such as freedom of the press, they simply emphasized others, such as good housing for all. And they argued that especially for poor or developing nations, all these rights – political as well as social and economic – were hard to achieve and would take many decades. In 1977, Secretary of State Vance spoke at the University of Georgia, where he said this:

> Let me define what we mean by "human rights."
>
> First, there is the right to be free from governmental violation of the integrity of the person. Such violations include torture; cruel, inhuman, or degrading treatment or punishment; and arbitrary arrest or imprisonment. And they include denial of fair public trial and invasion of the home.
>
> Second, there is the right to the fulfillment of such vital needs as food, shelter, health care, and education. We recognize that the fulfillment of this right will depend, in part, upon the stage of a nation's economic development. But we also know that this right can be violated by a government's action or inaction – for example, through corrupt official processes which divert resources to an elite at the expense of the needy or through indifference to the plight of the poor.
>
> Third, there is the right to enjoy civil and political liberties: freedom of thought, of religion, of assembly; freedom of speech; freedom of the press; freedom of movement both within and outside one's own country; freedom to take part in government.
>
> Our policy is to promote all these rights.[35]

His second definition came right out of the Russian playbook. And it was intellectually corrupting, we believed. The case of India was instructive: it was desperately poor, but democratic. It proved that no nation was too poor to be free. What did it even mean in a case like India's to say there was a "right" to shelter, when that right was impossible to fulfill? It meant that the Soviet argument was getting some intellectual support from flabby thinking in Washington. We believed there were social and economic *goals* and political *rights* – rights that no government could legitimately deny or violate whatever the country's stage of development. By corrupting the term "rights" and applying it to unattainable social and economic goals, the Carter administration was falling right into the Soviet trap and weakening the cause of human rights. (In the second annual human rights report of the Reagan administration, released in early 1983, we excised the term "economic and social rights" entirely.)

Finally and most crucially, we believed that Carter's human rights policy was tilted to the Left: he seemed unable to acknowledge that the main threat to freedom in the world was Soviet Communism. In his Notre Dame speech in May 1977 he had said, "We are now free of that inordinate fear of Communism which once led us to embrace any dictator who joined us in our fear."[36] But what kind of human rights policy could one have in the 1970s that did not put the Soviet Union and Communism at its heart? Jeane Kirkpatrick answered the question in 1982, just two years after Carter left office: "as it evolved under the Carter administration, the thrust of U.S. human rights policy was directed against U.S. allies. Instead of using the issue of human rights to place the totalitarian states on the defensive, the U.S. frequently joined the totalitarians in attacking pro-Western authoritarian states."[37]

Carter would have had difficulty pleading "not guilty" to that charge: in March 1977 he told a press conference, "I have tried to make sure that the world knows that we are not singling out the Soviet Union for abuse or criticism,"[38] and in June of that year, he said, "We have not singled out the Soviet Union for criticism, and I have never tried to inject myself into the internal affairs of the Soviet Union."[39] He seemed adamant that human rights would not be applied as an issue against the Soviets nor against other Communist dictators. In December 1977 he visited Warsaw, Poland, and whatever he may have said privately about human rights, in public he said, "Old ideological labels have lost their meaning."[40] If so, why worry about Communism at all? This looked like stumbling into a rough "moral equivalence" between the two sides in the Cold War, between our system and the other side's.

In his first days in office Carter had appointed Paul Warnke to lead the Arms Control and Disarmament Agency and be the chief U.S. negotiator in arms talks with the Soviets, an appointment that became an ideological battle for those of us on the neocon side. Forty senators voted against his confirmation, and they were not all Republicans: Jackson, as well as Daniel P. Moynihan, who had been elected in 1976 and whose staff I had joined the day he joined the Senate, also voted no. In fact his speech opposing the confirmation of Warnke was Moynihan's maiden effort on the Senate floor.

Warnke, who had been the key foreign policy and national security adviser to George McGovern during the 1972 campaign, had in 1975 written an article in *Foreign Policy* about the Cold War arms race titled "Apes on a Treadmill": the apes were, of course, the United States and the Soviet Union.[41] This was moral equivalence with a vengeance, and Moynihan rejected it both when it came to strategic arms and more broadly when it came to the Soviet regime. In that article Warnke had said that American strategic restraint would be met and matched by Soviet restraint; Moynihan rejected that claim and said, as I recall it, "When we build, they build. When we cut, they build." As to the nature of our adversaries, Moynihan had a remarkable colloquy with Sen. Frank Church, who asked him at one point if he thought the Soviet leaders would continue building their strategic forces, even if we cut ours, simply because they were insane. Moynihan replied, "No, sir, I do not think them to be mad: I think them to be evil and sane, and they seek to achieve a superiority, and they know what they will do with it. They will intimidate the world around them."[42]

It was this that the Carter administration appeared adamantly unwilling to admit: that instead of escaping an "inordinate fear of Communism," we needed to oppose Communist regimes and the doctrines they embraced because they were evil. If Carter's remarks in Warsaw had suggested moral equivalence, far worse were his comments in March 1978 when Marshal Tito, the Yugoslav dictator, visited Washington. "Perhaps as much as any person, he exemplifies in Yugoslavia the eagerness for freedom, independence, and liberty that exists throughout Eastern Europe and indeed throughout the world," Carter said of the Communist ruler.[43]

While Tito achieved some independence from the Soviet bloc, he ruled with an iron hand that allowed no space for freedom or liberty. Worst of all was what Carter said in welcoming the vicious Romanian Communist dictator Nicolae Ceausescu to the White House in April 1978. He called Ceausescu "a great leader" and said, "Our goals are also the same, to have a just system of economics and politics, to let the people of the world share in growth, in peace, and in personal freedom."[44] Like Tito, Ceausescu maintained some independence from the USSR, but he was an orthodox Stalinist who led a cruelly repressive regime. It was astonishing for Carter say that "our goals are the same," and it suggested that his vaunted message on human rights would be applied in one direction only.

Or so it seemed to us. In April 1978 Sen. Jackson spoke in Washington about human rights policy and said this:

> Many share my continuing dismay at the American policy on human rights that finds it convenient to criticize petty dictatorships, with which the world unhappily abounds, but inconvenient to speak out about the Soviet system that inspires repression around the world.... For too many officials, the intensity of the struggle for human rights abroad is inversely related to the power of the offender.[45]

As Jackson's biographer Robert Kaufman summed up his view,

> Jackson criticized Carter not for his emphasis on human rights but for the way his administration went about promoting them. Jackson had two principal objections to Carter's human rights policy. First, he faulted Carter for what he perceived to be the administration's selective application of human rights sanctions against less repressive right-wing authoritarian allies while slighting the violations of more repressive left-wing totalitarian adversaries such as the Soviet Union.... Second, Jackson faulted the Carter administration for slighting the imperatives of power and geopolitics in pursuit of its ideals. He thus described the "unsettling mixture of moralism, malaise, and retrenchment" that in his mind evoked contempt for U.S. weakness.[46]

The latter point is critical: Jackson believed that human rights would advance if American power advanced and would be undermined by

American weakness. He would have approved of and repeated the phrase Condoleezza Rice used in 2002: that a key American goal was "a balance of power that favors freedom."[47] Jackson and Moynihan believed Carter neither realized this nor understood that the Soviet gains of the late 1970s were undermining his own human rights goals. This idea that American power was a force for good in the world was a touchstone of Jackson's views and of neoconservative foreign policy and human rights policy. As Robert Kagan and William Kristol put it later, "Americans should understand that their support for American pre-eminence is as much a strike for international justice as any people is capable of making."[48]

Carter's view that our "inordinate fear of communism" had led to the United States backing all sorts of unattractive right-wing dictators, and that this must not be repeated, led him to watch as the shah of Iran fell. It is impossible to prove, of course, that tougher actions by the United States could have saved the shah or could have kept the military intact and prevented a takeover by the Ayatollah Khomeini. We will never know, because the United States did not undertake such an effort.

The same policy, seeking above all to avoid getting our hands dirty, was visible in Nicaragua, which fell to the Sandinistas in July 1979. Could Somoza have been forced out by the United States and some sort of provisional government put in place – which would soon call free elections and give way to a democratic government? The Carter White House would not undertake such an effort, Robert Pastor, the top official handling Latin America for the Carter National Security Council, later said, because "the age of U.S. unilateralism was past." As he explained, "Pete [Vaky, Assistant Secretary of State for Inter-American Affairs] felt that we could and should force Somoza out in the Fall of '78, and I felt that we couldn't and shouldn't.... I felt that Carter should not overthrow a government. I felt that we were in the business too long and it was time to get out of that business, regardless of what the circumstances were."[49] It seems clear that Carter agreed, though Pastor makes a very broad claim: "regardless of what the circumstances were," presumably including circumstances in which the alternative was a Communist regime tied to the Soviets and Cuba, and even in a situation where we could in fact successfully force Somoza out. The Carter administration's human rights chief, Pat Derian, felt the same way: a memo from June 1979 reads, "Assistant

Secretary Derian argued that supporting a non-Sandinista alternative would 'appear as our having opted for the status quo out of fear of social and political change.'"[50]

We, in the Jackson and neocon camp, had an entirely different analysis of the situation and one that led us to oppose Carter's policy vociferously. Jeane Kirkpatrick spelled it out in a landmark article in *Commentary* in November 1979.[51] It is worth examining at length, because it was one of the foundations of Reagan's human rights policy – and also because it proved to be a faulty foundation, at least as Jeane and many others interpreted it, and was sidelined after around 1983 or at least reinterpreted by those of us making human rights policy in the Reagan administration.

What was the problem that Jeane was addressing? "No problem of American foreign policy is more urgent," she wrote, "than that of formulating a morally and strategically acceptable, and politically realistic, program for dealing with non-democratic governments who are threatened by Soviet-sponsored subversion." And what was the Carter approach? "In the current year the United States has suffered two other major blows – in Iran and Nicaragua – of large and strategic significance. In each country, the Carter administration not only failed to prevent the undesired outcome, it actively collaborated in the replacement of moderate autocrats friendly to American interests with less friendly autocrats of extremist persuasion."

Unquestionably the United States favored reform in such countries (and she mentions others, such as Morocco, Guatemala, and El Salvador), but assisting in takeovers by groups worse than the incumbents was not reform. She found a

> suggestive similarity to our behavior in China before the fall of Chiang Kai-shek, in Cuba before the triumph of Castro, in certain crucial periods of the Vietnamese war, and, more recently, in Angola. In each of these countries, the American effort to impose liberalization and democratization on a government confronted with violent internal opposition not only failed, but actually assisted the coming to power of new regimes in which ordinary people enjoy fewer freedoms and less personal security than under the previous autocracy – regimes, moreover, hostile to American interests and policies.

So from the perspective of both American security interests and human rights, this policy was folly:

> [T]he U.S. will have been led by its own misunderstanding of the situation to assist actively in deposing an erstwhile friend and ally and installing a government hostile to American interests and policies in the world. At best we will have lost access to friendly territory. At worst the Soviets will have gained a new base. And everywhere our friends will have noted that the U.S. cannot be counted on in times of difficulty and our enemies will have observed that American support provides no security against the forward march of history.

She criticized the Carter administration's refusal to act in Iran, writing, "In Iran, the Carter administration's commitment to nonintervention proved stronger than strategic considerations or national pride." Nicaragua was an even worse case "both because the Cuban and Soviet roles were clearer and because U.S. officials were more intensely and publicly working against Somoza."

So what was Carter thinking, she asked. There were several assumptions behind Carter policy:

> [F]irst, the belief that there existed at the moment of crisis a democratic alternative to the incumbent government: second, the belief that the continuation of the status quo was not possible; third, the belief that any change, including the establishment of a government headed by self-styled Marxist revolutionaries, was preferable to the present government.

These assumptions were widely believed on the Left, but were all false, she wrote. The latter point engaged most attention:

> Although there is no instance of a revolutionary "socialist" or Communist society being democratized, right-wing autocracies do sometimes evolve into democracies – given time, propitious economic, social, and political circumstances, talented leaders, and a strong indigenous demand for representative government. Something of the kind is in progress on the Iberian peninsula and the first steps have been taken in Brazil. Something similar could conceivably have also occurred in Iran and Nicaragua if contestation and participation had been more gradually expanded.

But it seems clear that the architects of contemporary American foreign policy have little idea of how to go about encouraging the liberalization of an autocracy. In neither Nicaragua nor Iran did they realize that the
only likely result of an effort to replace an incumbent autocrat with one
of his moderate critics or a "broad-based coalition" would be to sap the
foundations of the existing regime without moving the nation any closer
to democracy.

Here Jeane was making "the totalitarian-authoritarian distinction,"
namely that authoritarian regimes such as those she referred to in Spain
or Portugal or Nicaragua or Iran might "evolve into democracies," but
Communist governments were not going to do so. To this she added the
criticism that the Carter administration did not know how to push the
authoritarians successfully into reform, but that critique was less important. The main point was that our right-wing allies could change, but
Marxist regimes would not. So replacing a friendly right-wing dictatorship with a Communist regime was damaging both to the United States
and to the people of that country, whose hopes for political progress were
now doomed.

Why would this be so? There were at least two major reasons. First, we
in the United States and "the West" or "Free World" *wanted* the regimes
to change. Their repression violated our principles and bothered our
consciences. If they were in the American camp they would be under
constant pressure to adhere more closely to our model. And while such
authoritarian regimes might defend their conduct as required to defeat
the Communist menace, there was no principled basis on which they
could defend repression. It was at best an expedient, a necessary evil.
In contrast, regimes that went into the Soviet camp would be pressed by
the Russians to hew more closely to their model, which provided ideological justification for the Leninist approach. Every form of repression
was excused and indeed glorified.

Second, there are "systemic differences between traditional and revolutionary autocracies that have a predictable effect on their degree
of repressiveness." Such regimes controlled the government – but not
the entire society. There was usually a free economy (which meant that

critics of the regime did not depend on it for their livelihood), freedom to travel, freedom of religion, some elements of free speech or free trade unions, and other bases on which a freer society could be built. In a Communist regime these bases were systematically attacked and eliminated.

As Jeane put it,

> Only intellectual fashion and the tyranny of Right/Left thinking prevent intelligent men of good will from perceiving the facts that traditional authoritarian governments are less repressive than revolutionary autocracies, that they are more susceptible of liberalization, and that they are more compatible with U.S. interests. The evidence on all these points is clear enough.
>
> Surely it is now beyond reasonable doubt that the present governments of Vietnam, Cambodia, Laos are much more repressive than those of the despised previous rulers; that the government of the People's Republic of China is more repressive than that of Taiwan, that North Korea is more repressive than South Korea, and so forth. This is the most important lesson of Vietnam and Cambodia. It is not new but it is a gruesome reminder of harsh facts.

Jeane had one more major criticism, which we have seen from Jackson: the application of double standards (which gave the article its name). As she wrote,

> So far, assisting "change" has not led the Carter administration to undertake the destabilization of a Communist country. The principles of self-determination and nonintervention are thus both selectively applied. We seem to accept the status quo in Communist nations (in the name of "diversity" and national autonomy), but not in nations ruled by "right-wing" dictators or white oligarchies.... The administration's conception of national interest borders on doublethink: it finds friendly powers to be guilty representatives of the status quo and views the triumph of unfriendly groups as beneficial to America's "true interests...." The President continues to behave as before – not like a man who abhors autocrats but like one who abhors only right-wing autocrats.

So what U.S. policy did Jeane call for in this article?

> Since many traditional autocracies permit limited contestation and participation, it is not impossible that U.S. policy could effectively encourage this process of liberalization and democratization, provided that the effort is not made at a time when the incumbent government is fighting for its life against violent adversaries, and that proposed reforms are aimed at producing gradual change rather than perfect democracy overnight. To accomplish this, policymakers are needed who understand how actual democracies have actually come into being. History is a better guide than good intentions.
>
> A realistic policy which aims at protecting our own interest and assisting the capacities for self-determination of less developed nations will need to face the unpleasant fact that, if victorious, violent insurgency headed by Marxist revolutionaries is unlikely to lead to anything but totalitarian tyranny.

In the Jackson wing of the Democratic Party – and we were still Democrats, though increasingly critical of President Carter's foreign policy – these views were nearly universal. If reaction against the *realpolitik* of the Nixon/Ford/Kissinger days had produced the human rights policy of the Left, as seen in the Carter administration's approach, it had also produced the neocon approach. We attacked the Carter policy as it was implemented from 1977 to 1981 – and soon enough, in the Reagan years, the Left and the human rights movement would inspire most Democrats to attack ours.

This is not to suggest that there were no arguments on the Right or within the neoconservative movement itself. On the Right, there was in many places great enthusiasm for some of the pro-American right-wing regimes that was not linked to any desire or effort to see them liberalize. They were anti-Communist, and that was enough. This view became even stronger during the Carter years, when official American pressure for liberalization appeared to redound to the benefit of the Soviet Union and Cuba. And among neoconservatives there were always powerful voices that expressed great pessimism about the wisdom and effects of such pressures for liberalization in the real world.

Irving Kristol was such a skeptic. He certainly agreed with the "totalitarian-authoritarian distinction" that Jeane Kirkpatrick was making, writing in 1980 that "it is not a betrayal of the democratic idea to imply that some dictatorships are better than others." But he was skeptical of the ability of very many countries to attain democracy and respect for human rights as we practiced them in the United States: "It is the fundamental fallacy of American policy to believe, in the face of evidence, that all peoples, everywhere, are immediately 'entitled' to a liberal constitutional government – and a thoroughly democratic one at that." It was in the days of Woodrow Wilson, Kristol argued, that "American foreign policy began to disregard the obvious for the sake of the quixotic pursuit of impossible ideals" and the result is "a foreign policy that is intellectually disarmed before all those cases where a government is neither totalitarian nor democratic, but authoritarian."[52]

In that 1980 essay he argued against American guilt for allying with authoritarian regimes, both because "the world is heterogeneous and complex" and because we would be trying to move them toward more enlightened behavior. Kristol later added that we had a duty to help "peoples who are actively striving for a constitutional system against the oppression of their governments," such as was the case in Eastern Europe. And he acknowledged, "American foreign policy must be defensible in moral terms as well as expediential ones . . . . Pure, amoral *realpolitik* is no part of the American political tradition."[53]

But realism was a part of that tradition, and Kristol thought the effort to turn Third World countries into great democracies was very often unrealistic. He wrote in 1990,

> The only innovative trend in our foreign policy thinking at the moment derives from a relatively small group, consisting of both liberals and conservatives, who believe there is an "American mission" actively to promote democracy all over the world. This is a superficially attractive idea, but it takes only a few moments of thought to realize how empty of substance (and how full of presumption!) it is.
>
> In the entire history of the U.S., we have successfully "exported" our democratic institutions to only two nations – Japan and Germany, after war and an occupation . . . . Why should anyone think we can do so in

Eastern Europe or Southeast Asia? If these countries are to be functioning democracies, they will have to achieve it the old-fashioned way – by working at it. Free elections are only the beginning.[54]

In dozens of conversations with Irving over the course of the 1980s and 1990s, he continued to express such skepticism. In this he was joined by Jeane: they shared a pessimism about what change away from known, friendly, pro-American regimes would lead to, and about our ability to maneuver with sufficient skill to liberalize an autocracy or replace it with an equally friendly, pro-American liberal democracy. In her famous article, Jeane had already attacked "the belief that it is possible to democratize governments, anytime, anywhere, under any circumstances" when on the contrary "democratic institutions are especially difficult to establish and maintain – because they make heavy demands on all portions of a population and because they depend on complex social, cultural, and economic conditions."

This debate became hotter and heavier among neoconservatives in the 1990s after the fall of the Soviet Union. As Justin Vaisse notes in his excellent analysis, *Neoconservatism: The Biography of a Movement*, most of us (certainly including me) believed that "the contest with the Soviets had been above all ideological, and the defense of democracy had not been just a byproduct of the containment of Communism but its very *raison d'être*."[55] But such differences among neocons were already apparent even in the 1970s and early 1980s, because while the struggle against Soviet- and Cuban-backed guerrillas was intense in some places, in others it was plainly over and was being used as an excuse for tyranny.

Where we all tended to agree was in the cases where a right-wing military regime was under immediate threat from a Cuban- and Soviet-backed guerrilla movement, such as in El Salvador or Nicaragua. Surely there was no human rights argument for permitting the Communist guerrillas – the FMLN in El Salvador, the Sandinistas in Nicaragua, and similar groups in Honduras and Guatemala – from seizing power. That would be the end, we believed, of hope for democracy. Where we parted company from each other was in the many cases where there did not seem (to me, in any event) to be such a threat: in Paraguay, Chile, and Argentina, or in South Korea and the Philippines, where military regimes

34

(and in the last case an old-fashioned authoritarian dictator) ruled and did not liberalize. By the time Reagan came to office these countries faced no real Communist guerrilla threat, if they ever had – and anyway continuing repression was likely to increase support for the hard Left. It seemed to me that Jeane's arguments in "Dictatorships and Double Standards" or Irving's in his essays acknowledged that, in such cases, the United States should be pushing hard for change. But they were unenthusiastic about doing so, and when in the Reagan years I led our human rights efforts this caused a real break with Jeane – though with Irving, who was of course not inside the administration serving as an official, fighting over policy choices never led to more (or, perhaps more accurately, anything less) than good arguments over good meals.

When Ronald Reagan defeated Jimmy Carter in the 1980 election, such debates in magazines and newspapers and over dinner became more consequential. For Reagan, a product of the conservative movement who brought into his administration a number of neoconservative Democrats, now had to decide what his human rights policy would be.

Those of us who supported Scoop Jackson and his approach to foreign policy and, more specifically, to human rights policy could not support Jimmy Carter's reelection. On January 31, 1980, a group of us, including Jeane Kirkpatrick, Max Kampelman, Ben Wattenberg, Norman Podhoretz, Midge Decter, and Admiral Elmo Zumwalt, were invited to meet with Carter in the White House Cabinet Room adjacent to the Oval Office. We were representatives of the Coalition for a Democratic Majority, a group founded in 1972 after the McGovern nomination (with Jackson as its patron saint), with the goal of returning the Democratic Party to its more traditional, centrist foreign policy stance. The setting for the Carter meeting was impressive, and I had been to the White House only one previous time. The idea was that Vice President Mondale and President Carter would play on the "mystic chords of memory" and remind us of our loyalty to the Democratic Party.

Mondale did an excellent job at this, and when Carter entered the room, our agreed spokesman, Austin Ranney of the American Political Science Association, told the president that we all wanted to be able to support him. And, Ranney said, we were encouraged by the new foreign policy approach toward the Soviets he was taking since the 1979 invasion of Afghanistan. He did not describe the many incidents that had bothered us (such as Ambassador to the United Nations Andrew Young's description of the Cuban troops in Angola as "a force for stability"), but said this new foreign policy approach was one we supported. Carter interrupted Ranney at that point and said he did not have two foreign policies and that his approach had not changed – and would not change. The meeting might as well have ended right then, and everything else Carter said only deepened the conclusion almost all of us reached that he was not someone for whom we could vote. And several of us, including Max Kampelman, Jeane Kirkpatrick, and me, later joined the Reagan administration.

Reagan's campaign had been strong on anti-Communism and advancing the argument that Soviet power was rising while American power in the world appeared to be declining. The Sandinista takeover in Nicaragua, the fall of the shah to a hostile regime, and the Soviet invasion of Afghanistan were prime examples. On human rights policy per se there was little debate, although Jeane Kirkpatrick's "Dictatorships and Double Standards" was gaining attention throughout 1980. It was in fact that article that brought her to Reagan's attention and led to her selection as ambassador to the United Nations when he won the presidency. Most conservatives and neoconservatives could agree on the central importance of anti-Communism to any human rights policy and on the critique of Carter policy for attacking right-wing allies far more than left-wing enemy regimes. We could also all agree that right-wing authoritarian regimes were in one key way preferable to totalitarian Communist regimes: they were susceptible to change, as Jeane had explained.

Reagan had said little about all of this except for his answer to one question in the first presidential debate in 1980. He was asked, "Do we back unpopular regimes whose major merit is that they are friendly to the United States?" He answered that replacing an authoritarian regime with a totalitarian one

> makes one wonder whether you are being helpful to the people. And we've been guilty of that. Because someone didn't meet exactly our standards of human rights, even though they were an ally of ours, instead of trying

patiently to persuade them to change their ways, we have, in a number
of instances, aided a revolutionary overthrow which results in complete
totalitarianism, instead, for those people. I think that this is a kind of a
hypocritical policy when, at the same time, we're maintaining a detente
with the one nation in the world where there are no human rights at all –
the Soviet Union.[56]

Reagan was, here, viewing human rights policy through the prism Jeane
had designed and underlining the special case of the Soviet Union. But
he was not abandoning the cause of human rights or suggesting it was an
unhealthy Carter invention; instead he seemed to espouse the need to
persuade allies who were human rights offenders "to change their ways."
And he was urging pragmatism: it could never be right to replace a bad
regime with a worse one – in the name of human rights.

Where the neocons and the "paleocons" (as members of the traditional conservative movement, from Barry Goldwater to William F. Buckley, to their many political descendants, came to be called) split was in
applying these views to actual cases. Only time could tell where Reagan
might come out on specific countries. It was one thing to say totalitarian
regimes were worse than authoritarian ones, which seemed to most of
us quite obvious. It was another to appear indifferent to the crimes of
authoritarian regimes or even to celebrate them because they were part
of a policy of "resisting Communism" or "defeating Marxist guerrillas."
And even worse was an approach that opposed *any* American support for
human rights, or *any* criticism of the abuses of friendly regimes, as an
unwarranted intervention in the internal affairs of a foreign state. This
was repeating the Kissinger/Nixon approach to human rights policy and
was bound not simply to evoke neocon disagreement but also to arouse
real hostility in Congress and in the human rights movement.

In his first press conference as the new secretary of state, Alexander
Haig stated, "International terrorism will take the place of human rights
in our concern because it is the ultimate of abuse of human rights."[57]
Haig was neither a neocon nor a paleocon: he had worked for Henry
Kissinger in the Nixon White House and was much closer to Kissinger's
realpolitik than to Reagan's far more ideological views of American foreign
policy. His press conference statement seemed to suggest that those who

wanted some sort of support for human rights were correct in fearing the new Reagan administration might simply jettison the entire policy.

Then in February 1981 President Reagan chose his nominee for Assistant Secretary of State for Human Rights: Ernest Lefever. Ernie was president of the Ethics and Public Policy Center, a Washington think tank. In a quirk of fate, I was to be not only his successor as the nominee for the human rights post at State but also his successor (once removed) as president of the Ethics and Public Policy Center. Ernie was an academic and foreign policy expert with a doctorate in Christian ethics from Yale and a lovely person, but was a terrible nominee. Democrats on the Hill, still smarting from Reagan's victory, attacked his use of the totalitarian-authoritarian distinction as a guide to human rights policy, and in this they were wrong. But Ernie had gone far beyond this in previous writings and statements. In 1979 testimony to Congress, he had said, "In a formal and legal sense the U.S. government has no responsibility – and certainly no authority – to promote human rights in other sovereign states" and had called for repealing most human rights statutes.[58] The Senate Foreign Relations Committee concluded that Ernie opposed human rights policy almost as a matter of principle and so rejected his nomination. The human rights post would remain vacant for the first eleven months of the Reagan administration.

In reality the policy being pursued by the new Reagan administration was not as different from Carter's as one might have thought – both because the administration was not entirely blind to human rights concerns or the support for them in Washington, and because the Carter administration had not been blind to the requirements of American security. In a 1978 internal memo about human rights policy under Carter, from Director of Policy Planning Anthony Lake to Secretary of State Cyrus Vance, Lake had asked, "Are We Being Consistent?" and had answered, "No. And we should not try to be completely so. There are times when security considerations, or broader political factors, lead us to be 'softer' on some countries' human rights performance than others."[59] So the differences between Carter and Reagan policy on the ground around the world were not black and white.

Reagan's support for the military regime in El Salvador, for example, was a continuation of Carter's policy rather than a contradiction or abandonment of it. As Hal Brands writes in his history of the latter years of the Cold War, "By the end of the Carter era, the U.S. posture was stiffening.... Carter's team laid the foundation for the Reagan Doctrine by initiating covert support for anticommunist movements and governments in countries such as Nicaragua [and] El Salvador."[60] Reagan's "infusion of emergency military aid to defeat a rebel 'final offensive' in early 1981" was, Brands notes, "building on an initiative from the last days of Carter's presidency."[61] In fact, in December 1980 when four American Catholic missionary women were raped and murdered in El Salvador by National Guardsmen, Carter nevertheless went forward with $5.9 million in military aid to the military regime there. Republicans were loathe to acknowledge this and Democrats to admit it, but Carter did not abandon all security considerations in the name of human rights, and Reagan's injection of security matters into human rights policy was not revolutionary.

But in 1981, it sometimes appeared so. After Ernie Lefever's nomination was defeated in early June 1981, the administration simply had no stated human rights policy. Neither the Department of State nor the White House was certain what to do. In the course of the summer many options were debated, including abolishing the human rights bureau entirely. That was impractical because Congress would need to agree to its abolition, but surely would not do so, and the fight over such a move would be terribly damaging to the administration. Perhaps the bureau could be combined with another one, others thought. But besides these bureaucratic issues, what would a Reagan human rights policy look like?

During that summer, Deputy Secretary of State William Clark approached me. We had only worked together for seven or eight months, but confidence between us had grown – which was important because Clark was one of the president's closest friends and advisers. Clark told me of the debate inside the administration about human rights policy and asked my advice. He thought that killing the bureau was nuts and was instead looking for a candidate to succeed Ernie. I was at the time Assistant Secretary of State for International Organization Affairs, meaning I was the man at Foggy Bottom handling the United Nations. And by the summer, only a few months in the job, I had already concluded that, while the rank was a great honor, the job was impossible. UN affairs were in truth handled by Jeane Kirkpatrick, who had cabinet rank and a close relationship with the president. She and Haig did not get along, and he saw every move she made as an effort to erode his prestige and authority as the "vicar" of American foreign policy (a term Haig himself had used). That left me caught between them, literally day after day, and it very quickly soured my relationship with Jeane and left me with minimal influence.

As I thought about Bill Clark's request, it seemed to me there was a great opportunity here – to escape the vise I was in, to be sure, but also to be of far greater value to the president. Working for Jackson and then Moynihan I had heard a lot and thought a lot about human rights and foreign policy. So after consultations with my wife, I went back to Clark and told him I had an obscure candidate in mind, whom I then described in extremely glowing terms. He got the joke quickly and asked if I were serious. I said yes. Clark said, "OK, write it up: tell me what a Reagan human rights policy should be like, and I'll show it to the president."

I then wrote what was later called the "Kennedy-Clark Memorandum," because Bill Clark and Undersecretary of State for Management Richard Kennedy enclosed my text in a memo dated October 26, 1981, that added their bureaucratic suggestions – including my selection for the position. Here is the text I wrote, with the original underscoring:

HUMAN RIGHTS POLICY

Overall Political Goals

Human rights is at the core of our foreign policy, because it is central to America's conception of itself. This nation did not "develop." It was created, with specific political purposes in mind. It is true that as much as America invented "human rights," conceptions of liberty invented America. It follows that "human rights" isn't something we add on to our foreign policy, but is its very purpose: the defense and promotion of liberty in the world. This is not merely a rhetorical point: We will never maintain wide public support for our foreign policy unless we can relate it to American ideals and to the defense of freedom. Congressional belief that we have no consistent human rights policy threatens to disrupt important foreign policy initiatives, such as aid to El Salvador. In fact, human rights has been one of the main directions of domestic attack on the administration's foreign policy.

East-West Relations and the Battle for Western Opinion

> "Americans don't fight and die for a second car or fancy refrigerator. They will fight for ideas, for the idea of freedom."
>
> Representative Millicent Fenwick

"Human Rights" meaning political rights and civil liberties gives us the best opportunity to convey what is ultimately at issue in our contest with the Soviet bloc. The fundamental difference between us is not in economic or social policy, but in our attitudes toward freedom. Our ability to-resist the Soviets around the world depends in part on our ability to draw this distinction and persuade others of it.

Neutralism in Europe or Japan, or a sagging of spirit here at home, results in part from fear of Soviet military might and fear that we do not or will not have the power to resist. But – particularly in the younger generation – its cause lies even more in relativism, in a refusal to acknowledge the distinctions between them. Why arm, and why fight, if the two superpowers are morally equal? Our human rights policy is at the center of our response, and its audience is not only at home but in Western Europe and Japan, and among electorates elsewhere. We must continue to draw that central distinction in international politics – between free nations and those that are not free. To fail at this will ultimately mean failure in staving off movement toward neutralism in many parts of the West. That is why a credible US policy in this area is so vitally important. Our new policy should convey a sense that US foreign policy as a whole is a positive force for freedom and decency in the long run.

Two-Track Policy

I recommend a two-track policy, positive as well as negative, to guide our rhetoric and our policy choices. On the positive side we should take the offensive:

– Expounding our beliefs and opposing the USSR in the UN, CSCE and other bodies;
– Hitting hard at abuses of freedom and decency by communist nations;
– Reinforcing international moral and legal standards whenever possible. (We can help by responding strongly to outrages against our citizens

and diplomats and by undertaking a serious program against terrorism.)

– Restoring our reputation as a reliable partner for our friends, so as to
maximize the influence of our quiet diplomacy.

On the <u>negative track, we must respond to serious abuses</u>. It is clear that
human rights is not the largest element in bilateral relations. It must be
balanced against US economic and security interests. It must take into
account the pressures a regime is under and the nature of its enemies.
We must be <u>honest</u> about this. We should not, if Pakistan or Argentina
is abridging freedom, say it is not; we should instead say (if it is) that it
<u>is</u> and that we regret it and oppose it. Then we can add that in the case
in question, terrorism or revolution or US security interests, or whatever,
are present and make a cutoff of aid or arms or relations a bad idea. We
should note the words the Hippocratic oath addresses to would-be inter-
venors, "First do no harm." It does not help human rights to replace a bad
regime with a worse one, or a corrupt dictator with a zealous Communist
politburo.

<u>We have to be prepared to pay a price</u>. In most <u>specific</u> cases taken
alone, the need for good bilateral relations will seem to outweigh our
broad concerns for freedom and decency. Nevertheless, it is a major error
to subordinate these considerations in each case – because <u>taken together</u>
these decisions will destroy our policy. They will therefore feed the view
that we don't care about violations of human rights and will undercut our
efforts to sway public opinion at home and abroad. <u>If we act as if offenses</u>
<u>against freedom don't matter in countries friendly to us, no one will take</u>
<u>seriously our words about Communist violations</u>, and few abroad will take
seriously our argument that our society (and our military effort) are dedicated to preserving freedom.

In practice this means that we must, in the MDBs,[62] abstain or vote
against friendly countries on human rights grounds if their conduct mer-
its it, although we should also motivate further improvement by voting
"yes" when there has been substantial progress. It also means that in highly
controversial areas such as crime control equipment, we should not issue
licenses in questionable cases. (While there will be exceptions, this is a
political rather than security issue: this equipment is readily available on

the market and those who need it can get it, so that our decision will not hurt other nations' security but can powerfully undercut our human rights policy.

Dealing with the Soviets

We must also be prepared to give human rights considerations serious weight in our dealings with the Soviet Union. The Soviets are a special case, for they are the major threat to liberty in the world. Human rights must be central to our assault on them, if we are to rally Americans and foreigners to resist Soviet blandishments or fight Soviet aggression. But to be seen as serious we must raise human rights issues in our discussions with the Soviets. In forums such as the UN, we must address issues such as abuse of psychiatry and restrictions on emigration. With Soviet or Soviet-sponsored invasions (in Afghanistan and Kampuchea) under attack in the UN, with Poles demanding political freedom, with Soviet CW [chemical weapons] violations coming to light, now is the time to press the issue of Soviet human rights violations.

A human rights policy means trouble, for it means hard choices which may adversely affect certain bilateral relations. At the very least, we will have to speak honestly about our friends' human rights violations and justify any decision that other considerations (economic, military, etc.) are determinative. There is no escaping this without destroying the policy, for otherwise what would be left is simply coddling friends and criticizing foes. Despite the costs of such a real human rights policy, it is worth doing and indeed it is essential. We need not only a military response to the Soviets, which can reassure European and Asian allies and various friends around the world. We also need an ideological response, which reminds our citizens and theirs what the game is all about and why it is worth the effort. We aren't struggling for oil or wheat or territory but for political liberty. The goal of human rights policy is to improve human rights performance whenever we sensibly can; and to demonstrate, by acting to defend liberty and speaking honestly about its enemies, that the difference between East and Went is the crucial political distinction of our times.

It seems that Clark and whoever else made the decision – perhaps the president – liked the memo, and I took the job. I was sworn in as

Assistant Secretary of State for Human Rights and Humanitarian Affairs on Human Rights Day, December 10, 1981.

The memo was in many ways a summary of neocon foreign policy as it then stood – the policy Jackson and Moynihan had been developing over the previous decade. It declared immediately that "human rights is at the core of our foreign policy" because of the nature of American society, history, and politics. Taking on skeptics (and I knew Haig to be one), it argued that a human rights policy was a critical tool in our struggle against both Soviet imperialism and European-style neutralism, and moreover that we would never attain public support for our foreign policy if it lacked this central component. So the argument was both pragmatic and ideological.

But I wanted to be clear that "a human rights policy means trouble" and that criticism of friendly despots was essential. Whatever errors Carter had made in directing his fire against them and despite our belief in the totalitarian-authoritarian distinction, none of that meant either silence or pulling too many punches: doing either would "destroy our policy." I also wanted to be clear that human rights policy could not be corralled off for use against small and weak countries; it needed to be central in our policy toward the Soviets too. This was of course pure Jackson, an effort to be sure there would be no temptation to undermine or abandon the Jackson Amendment or more generally our ideological struggle with the Soviets. Jackson's biographer was later to write, "Under the guidance of Assistant Secretary of State Elliott Abrams, the Reagan administration eventually pursued a human rights policy such as Jackson had originally envisaged and articulated in the 1970s."[63] But in January 1982 we were just beginning the effort to articulate a new Reagan human rights policy, and this memo was a first step.

I did not know what Haig would make of all this, but I thought Reagan would agree with it. So it seemed, for the moment at least. An argument that combined practical politics, love of America's unique past and unique role in the world, and fierce anti-Communism would be right up his alley; it was what had made me a Reaganite and had gotten me to campaign for him as part of "Democrats for Reagan." Now the task was to see if that memo could be turned into an actual policy.

At the State Department, each year's *Country Reports on Human Rights Practices* book began with an introduction. Drafting the text with one of my deputy assistant secretaries, Charles Fairbanks, we wrote the introduction to the volume covering 1981, which was released in early 1982.[64] There we repeated some of the themes from my memo and broached some new ones. It would have been too much to say we were explaining Reagan human rights policy; more accurately, we were partly explaining and defending existing policy, and partly arguing for what we hoped would *become* policy. The 1981 introduction noted and criticized the "double standard" in international fora "which focuses solely on certain countries, almost ignoring the violations of human rights in Communist lands." This was carrying forward the contribution of Pat Moynihan when he was envoy to the UN. We then noted some fundamental problems of modern human rights policy:

> [I]t aims at affecting the domestic behavior of other countries, while governments are reluctant to alter their nation's political system for foreign policy reasons. The leverage that the United States does have is strongest in friendly countries, where we have more access and influence. Such influence is an important resource in pursuing human rights, but its concentration in friendly countries creates a danger: human rights policy might highlight and punish human rights violations in friendly countries, while giving unfriendly countries immunity...a nation that came to display a general pattern of undermining or estranging friendly governments would obviously limit its future influence over them, including its influence over their human rights behavior. This is a second problem of human rights – the need to avoid pressing only where our influence is greatest rather than where the abuses are greatest.

This was, we hoped, a way of criticizing Carter's policy without attacking the intentions of the Carter-era officials. We then turned to another key criticism of the former president's policy: that it had focused on individual abuses rather than systemic change. We argued for setting our goals higher:

> There is a danger that human rights policy will become like the labor of Sisyphus because it deals only with effects and not with their causes. To take

an example, it is important not only to free political prisoners but also to encourage conditions in which new political prisoners are not taken .... It would narrow the range of action of our human rights policy excessively to limit it to responding to individual violations of human rights when they appear. This "reactive" aspect of human rights policy is essential. But it must be accompanied by a second track of positive policy with a bolder long-term aim: to assist in the gradual emergence of free political systems. It is in such systems that we most realistically expect the observance of human rights across the board.

We noted the various tools that a human rights policy can use, publicly and privately, and wrote that we should be guided by the "criterion of effectiveness." We then argued that human rights must be a key element of American foreign policy, that American power is a key asset of global human rights, that both the Soviet bloc and friendly countries must be criticized fairly, and finally that a consistent policy is both necessary and – to use that word again – trouble:

> This Administration believes that human rights is an issue of central impor-
> tance both to relieve suffering and injustice and to link foreign policy with
> the traditions of the American people .... The strength and prestige of
> the most powerful democratic nation is inevitably important for human
> rights .... A consistent and serious policy for human rights in the world
> must counter the USSR politically and bring Soviet bloc human rights vio-
> lations to the attention of the world over and over again.
>
> At the same time, the United States must continue to respond to serious
> human rights problems in friendly countries. U.S. human rights policy will
> not pursue a policy of selective indignation.
>
> [H]uman rights policy will sometimes be very troubling. We will some-
> times be forced to make hard choices between the need to answer human
> rights violations and other foreign policy interests, such as trade or secu-
> rity. In some cases we will have to accept the fact that bilateral relations with
> a friendly country may be damaged because of our human rights concern.
> This is an unavoidable price of a consistent policy.

Everything stated in that introduction to the 1981 *Country Reports* volume, which ran to ten pages, was consistent with the views expressed in my memo, but this was not a private document setting out my personal view: it was a publication of the Department of State ostensibly explaining the actual policy of the Reagan administration. It would go too far to say that by early 1982 the battle to introduce such a policy had been won, but soon there came real proof that the president agreed with these views and would push them forward. On June 8, 1982, President Reagan addressed the British Parliament and embraced the need for a human rights policy and for promotion of systemic change:

> No, democracy is not a fragile flower. Still it needs cultivating. If the rest of this century is to witness the gradual growth of freedom and democratic ideals, we must take actions to assist the campaign for democracy.
>
> While we must be cautious about forcing the pace of change, we must not hesitate to declare our ultimate objectives and to take concrete actions to move toward them. We must be staunch in our conviction that freedom is not the sole prerogative of a lucky few, but the inalienable and universal right of all human beings. So states the United Nations Universal Declaration of Human Rights, which, among other things, guarantees free elections.
>
> The objective I propose is quite simple to state: to foster the infrastructure of democracy, the system of a free press, unions, political parties, universities, which allows a people to choose their own way to develop their own culture, to reconcile their own differences through peaceful means.
>
> We in America now intend to take additional steps, as many of our allies have already done, toward realizing this same goal. The chairmen and other leaders of the national Republican and Democratic Party organizations are initiating a study with the bipartisan American political foundation to determine how the United States can best contribute as a nation to the global campaign for democracy now gathering force. They will have the cooperation of congressional leaders of both parties, along with representatives of business, labor, and other major institutions in our society. I look forward to receiving their recommendations and to working with these institutions and the Congress in the common task of strengthening democracy throughout the world.
>
> It is time that we committed ourselves as a nation – in both the pubic and private sectors – to assisting democratic development.[65]

I had had almost nothing to do with the drafting of this speech, which was great news: it meant that elsewhere in the administration and indeed at its top the same thoughts about democracy and human rights were shared. Here Reagan was not only making this a central element of his foreign policy but he was also adopting the view that systemic change toward democracy was the key. This speech led to the creation in 1983 of the National Endowment for Democracy (on whose board I now serve) to achieve precisely these goals, as well as the creation of four related institutes – what are now called the Solidarity Center and the Center for International Private Enterprise to represent labor and business, and the two party organizations, the International Republican Institute and the National Democratic Institute.

The reaction to the new Reagan policy on the Left and among human rights groups was pretty sour: one analyst wrote that "many human rights activists were traumatized to see a human rights policy, which was barely institutionalized by the late 1970s, being hijacked by the conservative camp of President Ronald Reagan under the label of 'democratization.'"[66] An article in *Foreign Affairs* explained the critique more carefully: "the civil libertarians who dominate the leading human rights monitoring groups also felt the focus on democracy was a way of evading many of the human rights concerns that had prevailed in international forums and in the Carter years: by emphasizing political rights and democratic institutions, it was felt, the Reagan Administration has effectively downplayed more fundamental rights associated with what is called 'the integrity of the person' – the right not to be killed, tortured or imprisoned at will."[67]

Moreover, the human rights organizations were offended when we began reporting on human rights violations by the guerrilla groups that were often fighting governments aligned with the United States. As Charles Fairbanks and I wrote in the introduction to the 1982 edition of *Country Reports on Human Rights Practices*, published in February 1983, "It is important for the comprehensiveness of these reports that they include significant violations not only by the government but also by opposition or insurgent groups, including terrorists. An attempt has been made to portray the wider context of the human rights situation, including threats from hostile powers of guerrilla insurgencies. Such pressures on a government or society do not excuse human rights violations, but an awareness of them is vital to a full understanding of the human rights situation."[68] To most of the human rights groups, this – like our commitment to democracy – was just another evasion and another way to criticize leftist groups while reducing criticism of right-wing governments. We did not agree, but our practice was a bone of contention.

In any event these "traumas" for human rights activists led to insistent, repeated attacks on Reagan administration policy (and on me), and while some criticism was no doubt fully justified, much of it seemed to us political: left against right. Moreover, we were being hit for doing some of the same things Carter had done: taking into account not only human rights matters but also American security and economic interests. We were not entirely consistent, but as Tony Lake had written to Vance, complete consistency was impossible.

Within the State Department I found myself in a series of fights after taking over the Human Rights Bureau in December 1981. The Bureau itself was at that point the State Department's weakest one. It is always the case that the geographical bureaus – Latin America, Europe, Asia, and so on – are the real "dukedoms," the real powerhouses. They are the contacts with and, to some extent, in control of our embassies around the world, and their influence over assignments to those embassies (and promotions within them) means that Foreign Service Officers wanted to be in those geographic bureaus. But the Human Rights Bureau was in real trouble even when compared with other "functional" bureaus such as economics, narcotics, and, for that matter, the International Organizations Bureau I had just left (against the advice of many friends and colleagues). Many bureaus had hundreds of employees; we had about thirty.

Moreover, it was difficult to recruit first-rate people for the bureau. There were many reasons for this: it was a very small shop, its future had been in doubt, it had been without a leader for nearly a year, functional bureaus always have more trouble recruiting staff, and we had little clout on the seventh floor, the area of the department where the top officials worked. But it was also, I thought, due in part to my predecessor Pat Derian's style of leadership. She seemed to me to believe that she was fighting not only human rights abuses but also every other bureau in the Department of State. Top-flight Foreign Service Officers would not sign up to be put in combat with the regional bureaus that would determine whether they got the future assignments they sought. And that combative approach seemed to me doomed anyway, so I tried a different one. As one critic of Reagan policy later wrote, "Not for him Derian's exhausting guerrilla warfare with the ARA [Latin America] regional bureau over arms sales."[69] It was better, I thought, to make common cause with the regional bureaus when possible and, when it was not, to use arguments they would have to respect even if they did not like them. For example, lectures about human rights would not make converts, but I recall winning an argument regarding Guatemala by pointing out that a particular arms sale would never get through; it would be blocked on the Hill, and pushing it was foolish because we would just end up being defeated, and looking bad, after a lot of wasted effort. So the choice, I argued, was not between selling arms and not selling arms, but between saying no, and claiming the high ground, or saying yes, losing anyway, and seeming indifferent to human rights. Easy choice, I said – and though the argument was not made at the level of high principle, it was important that the Human Rights Bureau win a few.

These were the only arguments that could succeed at that point because the regional bureaus did not have to listen to me. If we disagreed, my only recourse was to go upstairs and try to take the argument to Secretary Haig. My problem was that I never had the impression I would win if I did so – nor did anyone in the regional bureaus.

But on July 16, 1982 a new Secretary of State arrived, George P. Shultz. We had never met before he arrived at State, but it became instantly clear to me, and to everyone else in the building, that he cared about human rights. A couple of months later he attended a conference on democratization of Communist countries, at which he said, "Support for democracy is not simply a policy of the American government. It is basic to our history and world view."[70] This was music to my ears, and over the next six-and-a-half years he proved that he meant it.

At my first meeting with him I told him about the shabby physical condition and cramped quarters of my bureau, and to everyone's surprise he came down for a visit. To see the new secretary in our bureau did wonders for morale, and he soon took steps to improve our physical situation. Word of all this quickly spread in the building, and all of a sudden we were on the map bureaucratically. Now the regional bureaus had to start bargaining with me, because they knew that if a dispute were elevated to the secretary, he just might rule for the Human Rights bureau.

Shultz had a Reaganite, not Carterite, view of human rights policy and seemed entirely comfortable with my 1981 memo and Reagan's 1982 speech to Parliament. What is so striking now about the dichotomy between the Carter approach and the Reagan/Shultz policy, in my view, is that many of the key elements reappeared in the differences between George W. Bush's and Barack Obama's human rights policies. Bush's views were almost indistinguishable from Reagan/Shultz policy, and Obama's approach to human rights was reminiscent of that taken by Carter. Almost all the arguments of the 1970s and 1980s returned in the period from 2001 to 2017, as we shall see. Shultz did not see human rights policy as an occasional add-on to American foreign policy but as a central theme and goal. He did not see it as a form of foreign aid meant to compensate for various crimes committed by the United States in the past, a kind of apology for American history. He saw the advance of human rights as tied to the growth and use of American power, rather than as a way to limit American power, and did not shy away from interventions that could advance the cause because we had to "get out of that business." He believed in promoting systemic change, not individual interventions that became "casework." He believed our policy had to focus on helping the people who lived under tyranny, not the regimes that oppressed them. He was a pragmatist – an ex-Marine, an economist, a former labor negotiator, a former head of the Office of Management and Budget and of the Treasury and Labor Departments – but that pragmatism was harnessed to a deep and principled belief that American power was the greatest force for good in world politics and should be used to advance the cause of freedom.

Shultz's role is worth stressing, for he had enormous influence on President Reagan and led him to overcome his doubts and even his prejudices in numerous cases. In El Salvador, a policy (begun under Carter in 1980) of preventing a Communist victory became a highly interventionist push for democratization. "Democracy is what we want" in El Salvador, Reagan told the National Association of Manufacturers in 1983.[71] To get it, we were willing to use enormous pressure on the Salvadoran military and to back the Christian Democratic Party and its candidate for president, Jose Napoleon Duarte. As Shultz put it in his memoirs,

> The death squads and other violations of human rights were intolerable, and with pressure from the United States and from the president himself, progress was being made in correcting these problems. In December 1983, Vice President Bush came down hard on human rights abuses during a visit to El Salvador: U.S. support absolutely would not continue unless El Salvador dealt decisively with this problem. I pounded on this same necessity in visits to El Salvador and in sessions with its leaders visiting Washington.[72]

That pressure meant working with elements of the military, for which we were often abused by human rights groups: how could we be assisting a military that contained vicious "death squads?" Of course, these groups had not been so critical when Carter increased U.S. military aid to El Salvador in 1979 and 1980 with no push for democratization, but in any event we did not blush at those relationships. We believed that a failure of U.S. policy meant an FMLN takeover and the end of any hope for human rights and democracy in El Salvador.

As Assistant Secretary for Human Rights and later Assistant Secretary for Inter-American Affairs, I worked hard to advance our El Salvador policy. When I traveled to San Salvador, I met with heads of its various military and police organizations – some of whom were complicit in awful crimes and simply lied about their roles. I recall a long meeting with the head of the Treasury Police, one of the worst abusers of human rights, where I told him that none of his policemen were ever punished for such conduct. "Oh, they are," he replied, so I responded that we never saw any reports of this punishment. What are the numbers – how many cases? I could see the lightbulb go on over his head: "the Americans want numbers, so I will just have to give them some. Won't be hard; we can make them up tonight." But over time the intense American pressure worked: death squad killings came down by 90 percent, and Duarte won wide support at home and in the United States.

I testified in Congress many times about El Salvador, and we found substantial support for Duarte, and our policy, among Democrats (partly because of the AFL-CIO's strong backing for him). My main argument was simple: that abandoning El Salvador to the FMLN, backed by Cuba, Russia, and Nicaragua, could not possibly advance the cause of human rights.

That approach, promoting democracy to prevent Communist victory, meant different things in different cases: as the historian Hal Brands puts it, "If the United States pursued democracy via reform and stabilization in El Salvador, it . . . sought democratization through coercion and destabilization in Nicaragua." Brands is also correct in writing that the "anti-Sandinista campaign fused Reagan's pro-democracy sentiments to his anti-communism."[73] Despite the spectacular controversy that attended our policy in Nicaragua, we did not see the moral issue as a complicated one: we were trying to stop a pro-Soviet Marxist group from consolidating power it would then use not only to create a dictatorship at home but also to destabilize its neighbors so as to install similar regimes throughout the region. Allowing the Soviets to expand from their colony in Cuba to establish a foothold on the mainland of North America was unacceptable from a national security viewpoint – and also from a human rights standpoint. Again, anti-Communist ideology, national security, and human rights policy coincided.

The same was true throughout Latin America, where Reagan policy turned against the old dictator, Alfredo Stroessner, in Paraguay, and against the military juntas throughout the region. On dozens of occasions in countries such as Peru, Argentina, and Bolivia, we intervened to stop coups before they started –out of both a commitment to democratic change and the conviction that only the Communists would ultimately benefit from military repression.

In Haiti in 1985 we successfully pressed Jean-Claude "Baby Doc" Duvalier, inheritor of his father's vicious dictatorship, to leave power and to leave Haiti. I was newly installed in the Bureau of Inter-American Affairs then, when a representative of Duvalier came to see me. Opposition to Duvalier was spreading; what did we want of him? We want him to leave, I replied, and Shultz soon said precisely that on television. We wanted Haiti to move on from the Duvaliers toward democracy. Such was Reagan's influence at that point that "Baby Doc" did not resist: Duvalier's only request was that the United States get him to the airport and pull him out on an American plane, so that he could go into exile in one piece. The Haiti case had little impact in Latin America, but was, for us, another step toward ridding the entire hemisphere of dictators.

To take one case that was a success story and had interesting ideological implications, the administration was extremely active in Chile against the Pinochet regime, despite internal strife over Chile policy. Secretary Shultz knew many of the Pinochet regime's extremely successful economic officials, having taught these "Chicago Boys" as a professor at the University of Chicago, and both he and the president greatly admired their policy successes. But that did not stop Shultz from tightening the pressure on them, including through opposing or conditioning loans from international financial institutions. And in the end, we pressed hard to force Pinochet to hold a 1988 plebiscite on his rule that he lost – and then intervened again to prevent him from declaring martial law and dismissing the results of that election.[74] One student of the period, Hal Brands, argues, "Reagan's policy evolved so much that it became almost unrecognizable."[75]

But there was considerable opposition to this policy, externally from Henry Kissinger, Jeane Kirkpatrick (who had left the administration in 1985), and other critics, and internally from CIA director William Casey and the staff of the National Security Council (NSC). An NSC internal memo to National Security Adviser John Poindexter, dated November 1986, complained that "the focus of our Chile policy for about the last year has been against Pinochet and becoming the champions of the democratic opposition," said this was the wrong approach, and concluded that "our policy needs to move in a different direction."[76] These critics influenced Reagan's view, and opposing Pinochet did not come at all easily to him: he admired Pinochet's anti-Communism and his free-market economic reforms. At a key National Security Council meeting on November 18, 1986, he said that Pinochet had "saved his country" and suggested inviting him to Washington for a state visit. Shultz immediately rejected that idea with horror, saying, "No way; his hands are covered with blood." Shultz then went on to reject softer diplomatic approaches and said, "I don't think we can just try persuasion. We have to use some muscle or he won't change."[77]

Some of the critics of the tougher line against Pinochet argued about tactics, but more fundamentally the issue was the totalitarian-authoritarian distinction: were we repeating Carter's errors in Nicaragua and Iran, and would we see a friendly dictator replaced by an unfriendly and even more repressive leftist regime? My answer was no, and not only because regimes like those of Pinochet and Stroessner would ultimately radicalize the opposition to their crimes and strengthen the extreme Left. The totalitarian-authoritarian distinction suggested that we had to tolerate authoritarians if and when the alternative was worse, but in Chile in the 1980s it was not worse: it was far better. It was a Christian Democratic Party electoral victory followed by democratic government, and indeed in Reagan's second term, when I was Assistant Secretary of State for Inter-American Affairs, all the major Christian Democratic Party and Socialist Party leaders passed through my office – and I introduced a number of them to Shultz.

I agreed fully in theory that geopolitical and human rights concerns were intertwined, as Jeane had argued. I was quoted in a 1986 *Foreign Affairs* article on Reagan policy saying that "it is not enough to ask who is in power and what is he like. We also have to ask what is the alternative, what are the likely prospects for improvement," and "we do not betray the cause of human rights when we make prudential judgments about what can and can't be done in one place at one time."[78] But those were arguments, not excuses: when the facts justified acting to replace a repressive regime with a more democratic one, I felt we should act – and I argued forcefully for action.

The policy I was urging, and Secretary Shultz was supporting, was attacked from both the Left and the Right. On the Right we were accused of naivete and of repeating all Carter's dangerous mistakes; on the Left, of making human rights a handmaiden to strategic concerns. To the Right's critique the reply was factual: if our ideological "line" was correct, it had to be applied in real-world cases – and we knew which were the appropriate cases. To the Left the reply was more ideological. While that article in *Foreign Affairs* described the human rights groups as having "a more idealistic view – that human rights should be based on strictly humanitarian concerns" – we did not see that position as "more idealistic," but simply as absurd and unrealistic, and likely to produce setbacks for human rights – in the name of advancing human rights.[79] I would repeat my argument that a government is not an NGO and almost *never* acts out of strictly humanitarian concerns. To ignore the context of actions and their likely impact, as I often felt the human rights groups were doing, was either leftist politics masquerading as idealism, or it was idealism unlinked to any realistic notion of how the world works.

In the Chile case, we did help "destabilize" a friendly regime – because we believed the alternatives were far better, and we were correct. Chile has enjoyed democratic government steadily since the day Pinochet lost power. The refusal of conservative critics of our policy to acknowledge this – in the late 1980s and later – suggests that their interpretation of the totalitarian-authoritarian distinction veered off into simple support for friendly right-wing regimes. The standard of proof they seemed to demand for opposing such regimes – some kind of absolute assurance that a successor government would be equally pro-American and more democratic forever – could never be met in international politics. Thus they would have left us with a declaratory human rights policy that could not be applied in any real-world cases. No doubt they were right to worry, at the height of the Cold War, about the outcome of regime change, and we saw the same worries affect American policy when it came, for example, to the Mubarak regime in Egypt in 2012: when a friendly dictator was challenged by massive demonstrations, the Obama administration took the same position that Kissinger had suggested regarding Chile a quarter-century earlier. It was "better the devil you know" than the risk of change. Once again, the human rights policy debates of the 1980s illuminated policy choices decades later.

But Reagan human rights policy did not apply only to Latin America. A similar evolution of policy took place regarding South Korea and the Philippines. As is described later in Chapter 4, the administration used a sophisticated combination of public and private pressures and mechanisms to persuade South Korea's military ruler, Chun Doo Hwan, to allow a free election and to leave power. As to the Philippines, in 1982 Reagan hosted the dictator Ferdinand Marcos for a state visit and expressed considerable sympathy and support for him. The policy shift began in 1983, and it reflected both events in that country – such as the 1983 murder of opposition leader Benigno Aquino – and personnel changes in Washington, including Shultz's arrival and the appointment of Paul Wolfowitz as Assistant Secretary of State for East Asia. Paul and I were friends and colleagues, and on the day of his appointment I called to congratulate him and to ask, "How are we going to get rid of Marcos?"

That policy shift came hard to the president, and in many ways he remained committed to the fundamental argument of Jeane's famous article. In the 1984 presidential debates, he responded to a question about human rights policy by asking whether with the downfall of the shah, "Have things gotten better?" The alternative to right-wing dictators, he suggested in response to a question about Nicaragua, was likely worse:

> [M]any times – and this has to do with the Philippines, also, I know there are things there in the Philippines that do not look good to us from the standpoint right now of democratic rights, but what is the alternative? It is a large Communist movement to take over the Philippines. They have been our friend since their inception as a nation. And I think that we've had enough of a record of letting – under the guise of revolution – someone that we thought was a little more right than we would be, letting that person go, and then winding up with totalitarianism, pure and simple, as the alternative. And I think that we're better off, for example with the Philippines, of trying to retain our friendship and help them right the wrongs we see, rather than throwing them to the wolves and then facing a Communist power in the Pacific.[80]

That was the president's visceral reaction in almost every case, and it took hard evidence, plus strong arguments primarily from Secretary Shultz, to persuade him in case after case that, in fact, we and the people of the country would be far better off as soon as the dictator was removed. By 1985, he was persuaded in the case of the Philippines, and the administration undertook an orchestrated campaign to remove Marcos. Here again Reagan and Shultz used a combination of pressures, including a visit there from the president's close friend Sen. Paul Laxalt and direct communications from Reagan to Marcos. In February 1986 a presidential directive called for a transition there, and Laxalt called Marcos to say the United States wanted him "to cut and cut cleanly" and to offer him exile in the United States.

Success bred confidence that our policy was right in Latin America and in East Asia as well: "within the Reagan administration, the experience of East Asia during the 1980s vindicated the key ideas behind the growing emphasis on democracy promotion in U.S. foreign policy."[81] We used every weapon in the arsenal – from military invasion (in Grenada in 1983) and military pressure (against the Sandinistas in Nicaragua, via the Contras); to diplomatic pressure through private and public communications; economic pressure through granting, conditioning, or withholding of foreign aid and loans from international financial institutions; and coordination with other governments willing and able to join in the effort to promote democracy. By 1988 even the hostile *New York Times* wrote in an editorial titled "Mr. Reagan's Human Rights Conversion" that we had "made useful trouble with 'friendly' dictators."[82]

Reagan remained staunchly anti-Communist, as indeed we all were, and that led to extremely active opposition to the Soviet Union and its satellites. As an example, we pushed Romania hard to permit an increase in emigration, using the Jackson Amendment – which applied to all non-market economy countries – to force concessions. I visited Bucharest in 1983 to discuss these issues and to hold a "human rights dialogue" with the regime, a useless gesture, and when I returned I stated on Radio Free Europe that the Ceausescu regime was "an extremely oppressive Communist dictatorship" with a "deplorable, terrible" human rights record.[83] While the regime objected to those comments, I heard no criticism from within the administration for the use of such rhetoric.

Secretary Shultz's role was central when it came to the Soviet Union and other Communist nations as well. It would have been easy to disinter the old argument that, in the Soviet case, human rights issues simply had to give way to national security concerns. Shultz took the contrary view – that the importance of the bilateral relationship meant human rights concerns were especially vital. In meetings with the Soviets, as he wrote in his memoirs, "I pounded on the subject at every opportunity."[84] That was quite accurate. While every secretary of state makes a couple of good speeches about human rights, those are often throwaway lines even if accompanied by a small program or a gesture or two. Not for Shultz.

He believed that "human rights had to be on the top of our agenda" because "only when the Soviets changed human rights practices and recognized the importance of these rights to their own society could Soviet-American relations change at the deepest level." So when he met with Soviet foreign minister Eduard Shevardnadze, he recalled, "I raised the issue of human rights first."[85] It was the first subject for Shultz, not an add-on late in any meeting or simply a box to be checked – which was something the Soviets obviously noticed. Similarly, it was typical of Shultz to include in a visit to Moscow in April 1987 a Passover seder at the U.S. ambassador's residence for prominent Soviet Jewish "refuseniks." He reassured them, telling them, "You are on our minds; you are in our hearts. We never give up, we never stop trying" to help you, "but never give up, never give up" – and meeting them affected him: "I came away inspired by the courage and the strength of spirit of these men and women."[86]

There was a very large program of support for Poland's emerging democratic forces after the declaration of martial law in December 1981, including cash support for the Solidarity movement and close collaboration with the Vatican. Reagan's rhetoric was unwaveringly tough, and in his famous 1983 speech to the National Association of Evangelicals, he called the Soviet Union an "evil empire," said "communism is another sad, bizarre chapter in human history whose last pages even now are being written," and termed it "the focus of evil in the modern world."[87] In 1987, in one of his greatest speeches, he told Berliners at the Brandenburg Gate of a challenge to the new Soviet leader: "Come here to this gate! Mr. Gorbachev, open this gate! Mr. Gorbachev, tear down this wall!" He assured them, "Yes, across Europe, this wall will fall. For it cannot withstand faith; it cannot withstand truth. The wall cannot withstand freedom."[88]

What is notable about such remarks is their reach. He did not just call for improved respect for human rights nor merely for increased cooperation and less Cold War tension. His denunciations were fierce and ideological with no holds barred, and his goals were transformative: the end of the Cold War and the demise of Soviet Communism. Here again we see the dramatic differences between what I would call the Reagan and George W. Bush approach, which was transformation of "evil" states into democracies through the unapologetic use of American power and influence, and the Carter and Obama approach, where human rights goals were far more limited and in fact appeared to be the product of a desire to limit American power and its use abroad – and to remedy and rectify past errors of U.S. foreign policy.

When Reagan left office, it is fair to say there was an ambitious American human rights policy aimed at spreading democracy. It viewed the Soviet empire as the worst enemy of human rights, saw friendly authoritarian regimes as good targets for American pressure, and considered U.S. power the critical element in the expansion of democracy in the world.

Because I did not participate in the George H. W. Bush or Bill Clinton administrations, this introduction will not examine their human rights policies in any depth. For me and for others who wanted the United States to promote the expansion of democracy and respect for human rights, the question was whether the Jackson/Reagan/Shultz policies would be followed once Reagan was out of office.

The George H. W. Bush period, only four years, was marked above all by the collapse of the Soviet Union – a giant and historic gain for human rights in the world, which permitted the spread of democracy to the three Baltic and to many Eastern and Central European nations. Bush did not, however, much celebrate this expansion of freedom: when the Berlin Wall fell in 1989 he said, "I'm very pleased," and left it at that; when asked why he did not say more about the collapse of what had surely been an "evil empire," he replied, "I am not an emotional kind of guy."[89] The soaring rhetoric about freedom was a thing of the past. The same *realpolitik* approach was visible in 1991 when Bush visited Kiev, the capital of Ukraine, just months before it would have a referendum on withdrawing from the Soviet Union. In his speech he warned of "suicidal nationalism," disappointing not only Ukrainian nationalists but also many other critics who saw it is an unrealistic form of *realpolitik* not to acknowledge that Ukraine would inevitably seek independence.

This was a return to the Nixon/Ford/Kissinger policy of *realpolitik*. Bush's invasion of Panama in 1989 was reminiscent of Reagan's invasion of Grenada in that it left behind a working democracy that (however imperfect) continues to this day. The invasion of Iraq in 1991, however, left behind the same dictator and the same vicious system of human rights abuses; this was a victory for *realpolitik* rather than human rights policy or the spread of democracy. The Westphalian state system was defended: cross-border invasions to seize land, or an entire country, were not tolerable, but any amount of mass murder inside the borders of a state apparently was. The goal of the war was removing Saddam Hussein's forces from Kuwait – period. Similarly, when fighting broke out in the former Yugoslavia in 1992, Secretary of State Baker coldly declared that the United States "had no dog in this fight."[90]

The administration's reaction to the massacre in Tienanmen Square in 1989 was intellectually consistent with its Iraq and Balkans policy: pure *realpolitik* without a significant human rights element. Just weeks after tanks crushed demonstrators, Bush sent National Security Advisor Brent Scowcroft and Under Secretary of State Lawrence Eagleburger to Beijing to smooth relations, and State Department talking points for that trip refer to the massacre as "an internal affair."[91]

As the brief summary of the George H. W. Bush foreign affairs record by the University of Virginia's Miller Center says, "Realists complained that it was hard to justify U.S. involvement in situations without a clear national interest. But others felt that once the Cold War ended, the United States had to take on a large role as a world leader to guard against human rights abuses, defend democratic regimes, and lead humanitarian efforts."[92] That is a fair statement of the change from Reagan to Bush: the president and his closest advisers, Secretary of State Baker and National Security Adviser Scowcroft, were indeed realists; not just the rhetoric but also the entire approach of the Reagan years – growing out of the fusion of the Jackson and neocon policies with the anti-Communism of the conservative movement – were out. The collapse of the Soviet Union meant that neither the doctrine of containment nor Reagan's moral and strategic objective of winning the Cold War would any longer be a guide to American foreign policy. What should replace it? The administration, of course, favored in principle the expansion of democracy, but the sense that it should be at the core of foreign policy was gone, replaced by a more pragmatic desire to manage events in what was admittedly a very fast-changing international system.

The first fully post–Cold War presidency was that of Bill Clinton, and it necessarily grappled with the same questions. Did the Soviet collapse mean there could (and should) be far *less* American activism on behalf of human rights and democracy, because the Soviet threat to them was diminished, or far *more*, because the opportunities were greater – and because the threat that some American action would evoke a Soviet response was gone?

Clinton was writing on a newly blank slate, and his rhetoric was soaring. "No national security issue is more urgent than securing democracy's triumph around the world," Clinton said during the 1992 campaign – as part of his criticism of the Bush administration's apparent indifference to human rights matters and particularly of its inaction when the collapse of Yugoslavia after 1991 led to mass violence.[93] In campaign speeches he said President Bush "seems too often to prefer a foreign policy that embraces stability at the expense of freedom" and attacked what he called Bush's "ambivalence about supporting democracy."[94]

In Clinton's first inaugural address, in 1993, he said, "When our vital interests are challenged or the will and conscience of the international community is defied, we will act, with peaceful diplomacy whenever possible, with force when necessary." To use American military power when the "conscience of the international community" – whatever that means – is "defied," another ambiguous term, was biting off a lot to chew. As Susan Woodward writes, "The end of the Cold War meant the end of restrictions on the use of American military power.... The restraint or excuse not to act that came from the threat of Soviet response was gone.... The international role of the United States also changed, from defender of the free world and its principles to an unlimited guardian of global order and morality."[95] That formulation goes too far, but the later reach of George W. Bush's rhetoric about American support for the expansion of democracy was criticized on precisely these grounds: that, like Clinton's campaign and inaugural rhetoric, it included no inherent limits.

But, of course, there were limits, and a good example is Clinton's 1994 decision to renew most-favored-nation tariff status for China, despite the human rights abuses there. Clinton had supported linking trade benefits to China's human rights record when he was campaigning for president, but now saw strategic and economic reasons to drop the link. As was true of his predecessors and his successors, his rhetoric may have suggested the universal and limitless priority of human rights matters, but this was not his actual policy.

The most significant part of the Clinton record was the story of military intervention (and the failure to intervene). To be sure, the expansion of NATO and the European Union meant that the frontiers of freedom were also expanding, and the political tests imposed on would-be members emerging from the Soviet empire were powerful inducements to move toward democracy. But the new development in the Clinton years was what came to be called "humanitarian intervention" to prevent mass murder, rather than the sort of democracy promotion Reagan had championed. Two signal events, the Rwandan genocide in 1994 and the Srebenica massacre in 1995, led to a growing consensus that intervention to avoid mass killing was morally obligatory and overrode traditional Westphalian notions of the inviolability of state sovereignty. In 2005 this consensus led finally to the adoption by the UN General Assembly of the doctrine called "R2P" or "Responsibility to Protect." The key paragraph in the 2005 World Summit's Outcome Document reads,

> Each individual State has the responsibility to protect its populations from genocide, war crimes, ethnic cleansing and crimes against humanity.... The international community, through the United Nations, also has the responsibility to use appropriate diplomatic, humanitarian and other peaceful means, in accordance with Chapters VI and VIII of the Charter, to help protect populations from genocide, war crimes, ethnic cleansing and crimes against humanity. In this context, we are prepared to take collective action, in a timely and decisive manner, through the Security Council, in accordance with the Charter, including Chapter VII, on a case-by-case basis and in cooperation with relevant regional organizations as appropriate, should peaceful means be inadequate and national authorities manifestly fail to protect their populations from genocide, war crimes, ethnic cleansing and crimes against humanity.[96]

Translated from UN language to English, military action against a regime attacking or failing to protect its own populace was possible and could be morally required.

In Rwanda in April 1994, the mass murder of Tutsis began, and an estimated 800,000 were soon killed (and two million turned into refugees). The United States did not act and indeed refused to call the mass murder "genocide," which it clearly was.[97] A decade later Clinton said "his inaction in Rwanda was the worst foreign-policy mistake of his Administration," and he told a reporter, "It is inexplicable to me looking back, but...we just blew it. I blew it. I just, I feel terrible about it."[98] R2P was in substantial measure the world's reaction to Rwanda.

Of less significance to U.S. foreign policy, and to the administration, was Sudan. There, the Muslim Arab regime in Khartoum carried on a long policy (beginning in 1983) of forced Islamization and of oppression in the south of the country, which was Christian and African, not Arab. Over time millions of Sudanese were displaced or died as a result of this civil war. The United States did not intervene, but the issue led to formation of a novel human rights alliance: As Alan Hertzke wrote, "Sometimes miscast as a parochial cause of the Christian Right, the Sudan cause weaves evangelicals into a coalition with the Congressional Black Caucus, Catholic Bishops, Jews, Episcopalians, and secular activists appalled by the indifference of the West toward this humanitarian tragedy."[99] I was a part of the alliance, speaking at conferences and press events and meeting with administration officials. But we lacked the clout, despite the breadth of the alliance, to change American foreign policy. For most of those in this alliance, the cause was just, but was not central to their political activities in the way that Soviet Jewry had been for so many American Jews and their organizations. So the pressure generated was simply not enough to move the administration, and while President Clinton made some statements of support for the southern Sudanese separatists he did not act.

But in the Balkans he did act, even if belatedly. Fighting between Serbs, Croats, and Muslim "Bosniaks" began in 1992, but the United States did not intervene, despite a death toll that reached roughly 100,000. In July 1995 Bosnian Serbs assaulted what had been the UN safe haven for Muslims at Srebenica and killed 7,000. Led by the United States, a three-week bombing campaign in response finally resulted in a peace agreement and a NATO peacekeeping force that included 20,000 U.S. troops. The United States intervened militarily again in the former

Yugoslavia in 1999, this time in a far larger, three-month NATO air campaign (NATO's first military intervention in its then-fifty-year history) to stop "ethnic cleansing" in Kosovo. But the more critical turning point was the first decision to use force, in 1995, and it was in good part a reaction to the massacre in Srebenica. More broadly, it can be called humanitarian intervention for traditional foreign policy reasons: to sustain American credibility. As Ivo Daalder has written, "The real reason was the palpable sense that Bosnia was the cancer eating away at American foreign policy, in the words of Anthony Lake, Clinton's National Security Adviser. U.S. credibility abroad was being undermined perceptibly by what was happening in Bosnia, and by the America's and NATO's failure to end it."[100]

All administrations must grapple with traditional national security challenges and must balance many and varied national interests, from economic, financial, and commercial to military to what might be termed reputational. Human rights and democracy can never be the sole objective of American foreign policy, but the end of the Cold War once again posed familiar questions. How central are human rights and promoting democracy, and what risks should we take to advance them? Are they at the heart of foreign policy or at its periphery? Carter and Reagan had in their very different ways answered that they were central to American foreign policy, though this led to very different foreign policies. George H. W. Bush had returned to the more traditional view that took states as we found them and viewed their internal arrangements as largely their own business. Clinton had rhetorically abandoned that approach and, by the time he left office, had shown both that military intervention could lead to real improvements in the human rights situation (the Balkans) – and that the failure to intervene could lead to immense tragedy (Rwanda).

It has been said that, between the fall of the Soviet Union in 1991 and the 9/11 attacks of 2001, the United States enjoyed a holiday from history. This is, of course, an exaggeration, but it is certainly true that the threats to the country appeared far lower to most Americans and no doubt to the Clinton administration. The difficulty of making foreign policy was due less to the constraints we faced than the lack or, at least, the weakness of constraints. As the Clinton years passed, criticism arose among some conservatives, and especially neoconservatives, that the opportunities of the 1990s were being squandered – and not least the opportunity to spread democracy more widely in the world. Robert Kagan and William Kristol was summarized the argument as early as 1996 by in an article in *Foreign Affairs* titled "Toward a Neo-Reaganite Foreign Policy."[101] They urged that conservatives should not "accede to ... today's lukewarm consensus about America's reduced role in a post Cold-War world," but should instead aspire to a "benevolent hegemony" by the United States in world affairs. Why? Because "American hegemony is the only reliable defense against a breakdown of peace and international order." They continued,

> American foreign policy should be informed with a clear moral purpose.... The United States achieved its present position of strength not by practicing a foreign policy of live and let live, nor by passively waiting for threats to arise, but by actively promoting American principles of governance abroad – democracy, free markets, respect for liberty. During the Reagan years, the United States pressed for changes in right-wing and left-wing dictatorships alike, among both friends and foes – in the Philippines, South Korea, Eastern Europe and even the Soviet Union. The purpose was not Wilsonian idealistic whimsy. The policy of putting pressure on authoritarian and totalitarian regimes had practical aims and, in the end, delivered strategic benefits.

These views were spelled out in much greater detail in a 2000 book called *Present Dangers*, edited by Kagan and Kristol, who were both close friends of mine. I contributed a chapter. The book added an additional concept: regime change. They wrote, "An American strategy that included regime change as a central component would neither promise nor expect rapid transformations in every rogue state or threatening power." They argued that "the idea ... that the United States can 'do business' with any regime, no matter how odious and hostile to our basic principles, is both strategically unsound and unhistorical." Accordingly, "when it comes to dealing with tyrannical regimes ... the United States should seek not coexistence but transformation." They understood and replied to the likely criticism: "To many the idea of using American power to promote changes of regime in nations ruled by dictators rings of utopianism. But in fact, it is eminently realistic. There is something perverse in declaring the impossibility of promoting democratic change abroad in light of the record of the past three decades."[102]

This was not a call for endless military intervention, and the promotion of democratic change through the application of American power entailed all aspects of that power, not just U.S. troops. But in 2000, it seemed that George W. Bush was uninterested in or even opposed to that goal of "promoting democratic change." In the 2000 Republican primary race, Kristol, Kagan, and I supported John McCain, finding him much closer to the views expressed in all of our contributions to *Present Dangers*. The entire subject was not much discussed during the campaign, but it did arise in the second debate between Bush and Al Gore, on October 11, 2000. Asked about "guiding principles for exercising this enormous power" held by the United States, Gore replied, "I see our greatest... national strength coming from what we stand for in the world. I see it as a question of values," while Bush said the better question was "is it in our nation's interests?" Bush supported the Clinton intervention in the Balkans, but made a broader statement about American foreign policy:

> I'm not so sure the role of the United States is to go around the world and say this is the way it's got to be. We can help. And maybe it's just our difference in government, the way we view government. I want to empower the people. I want to help people help themselves, not have government tell people what to do. I just don't think it's the role of the United States to walk into a country and say, "we do it this way, so should you." I think we can help. I know we've got to encourage democracy in the marketplaces.... Now, we trust freedom. We know freedom is a powerful, powerful, powerful force, much bigger than the United States of America, as we saw recently in the Balkans. But maybe I misunderstand where you're coming from, Mr. Vice President, but I think the United States must be humble and must be proud and confident of our values, but humble in how we treat nations that are figuring out how to chart their own course.[103]

Bush seemed to be speaking from the tradition represented by his father, a hard-headed if not "realist" approach that lauded American views of freedom, but suggested that spreading it throughout the world was not our role. This appeared to be the outlook of the Bush camp (and indeed was one reason I supported McCain); indeed, Condoleezza Rice had written an important January 2000 article in *Foreign Affairs* titled "Campaign 2000: Promoting the National Interest."[104] There she wrote, "America's pursuit of the national interest will create conditions that promote freedom, markets, and peace. Its pursuit of national interests after World War II led to a more prosperous and democratic world. This can happen again." This line appeared to suggest that advances for human rights and democracy were the natural product of an American foreign policy founded in *realpolitik* and need not be pursued as a distinct policy objective.

Rice did argue that "American values are universal [and] the triumph of these values is most assuredly easier when the international balance of power favors those who believe in them." That was also a neocon view: we needed a balance of power favoring freedom. But Rice then added that "sometimes that favorable balance of power takes time to achieve, both internationally and within a society. And in the meantime, it is simply not possible to ignore and isolate other powerful states that do not share those values." Whether or not intended as a direct rejoinder to the foreign policy Kristol and Kagan had proposed, Rice's line was a clear contradiction of the proposal that values and democracy promotion be at the center of American foreign policy.

What happened that led Bush and his administration to the soaring rhetoric of his Second Inaugural and the "Freedom Agenda?" In Chapter 4 I discuss particular cases of Bush foreign (and democracy promotion) policy – toward Egypt or Tunisia, for example. Here my focus is ideological: how did Bush get from *realpolitik* to democracy promotion?

In a way the answer is simple: 9/11. He, Rice, and others understood that 9/11 was the turning point in his presidency, and they struggled to understand what had led to those attacks: why was the United States the target of this Arab hatred and terror? Bush and Rice came to believe that, as she put it later, "the culprit was a freedom gap in the Middle East that produced the kind of virulent hatred that exploded on our streets in New York and in the Pentagon."[105] Rice wrote later in her memoir, "The question 'Why do they hate us' was a complex one.... For many in the Arab world, the United States was associated with authoritarian regimes – not freedom, as in Eastern Europe."[106] From there it was a short jump to concluding that the Freedom Agenda was, as she called it, "the ultimate answer to terrorism."[107]

In a conversation in November 2016, Bush looked back on his attitude when coming to the White House and why it changed:

> I felt, given the circumstances then, that the job of the military ought to be to prevent war, not nation-build. Because I couldn't see the need to nation build. I didn't think at the time it was a military function. Then we get attacked and my whole outlook changed . . . the spread of democracy: the reason that became important is that what many in the world recognized is that we had an ideological conflict on our hands. It was not an isolated law enforcement call, it was a call to use all assets . . . to marginalize the ideology of the recruiters and the killers. And the only way to do it is to spread freedom. What makes this very frustrating for some is that the timelines are very different: The one timeline of holding a country to account – the Taliban happened very quickly; holding Saddam Hussein to account happened quite quickly – when the spread of democracy takes a long time. My attitude changed dramatically, just like the world changed dramatically on 9/11.[108]

Of course this progression was not so simple. First, it required rejecting or at least giving little weight to alternative theories – they hate us because we support Israel (a view that quickly emerged in the State Department); because we are rich or strong; because our treatment of women and sexuality offends them; or because we are free – and settling instead on a single central theory: the "freedom deficit" in Arab lands, as it was called in the 2002 *Arab Human Development Report* (discussed further in Chapter 1). This was not Bush's immediate reaction to 9/11, and in his speech to Congress on September 20, 2001, he said, "Americans are asking, why do they hate us? They hate what we see right here in this Chamber, a democratically elected government. Their leaders are self-appointed. They hate our freedoms – our freedom of religion, our freedom of speech, our freedom to vote and assemble and disagree with each other."[109] But this view was not incompatible with asserting that these countries' own "freedom deficit" was central, and this latter understanding came to be more important.

Next, the progression required advancing beyond a Carter-like concentration on human rights without seeking systemic change. This took time. In his 2002 State of the Union address, delivered four months after 9/11, Bush said, "America will always stand firm for the non-negotiable demands of human dignity: the rule of law; limits on the power of the state; respect for women; private property; free speech; equal justice; and religious tolerance."[110] This was not democracy promotion, but instead the insistence on basic human rights. Yet while these remarks were being written, American policy toward Afghanistan and toward the Palestinians was beginning to teach a different lesson: that "regime change" might be part of the answer. And these two cases also showed that regime change might be accomplished peacefully, through diplomatic pressure, or might sometimes be achieved through military force. The lesson of the Clinton years and of the very concept of R2P was surely that use of force was sometimes justifiable and perhaps even required.

Toward the Taliban regime in Afghanistan, Bush delivered an ultimatum in that September 20, 2001, address: "The Taliban must act and act immediately. They will hand over the terrorists, or they will share in their fate." There was no doubt that this meant the United States would invade and would replace the Afghan government. In his speech to the UN General Assembly on November, 10, 2001, to the session that had been postponed after the 9/11 attacks, Bush made the goal even clearer: "The Afghan people do not deserve their present rulers . . . . The Taliban's days of harboring terrorists and dealing in heroin and brutalizing women are drawing to a close. And when that regime is gone, the people of Afghanistan will say with the rest of the world, 'Good riddance.'"[111] The case of Afghanistan, and of course later Iraq, began the fateful association of democracy promotion with regime change – and indeed with regime change through the use of force. The lines were being fudged – between protection of human rights, promotion of democracy, R2P intervention in cases of "genocide, war crimes, ethnic cleansing and crimes against humanity," regime change through force, and the very traditional use of military force to protect the homeland and respond to an attack on it.

The Palestinian issue was very different, but equally complex from the standpoint of democracy policy. Bush had by the end of 2001 committed himself to promoting an independent Palestinian state. But on January 3, 2002, Israeli gunboats intercepted a ship, the *Karine A*, that turned out to be carrying weapons from Iran to the Palestinian leader Yasser Arafat.[112] This was proof that Arafat, who had practiced terrorism for decades, was still at it – even after 9/11! There was no way the United States could promote the creation of a terrorist state or new state led by a terrorist. How did we escape from that box?

The answer was to say the United States would support creation of a Palestinian state when it would be a democracy – and not before. In an April 2002 speech, Bush began to attack Arafat: "The chairman of the Palestinian Authority has not consistently opposed or confronted terrorists. At Oslo and elsewhere, Chairman Arafat renounced terror as an instrument of his cause, and he agreed to control it. He's not done so. The situation in which he finds himself today is largely of his own making. He's missed his opportunities and thereby betrayed the hopes of the people he is supposed to lead."[113] And two months later, he was ready to say Arafat had to be replaced so that a democracy could be created:

Peace requires a new and different Palestinian leadership, so that a Palestinian state can be born.

I call on the Palestinian people to elect new leaders, leaders not compromised by terror. I call upon them to build a practicing democracy, based on tolerance and liberty....

And when the Palestinian people have new leaders, new institutions and new security arrangements with their neighbors, the United States of America will support the creation of a Palestinian state....

Today, the elected Palestinian legislature has no authority, and power is concentrated in the hands of an unaccountable few. A Palestinian state can only serve its citizens with a new constitution which separates the powers of government. The Palestinian parliament should have the full authority of a legislative body. Local officials and government ministers need authority of their own and the independence to govern effectively.

The United States, along with the European Union and Arab states, will work with Palestinian leaders to create a new constitutional framework, and a working democracy for the Palestinian people....

If Palestinians embrace democracy, confront corruption and firmly reject terror, they can count on American support for the creation of a provisional state of Palestine....

If liberty can blossom in the rocky soil of the West Bank and Gaza, it will inspire millions of men and women around the globe who are equally weary of poverty and oppression, equally entitled to the benefits of democratic government.[114]

Here Bush had not only embraced the need for promoting democracy but even prescribed its elements: separation of powers, a parliament and constitution, free elections, and so on. Moreover, he had stated clearly that the Palestinian case was a model that could inspire others around the world who also deserved "democratic government."

This was another requirement for the progression toward the Freedom Agenda: a belief that democratic government was actually possible outside the confines of the North Atlantic and was adaptable to all cultures. Bush addressed this issue directly in a February 2003 speech to the American Enterprise Institute:

There was a time when many said that the cultures of Japan and Germany were incapable of sustaining democratic values. Well, they were wrong. Some say the same of Iraq today. They are mistaken. The nation of Iraq – with its proud heritage, abundant resources and skilled and educated people – is fully capable of moving toward democracy and living in freedom.

The world has a clear interest in the spread of democratic values, because stable and free nations do not breed the ideologies of murder. They encourage the peaceful pursuit of a better life. And there are hopeful signs of a desire for freedom in the Middle East. Arab intellectuals have called on Arab governments to address the "freedom gap" so their peoples can fully share in the progress of our times....

It is presumptuous and insulting to suggest that a whole region of the world – or the one-fifth of humanity that is Muslim – is somehow untouched by the most basic aspirations of life. Human cultures can be vastly different. Yet the human heart desires the same good things, everywhere on Earth. In our desire to be safe from brutal and bullying oppression, human beings are the same. In our desire to care for our children and give them a better life, we are the same. For these fundamental reasons, freedom and democracy will always and everywhere have greater appeal than the slogans of hatred and the tactics of terror.[115]

Nine months later, Bush spoke at the twentieth-anniversary celebrations of the National Endowment for Democracy.[116] Here he went further, and deeper, in explaining his "conversion" to the promotion of democracy. Speechwriters, of course, wrote the exact words of the speech, but it was clear to those around him that "the idea that a substantial part of the answer to the ideological problem in the war on terror is democracy is his idea."[117] Bush began by noting that Ronald Reagan's speech to the British Parliament, where he had spoken so optimistically about the expansion of democracy, had been regarded as naïve:

> In June of 1982, President Ronald Reagan spoke at Westminster Palace and declared, the turning point had arrived in history....
>
> President Reagan said that the day of Soviet tyranny was passing, that freedom had a momentum which would not be halted. He gave this organization its mandate: to add to the momentum of freedom across the world. Your mandate was important 20 years ago; it is equally important today. A number of critics were dismissive of that speech by the President. According to one editorial of the time, "It seems hard to be a sophisticated European and also an admirer of Ronald Reagan." Some observers on both sides of the Atlantic pronounced the speech simplistic and naive, and even dangerous. In fact, Ronald Reagan's words were courageous and optimistic and entirely correct.

So Bush wrapped himself in Reagan's mantle and took on the critics of democracy promotion. But what was the American role? A "mission to promote liberty":

> It is no accident that the rise of so many democracies took place in a time when the world's most influential nation was itself a democracy.
>
> The United States made military and moral commitments in Europe and Asia, which protected free nations from aggression, and created the conditions in which new democracies could flourish. As we provided security for whole nations, we also provided inspiration for oppressed peoples. In prison camps, in banned union meetings, in clandestine churches, men

and women knew that the whole world was not sharing their own night-mare. They knew of at least one place – a bright and hopeful land – where freedom was valued and secure. And they prayed that America would not forget them, or forget the mission to promote liberty around the world.

Reviewing the history of the twentieth century, including the collapse of the Soviet Union and the peace in Europe after World War II, Bush added, "Every nation has learned, or should have learned, an important lesson: Freedom is worth fighting for, dying for, and standing for – and the advance of freedom leads to peace. And now we must apply that lesson in our own time. We've reached another great turning point – and the resolve we show will shape the next stage of the world democratic movement."

Bush then addressed, again, the questions of whether democracy was culture bound or universal, and whether Islam was an insuperable barrier:

And the questions arise: Are the peoples of the Middle East somehow beyond the reach of liberty? Are millions of men and women and children condemned by history or culture to live in despotism? Are they alone never to know freedom, and never even to have a choice in the matter? I, for one, do not believe it. I believe every person has the ability and the right to be free.

Some skeptics of democracy assert that the traditions of Islam are inhos-pitable to the representative government. This "cultural condescension," as Ronald Reagan termed it, has a long history. After the Japanese surren-der in 1945, a so-called Japan expert asserted that democracy in that for-mer empire would "never work." Another observer declared the prospects for democracy in post-Hitler Germany are, and I quote, "most uncertain at best" – he made that claim in 1957. Seventy-four years ago, *The Sunday Lon-don Times* declared nine-tenths of the population of India to be "illiterates not caring a fig for politics." Yet when Indian democracy was imperiled in the 1970s, the Indian people showed their commitment to liberty in a national referendum that saved their form of government.

Time after time, observers have questioned whether this country, or that people, or this group, are "ready" for democracy – as if freedom were a prize you win for meeting our own Western standards of progress. In fact, the daily work of democracy itself is the path of progress. It teaches cooperation, the free exchange of ideas, and the peaceful resolution of differences. As men and women are showing, from Bangladesh to Botswana, to Mongolia, it is the practice of democracy that makes a nation ready for democracy, and every nation can start on this path.

It should be clear to all that Islam – the faith of one-fifth of humanity – is consistent with democratic rule. Democratic progress is found in many predominantly Muslim countries – in Turkey and Indonesia, and Senegal and Albania, Niger and Sierra Leone. Muslim men and women are good citizens of India and South Africa, of the nations of Western Europe, and of the United States of America.

Bush's argument for promoting democracy was, in his view, pragmatic and stemmed from his conclusions that the absence of freedom in the Arab world had contributed to the growth of resentment, violence, and terrorism, and that American support for oppressive regimes had meant that the terror would be directed in part at us:

> Sixty years of Western nations excusing and accommodating the lack of freedom in the Middle East did nothing to make us safe – because in the long run, stability cannot be purchased at the expense of liberty. As long as the Middle East remains a place where freedom does not flourish, it will remain a place of stagnation, resentment, and violence ready for export. And with the spread of weapons that can bring catastrophic harm to our country and to our friends, it would be reckless to accept the status quo.

With these conclusions in mind, it was not surprising that he viewed democracy promotion as central to U.S. foreign policy:

> Therefore, the United States has adopted a new policy, a forward strategy of freedom in the Middle East. This strategy requires the same persistence and energy and idealism we have shown before. And it will yield the same results. As in Europe, as in Asia, as in every region of the world, the advance of freedom leads to peace.
>
> The advance of freedom is the calling of our time; it is the calling of our country. From the Fourteen Points to the Four Freedoms, to the Speech at Westminster, America has put our power at the service of principle. We believe that liberty is the design of nature; we believe that liberty is

the direction of history. We believe that human fulfillment and excellence come in the responsible exercise of liberty. And we believe that freedom – the freedom we prize – is not for us alone; it is the right and the capacity of all mankind.

Working for the spread of freedom can be hard. Yet, America has accomplished hard tasks before. Our nation is strong; we're strong of heart. And we're not alone. Freedom is finding allies in every country; freedom finds allies in every culture. And as we meet the terror and violence of the world, we can be certain the author of freedom is not indifferent to the fate of freedom.

That final line, like some of the remarks to the American Enterprise Institute (AEI) months before, revealed the religious element in Bush's thinking. This issue has been completely misunderstood by some critics, who have alleged that Bush felt a theological requirement to spread democracy, even if it meant the use of force. That is wrong. What Bush argued, instead, had nothing to do with any particular American role; rather, his argument was that every individual had God-given rights. At the AEI he spoke of the desires of the "human heart" as universal; now he spoke of the "design of nature" and the "author of freedom." If all humankind was the creation of one "author," and all hearts fundamentally alike, then freedom could not rightly be denied to any man or woman on earth.

On November 2, 2004 President Bush was reelected for a second term. During that time Bush was reading Natan Sharansky's book *The Case for Democracy* and on November 15 he invited Sharansky to the White House. Sharansky's argument about "double think," tyranny as the real threat to peace, and the universal desire to escape regimes based on fear resounded with Bush. That is when he apparently made the decision to have democracy promotion at the center of his Second Inaugural Address: "Several weeks later, Bush told his chief speechwriter, Michael J. Gerson, that he wanted to make democracy promotion the centerpiece of his second inaugural address."[118]

In that speech he repeated certain themes, most importantly the link between freedom and American security, freedom and the fight against terror, and the universal appeal of freedom to people all around the globe. The rhetoric was soaring, but novel only to those who had not been paying attention.

First Bush argued that our security required this turn to promoting freedom:

> For as long as whole regions of the world simmer in resentment and tyranny, prone to ideologies that feed hatred and excuse murder, violence will gather and multiply in destructive power and cross the most defended borders and raise a mortal threat. There is only one force of history that can break the reign of hatred and resentment and expose the pretensions of tyrants and reward the hopes of the decent and tolerant, and that is the force of human freedom.
>
> We are led, by events and common sense, to one conclusion: The survival of liberty in our land increasingly depends on the success of liberty in other lands. The best hope for peace in our world is the expansion of freedom in all the world.

If that conclusion is right, then American foreign policy must reflect it:

> So it is the policy of the United States to seek and support the growth of democratic movements and institutions in every nation and culture, with the ultimate goal of ending tyranny in our world.

Again Bush stressed the universality of the call:

> Eventually, the call of freedom comes to every mind and every soul. We do not accept the existence of permanent tyranny because we do not accept the possibility of permanent slavery.
>
> When the Declaration of Independence was first read in public and the Liberty Bell was sounded in celebration, a witness said, "It rang as if it meant something." In our time, it means something still. America, in this young century, proclaims liberty throughout all the world and to all the inhabitants thereof.

He made one bow to pragmatism, noting, "The great objective of ending tyranny is the concentrated work of generations," not something that would be completed in his remaining years of office. Yet, he continued, "The difficulty of the task is no excuse for avoiding it." And it certainly seemed, in those days, that the difficulty of the task was not insuperable.

In Lebanon, the killing of Rafik Hariri on February 14, 2005, led to the withdrawal of Syrian troops after thirty years, to free elections in May and June, and to the establishment of an independent and democratic government led by Hariri's son, Saad. After Yasser Arafat's death in the fall of 2004, Palestinians held a free and competitive election on January 9, 2005, to choose his successor as president of the Palestinian Authority. On January 30, 2005, Iraq, freed of Saddam Hussein, held competitive elections for a transitional national assembly, and more than eight million Iraqis went to the polls.

Here it is worth noting that if American military force had brought about regime change in Iraq and Afghanistan, it had certainly not done so in the Palestinian Territories or Lebanon. For those of us in the Bush administration, the promotion of democracy, as Bush explained it, was not at all a formula for invasion after invasion. The Reagan example showed that American power could have enormous influence even if the use of military force was sparing, and the vast expansion of democracy around the globe in the 1980s was not the result of military action. The uses of force by Clinton in the Balkans and now by Bush in Afghanistan and Iraq were not undertaken out of a sudden concern for spreading democracy and were not R2P interventions motivated almost exclusively by humanitarian concerns. They were instead products of traditional security concerns (U.S. credibility and European stability for Clinton, attacks on the homeland and the possession by enemies of the United States of weapons of mass destruction for Bush). But it is fair to say that the combination of our Bush administration rhetoric with the cases of Afghanistan and Iraq led to the widespread conclusion that those invasions – what James Traub calls "transformation by warfare" – were closely related to and perhaps the inevitable product of the Freedom Agenda.[119]

That was certainly not the view we took inside the administration. We had in mind a variety of traditional and nontraditional efforts to press for change in the Middle East, and the "Broader Middle East and North Africa Initiative" adopted at the summit hosted by Bush at Sea Island, Georgia, in 2004 is an example. It led to an effort to institutionalize discussions of political change in what we called the "Forum for the Future," which met in Morocco in December 2004 and in Bahrain in November 2005. There the "Group of Eight" major economic powers (represented at the foreign minister level in many cases) met with Middle Eastern officials and civil society leaders to talk about reform. A group of small initiatives followed, including a "Democracy Assistance Dialogue" that included four conferences bringing together hundreds of democracy and civil society activists with government officials. The main goal of all this activity was to institutionalize discussion of the need for and the character of social and political change in the region. As Condi Rice later described the effort,

> Officials from the United States and Europe joined ministers from monarchies such as Jordan and Saudi Arabia and dictatorships such as Syria in sessions devoted to human rights and democracy. The goal was to push on different dimensions, supporting civil society and pressuring governments. The presentations at those sessions were, not surprisingly, sterile and sometimes even a little hostile toward us. Still the participants – representatives of governments and members of civil society – attended, and political reform was on the agenda at every meeting. In this we attempted to replicate the Conference on Security and Co-operation in Europe.[120]

And we had in mind the power of the American example in a world where the balance of power favored freedom, active promotion of democratic governance, use of the bully pulpit of the presidency, and the usual diplomatic and sometimes economic pressures on undemocratic governments and recalcitrant tyrants. One could see that approach throughout the Bush years toward countries as varied as Yemen, Burma, the Palestinian Territories, Lebanon, Belarus, Egypt, Tunisia, Cuba, Syria, and Venezuela. Of course the 9/11 attacks and the Taliban's protection of al-Qaeda had led to the Afghan regime's overthrow by invasion and military attack, and the belief that Saddam Hussein possessed weapons of mass destruction had led to his removal. What we did not then see was that the entire enterprise of promoting democracy would, in the minds of very many people who should have known better, be equated with a military program. What we saw as the exceptions and rare cases where force would be used, Bush's critics saw as the very essence of the Freedom Agenda: endless military engagements.

To reach that conclusion the critics would need to be guided by igno-rance of the arguments Bush was in fact making or by a personal antag-onism to him that led to dismissing those arguments – or both. It also required dismissing the entire history of democracy promotion, back to Cold War days and through the Reagan era, through the expansion of democracy in the 1980s and 1990s, and to those many cases where Bush promoted democracy through more traditional methods. And that is pre-cisely what happened: opposition to Bush and to the war in Iraq led to the equation of the war in Iraq with the Freedom Agenda. In fact not only democracy promotion but also humanitarian intervention became tarnished by the length and unpopularity of that war, and Obama and his team abandoned those efforts; as Anne Marie Slaughter wrote in late 2016, "Today, as the Obama administration nears its end, R2P has gone deeply out of fashion."[121]

For democracy promotion, 2005 was the high-water mark – for rhetoric and for hopes that the expansion of democracy and respect for human rights would continue. As I discuss in Chapter 4, this level of commitment to democracy and the Freedom Agenda was not main-tained throughout the administration during Bush's second term. Bush's own commitment did not change: his belief that promoting democracy was essential to American security remained, and he continued to meet with dissidents and to employ the same rhetoric. In June 2007, for exam-ple, he told a conference of dissidents and democracy activists in Prague that "pursuing stability at the expense of liberty does not lead to peace – it leads to September the 11th, 2001."[122] Throughout his years in office Bush paid close attention to Sudan and the effort of southern Sudanese to stop the terrible abuses by the Islamist regime in Khartoum: he "'could have been the desk officer' because he was so engaged on southern Sudan."[123] During an Asia trip in 2008, repression in Burma was "high on Bush's agenda," and he met with dissidents at the U.S. Embassy while First Lady Laura Bush visited refugee camps on the Thailand-Burma bor-der.[124] Policy toward Burma, which was personally overseen by the presi-dent and First Lady, used traditional foreign policy methods to pressure the regime there for a political opening. There are no speeches by Bush or other top officials that compromise the commitment he had made in the major democracy addresses or that suggest that new (or, more accurately, much older) foreign policy goals had taken the place of the Freedom Agenda.

In Bush's 2007 State of the Union message he said of the fight against terror, "This war is more than a clash of arms – it is a decisive ideological struggle.... What every terrorist fears most is human freedom.... Free people are not drawn to violent and malignant ideologies.... So we advance our own security interests by helping moderates and reformers and brave voices for democracy."[125] His final State of the Union speech, in January 2008, underlined the same themes a final time: "We are engaged in the defining ideological struggle of the 21st century," he said again. "In the long run, men and women who are free to determine their own destinies will reject terror and refuse to live in tyranny.... And that is why, for the security of America and the peace of the world, we are spreading the hope of freedom.[126]

But just as the world had changed on 9/11, so it had changed in the seven years between that day and the end of the Bush administration. The apparent good news from the Middle East in 2005 – democracy or at least political openings slowly spreading to Egypt, Palestine, Lebanon, and Iraq – was replaced by Mubarak's renewed crackdown, the Hamas victory in the 2006 Palestinian parliamentary elections, Hezbollah's takeover of Beirut in May 2008, and endless violence and turmoil in Iraq.

My own perspective was that the 2007–2008 effort to forge an Israeli-Palestinian peace agreement took a heavy toll on the Freedom Agenda in the Middle East.[127] Secretary of State Rice concluded, after the Lebanon (or Israel-Hezbollah) war in the summer of 2006 that Israeli prime minister Ehud Olmert – weakened by Israel's failure to win a victory in that conflict and to meet its own stated war aims – would not be able to lead the way to a peace agreement. She decided that the United States would have to take the lead and would need to enlist Arab nations, starting as usual with Egypt, in the effort. Surely the Bush administration's troubles in 2005–2006 – from the mishandling of Hurricane Katrina to losses in the mid-term elections to the deepening morass in Iraq – contributed to reaching that conclusion: she wanted an achievement in the Middle East for the president and the administration, and for the country. Moreover, her own term as secretary of state was half over, and quite naturally she wanted a major achievement for herself. The result was a perception, never stated in plain language, that pressure on the Arabs for internal reforms would have to take a back seat to "the Annapolis process," as the renewed effort on the Israeli-Palestinian front was called after the peace conference held in Annapolis in November 2007.

One can see this effect by comparing the language of Rice's own 2005 speech in Cairo (see Chapter 4), at the American University there, with language she used in later years. In February 2006 Rice visited Egypt again and met with Mubarak. Her language was then much softer, and Mubarak later said of their conversations that Rice "didn't bring up difficult issues or ask to change anything."[128] Of course Mubarak had reason to mislead about that, but as a participant in that visit I can attest that he was right.

President Bush visited Egypt in January 2008, and after a meeting with Mubarak pulled his punches in public when it came to discussing freedom and oppression there:

> Progress toward greater political openness is being led by the Egyptians themselves, by pioneering journalists – some of whom even may be here – bloggers or judges insisting on independence or other strong civic and religious leaders who love their country and are determined to build a democratic future.
>
> Because of the predominant role you play and because I strongly believe that Egypt can play a role in the freedom and justice movement, you and I have discussed the issue. You have taken steps toward economic openness, and I discussed that with your Prime Minister – and democratic reform. And my hope is that the Egyptian Government will build on these important steps and give the people of this proud nation a greater voice in your future. I think it will lead to peace, and I think it will lead to justice.[129]

During the preparations for that trip, Bush had told his speechwriting staff that "the Mubarak regime was his biggest disappointment. Bush had hoped that the country, with its educated, productive populace, might lead the way for democratic reform in the Middle East, but a crusty apparatchik stood in the way. Nothing was likely to change in Egypt, Bush said, until Mubarak was gone."[130] I had heard similar remarks from Bush:

that Mubarak (then age eighty) was too old to change. But that had not stopped the president, and Rice, from pressuring Mubarak and his regime in 2004–2005.

In his address to the World Economic Forum in Sharm el Sheik during a second visit to Egypt (in May 2008) Bush was unyielding in his general support for democracy: "Taking your place as a center of progress and achievement requires extending the reach of freedom.... Freedom is also the basis for a democratic system of government, which is the only fair and just ordering of society and the only way to guarantee the God-given rights of all people."[131] The word "only" must have been noticed by his listeners (many of them from Arab monarchies), and even at this distance its use is striking.

Moreover, Bush again discussed exactly what he meant by democracy, lest it be thought that he was accepting the standard Middle Eastern excuses as valid: "Some say any state that holds an election is a democracy. But true democracy requires vigorous political parties allowed to engage in free and lively debate. True democracy requires the establishment of civic institutions that ensure an election's legitimacy and hold leaders accountable. And true democracy requires competitive elections in which opposition candidates are allowed to campaign without fear or intimidation."

But when it came to Egypt, Bush softened the rhetoric: "Egypt ... has posted strong economic growth, developed some of the world's fastest growing telecommunications companies, and made major investments that will boost tourism and trade. In order for this economic progress to result in permanent prosperity and an Egypt that reaches its full potential, however, economic reform must be accompanied by political reform. And I continue to hope that Egypt can lead the region in political reform." Rice had spoken in 2005 of regime violence against reformers and the need to end rule by emergency decree in Egypt, and she had used the word "tyranny"; Bush's vague public call for "political reform" in Egypt was a weaker substitute.

Two days before, Bush had told reporters "that in a meeting with Mr. Mubarak, he specifically raised the case of Ayman Nour, Mr. Mubarak's main opponent in the 2005 elections, who was imprisoned on fraud charges that Mr. Nour's supporters regard as politically motivated. Mr. Bush has said before that he believes Mr. Nour has been 'unjustly imprisoned.'"[132]

But in his speech to the World Economic Forum in Sharm el Sheik, there was no public mention of Nour, and in fact what had been planned as a pointed speech dealing candidly with the need for freedom in Egypt had been whittled down. As one of Bush's speechwriters later wrote, the first draft – which had been approved – was much tougher; it included lines like "The only question left to be asked by the leaders and intellectuals of this region, and in this room, is this: Will you be left behind by this change – or will you choose to lead it?" More dramatically, "Bush would stand in Egypt and call directly for Mubarak to send a message of 'goodwill' to the world by ordering his guards to go to the prison where dissidents were held, open the door of the cell where his nemesis was held, and set free one of the world's most famous political prisoners: Ayman Nour, an Egyptian reformer whose only real crime was to challenge Mubarak in a 'free' presidential election."[133]

The government of Egypt was told about the speech and began to push back, including by getting the Saudis to advise against it. They changed the choreography to put Mubarak on the stage with Bush during the World Economic Forum speech, hoping that Bush would be too polite to criticize Mubarak to his face. Moreover, they began to spread the rumor that Nour was soon to be let free and that such a public challenge in the speech could actually delay his release date. Debates over the speech continued on Air Force One as we flew to the Middle East, but in the end Secretary of State Rice prevailed on the president to cut out all of what I, and the speechwriting staff led by Bill McGurn, considered the most important lines. So instead of a direct challenge to Mubarak or any other Arab regimes, there were the quoted sharp but quite general remarks on democracy, and their impact was much less than what some of us had wanted. One year before, in June 2007 at a conference of dissidents in Prague (see Chapter 4), Bush had said, "There are many dissidents who couldn't join us because they are being unjustly imprisoned or held under house arrest. I look forward to the day when a conference like this one include[s] Alexander Kozulin of Belarus, Aung San Suu Kyi of Burma, Oscar Elias Biscet of Cuba, Father Nguyen Van Ly of Vietnam,

Ayman Nour of Egypt."[134] When visiting Egypt twice in 2008, however, Bush did not mention Nour publicly. In the end Nour was not released until February 2009.

But in private Bush did press Mubarak on the subject of democracy. In late 2016 he gave this account of their May 2008 conversation:

> This was about the time it looked like he was going to shoehorn in [his son] Gamal. I was alone with him. And I said, "you know, I think it's a big mistake for you to put Gamal in power. I think you need to let the Egyptian people decide who the president's going to be." And he said, in a somewhat patronizing voice, basically, "young man, you don't understand. The Muslim Brotherhood will win." And I said, "well, President, why don't you figure out why the Muslim Brotherhood will win and do a better job of appealing to the people who decide?" I thought long and hard about that conversation, which by the way he was not interested in hearing. And I think the events after Tahrir Square bore out my thinking at the time – that the Muslim Brotherhood was a convenient straw man for Mubarak to trot out to Western leaders as a way to maintain his power, because he goes to his benefactors like the US and says, "don't press me on elections; otherwise, you'll have to be dealing with the Muslim Brotherhood!" Well, this overlooks who his constituency should have been. It's not the US. His constituency should have been those who ended up in Tahrir Square.[135]

As the rhetoric used during the two visits to Egypt in 2008 demonstrates, the criticism that Bush was a wild dreamer who lost touch with the realities of world politics is nonsense. The better criticism is that, by the end of the administration, the Freedom Agenda was more a personal cause of his and less a pervasive administration policy. To some extent this reflects the unavoidable arrival of lame-duck status, when the great bureaucracies of government begin to reassert themselves and impose their traditional views. Promoting democracy and protesting human rights abuses always creates problems (the "trouble" to which I had pointed in my memo of 1981) between U.S. government agencies – USAID and the State Department, especially – and the foreign governments with which they must deal each day, so the bureaucracy will always find good reasons to tone things down and pull back unless pushed from the top. As an administration nears its end, they push back against that pressure or try to ignore it. And in the Bush administration case in 2008, weariness with the wars in Iraq and Afghanistan and the association of those wars with the Freedom Agenda spurred a broader resistance to promoting democracy. It is fair to summarize by saying that George W. Bush never at any time abandoned the Freedom Agenda or diminished his belief in it, but by the end of 2008 the U.S. government had begun to turn back to more traditional diplomatic approaches focused on getting along with existing regimes. Once again the focus was moving toward dealing with governments, rather than helping their oppressed citizens, and that movement was greatly hastened by the Obama administration.

I thought and think this shift was a great mistake. I had joined the struggle over the role of human rights and democracy promotion in American foreign policy in the 1970s – working for Scoop Jackson against the Nixon/Kissinger version of *realpolitik*, which largely excluded human rights concerns, and the Carter version of human rights policy, which largely excluded promotion of democracy and criticism of what was then the greatest threat to freedom, Soviet Communism and the states it controlled.

The approach championed by Jackson and then Ronald Reagan was certainly not disconnected from American strategic concerns: both men were fierce anti-Communists who saw the Soviet Union as the greatest threat facing the United States, as well as the greatest enemy of liberty in the world. Both men saw promotion of democracy as a useful weapon in the struggle against Soviet Communism, a battle they understood was ideological as well as military. And both men understood that the human rights struggle could ultimately be won only by going further than case-by-case or issue-by-issue amelioration; both men would have understood Andrei Sakharov's view, as Sharansky explained it: "Sakharov agreed that it was important to change the regime." Sakharov was not urging or hoping for war any more than Jackson or Reagan was, but he was hoping for "regime change" and the end of the Leninist system that had ruled Russia since 1917.

To this end, Jackson and Reagan understood that all the traditional tools of American diplomacy and pressure must be used, but also saw that those tools were not enough. The central concern of the policy must be people and their rights, not regimes. Engagement with tyrannical regimes was necessary, but certainly not sufficient – and also morally hazardous unless it was combined with the clearest denunciations of the moral character of such regimes. And the end goal of American policy should also be clear – liberty, in a democratic political system – not a few more concessions to a dictator who remained in full control.

The end of the Cold War and the new (though as it turned out, brief) period of clear American supremacy as a world power presented new challenges, because the constraints presented by Soviet power were gone. This did not result in an American policy of overthrowing regimes all over the globe nor even in a particularly reenergized human rights policy, but that is understandable because in fact a spontaneous wave of democratization was occurring. Regime change was happening in many places once the USSR and its empire collapsed, and the American role was largely that of cheering and advising. The spread of democracy increased, because democracy appeared to be the clear winner in the political/ideological context just as the United States appeared to be the clear winner in the global military sweepstakes – and that connection is critical rather than fortuitous. What was new in the 1990s was acceptance and approval of "humanitarian intervention": the use of military power across international boundaries and in violation of Westphalian sovereignty principles, for largely humanitarian purposes, to prevent governments from killing their own people.

The George W. Bush administration inherited what appeared at first to be that new world of the 1990s, but our understanding of the real situation changed on 9/11. The threats we now saw ourselves facing were both physical – terrorism, including the prospect of terrorists armed with weapons of mass destruction – and once again ideological, this time not Communist ideology but violent extremism based in a radical version of Islam. We came to believe that repressive Muslim regimes could not win that fight and indeed fueled it, so once again – as during the Cold War – we were faced with a security threat that required an ideological and political as well as a military reaction. So the policy we adopted, which President Bush enunciated repeatedly, turned back to many of the arguments and tools of the previous Cold War struggle – sometimes knowingly and sometimes not. Human rights policy in the Carter sense was inadequate, and regime change – meaning the call for democratic government – became the stated goal. Condoleezza Rice has explained this evolution well:

> [T]he Freedom Agenda was not just a moral or idealistic cause; it was a redefinition of what constituted realism, a change in the way we viewed U.S. interests in the new circumstances forced on us by the attacks of that horrible day. We rather quickly arrived at the conclusion that U.S. interests and values could be linked together in a coherent way, forming what I came to call a distinctly American realism.... Only the emergence of democratic institutions and practices could defeat terrorism and radical political Islam. We knew that the path would not be easy and there would undoubtedly be trade-offs in the short term. The United States could not radically reorient its foreign policy, refusing to deal with friendly authoritarian regimes such as Saudi Arabia and Egypt on matters of strategic importance. The Freedom Agenda was meant to be a long-term strategic shift in the way we defined our interests, not just a genuflection toward our values.[136]

But human rights, democracy promotion, and even the goal of regime change did not imply the use of military power. Bush made it clear that this was "the work of generations," and in dozens of countries around the globe we used the traditional tools of international politics, from public statements to diplomatic pressure to economic leverage. Military power was used in two cases – Afghanistan, because it was the sanctuary of al-Qaeda, and Iraq, which all believed had weapons of mass destruction – but not in others, such as Sudan, where it might arguably have done some good. To us the cases of military intervention were necessary exceptions, so why did they in the following decade swallow the entire enterprise?

The costs of the Afghan and especially the Iraq wars – in dollars, in nearly 7,000 American dead and tens of thousands of Americans wounded, and in the sense that too little was gained to justify these very long conflicts – are of course the largest contributor to the aversion to such commitments. But Americans do understand the danger of terrorism and of hostile regimes such as those in Iran and Russia; using the military to fight the Islamic State, for example, always has had majority support. So why the widespread hostility to promoting democracy?

There are five explanations, in my view. First is the widespread conclusion that promoting democracy inevitably or very likely leads to war. This was the deduction made by some Americans who listened to presidents (especially George W. Bush) and other leaders talk about the need and the desire to promote democracy in Afghanistan and Iraq. But why did Americans understand that we did not go to war against Japan and Germany to install democracy in those countries, despite the fact that after winning World War II we did exactly that? Why did they separate in those cases what we did when we had won the war, and had the power to impose new political systems, from what drove us into war to begin with?

Pearl Harbor is a large part of the answer: we were attacked, and they chose war, so we had to fight and of course to win. Perhaps if there had been no Iraq war but only the Afghanistan effort this view might have prevailed. Al-Qaeda attacked us, the Taliban protected them, so we overthrew the regime – and then tried to impose democracy because that is the form of government we believe in. Iraq did not attack us, and when the weapons of mass destruction rationale for the invasion proved to be wrong it seemed that the only thing we were doing there was replacing a dictator with a better government. The use of force in Libya by the Obama administration deepened the sense that supporting better governance in foreign capitals meant a U.S. military attack. Thus the equation of democracy promotion with invasions.

Americans will never support such interventions, a conclusion I drew in writing about the subject in the 1990s. As I put it then, the American people will not support military intervention in which American national interests are vague or consist only of an inchoate interest in a better or more peaceful world, and whose beneficiary is "the international community" as an undifferentiated whole, rather than the United States in any identifiable sense. This is in good part because, for Americans, idealism about peace and democracy mingles with realism about the propensity of human beings to seek relief from work and sacrifice when others can be persuaded to undertake them. The American fear has been that the sacrifices required in the national efforts to make the world freer and more peaceful would be unfair, thankless, and endless.[137] So to the extent that promotion of democracy is seen as a slippery slope to military intervention, it will never win broad support.

Second, President Obama very often promoted this conclusion as part of a highly ideological foreign policy that sought to restrain the use of American power and frequently equated its use – past and present – with sins, crimes, and errors. In this he has had the support of a sizable number of scholars, commentators, and even political leaders on the Left, for example Bernie Sanders, who agree with his views. In this understanding of America and American history, we are not a "shining city on a hill" and we need to attend to solving our own problems rather than exporting them through the misbegotten use of our power.

Third, defenders of the traditional *realpolitik* approach to statesmanship have always frowned on democracy promotion and continue to make what are often pragmatic (though, in my view, in the end erroneous) arguments against it.

Fourth, there is particular pessimism about the possibility of success in the Middle East. The Arab nations seem especially resistant to democracy, and the record of the Arab Spring makes optimism easy to dismiss.

Finally, the champions of democracy promotion in American politics have been too few and too quiet since the Iraq war, allowing the misunderstanding to spread that promoting democracy is an essentially military task.

Could it have been otherwise, and can it be in the coming years? Can American foreign policy return to the views we associate with Jackson and Moynihan, and Reagan and Bush, about American moral and political leadership in the world and the association of the United States with the cause of freedom?

In my view, the belief that America has a special role in world affairs and that we are safest in a world where freedom is expanding should and will regain wide support. This will require leadership: when a president argues against it, the burden on those who seek to explain the special relationship between the United States and democracy in the world is much more difficult. And it will require statesmanship: the deeper understanding of where our long-term interests lie. Condoleezza Rice described this kind of statesmanship in the aftermath of World War II:

> Roosevelt didn't enter the war to democratize Germany and Japan. When the war was over, the Europeans, particularly Great Britain, cared less about the form of the new German government than about containing its power.... The Americans, though, had a different view. There was indeed a moral dimension to their insistence on democratic processes and institutions. But there was a practical reason as well: Truman, Acheson, Marshall, and others began to equate a new and stable order with a permanent change in the nature of the defeated regimes, a change that could be secured only with democracy. They believed that the balance of power could be improved in our favor if democratic states emerged in Europe. This linking of our interests (the balance of power) and our values (democracy) was at the core of our strategic thinking.[138]

So it was in the Bush years, when our strategic thinking led (in Rice's phrase) to "a distinctly American realism."

As we saw in the McGovern/Nixon and Carter/Reagan contests, the sense that America's power and prestige are slipping and are anyway undeserved does not sit well with Americans. Moreover, a policy that unduly restrains American power and ambitions leads to a more dangerous world, as we learned again through the experiment with that foreign policy approach during the Obama years. If as some argue there is a regular, pendulum-like movement in American foreign policy between retrenchment and expansion, the excessive movement under Obama toward retrenchment and the dangers it created will help propel movement back toward greater activism under his immediate successors.[139] And the struggles of individuals and movements dedicated to protecting basic human rights, political freedoms, and democratic systems will again attract greater American sympathy and support.

That is my view and my hope.

CHAPTER 1

The Arab Spring

THE ARAB SPRING WAS A SURPRISE. The third wave of global democratization, dated from Portugal's political change in 1974, appeared to have washed over the Arab world without much impact. Ruling royal families remained in place in the new twenty-first century, and strongmen like Ben Ali, Mubarak, Qadhafi, and Hafez al-Assad and his son Bashar made the occasional remarks about change, but then worked to be sure that it never came. And it never did.

The longevity of Arab regimes, not freedom in the Arab world, was the focus of academic inquiry. Among academic and think tank specialists, it became an article of faith that change would not come to the Arab world any time soon. As Marc Lynch of George Washington University puts it, "The uprisings destabilized not only the regimes themselves but also the findings of a sophisticated literature that developed over the previous decade to explain the resilience of authoritarian Arab states."[1] Like the Soviet collapse, the collapse of several Arab regimes was unforeseen by the most renowned experts. At a lunch I hosted at the Council on Foreign Relations in 2011, I asked Sir John Sawers, at that time the head of MI6, the British Secret Intelligence Service, whether he was not embarrassed that neither his intelligence agency nor any other had predicted the Arab Spring uprisings. He replied "Elliott, are you not embarrassed that neither your think tank nor any other predicted the Arab Spring uprisings?" Touché.

THE FREEDOM DEFICIT

This is not to say that no one mentioned freedom. In the first decade of the century, the president of the United States mentioned it repeatedly.

In a famous 2003 speech celebrating the twentieth anniversary of Ronald Reagan's creation of the National Endowment for Democracy, George W. Bush derided those who said Arabs would never gain freedom:

> Some skeptics of democracy assert that the traditions of Islam are inhospitable to the representative government. This "cultural condescension," as Ronald Reagan termed it, has a long history. After the Japanese surrender in 1945, a so-called Japan expert asserted that democracy in that former empire would "never work." Another observer declared the prospects for democracy in post-Hitler Germany are, and I quote, "most uncertain at best" – he made that claim in 1957. Seventy-four years ago, *The Sunday London Times* declared nine-tenths of the population of India to be "illiterates not caring a fig for politics." Yet when Indian democracy was imperiled in the 1970s, the Indian people showed their commitment to liberty in a national referendum that saved their form of government.[2]

Bush made his own conclusions clear:

> In many nations of the Middle East – countries of great strategic importance – democracy has not yet taken root. And the questions arise: Are the peoples of the Middle East somehow beyond the reach of liberty? Are millions of men and women and children condemned by history or culture to live in despotism? Are they alone never to know freedom, and never even to have a choice in the matter? I, for one, do not believe it.

Bush was not alone in discussing the necessity of expanding freedom in the Arab world. In 2002, the United Nations Development Program issued its annual *Human Development Report* for the seventeen Arab states. Written by Arab intellectuals, this report could not be subjected to the criticism Bush's speech later aroused: it was not political, could not be called an effort to justify invading Afghanistan or Iraq, and was not the voice of outsiders. In a passage that reverberated widely, the authors made freedom central to their analysis of Arab underdevelopment:

> There is a substantial lag between Arab countries and other regions in terms of participatory governance. The wave of democracy that transformed governance in most of Latin America and East Asia in the 1980s and Eastern Europe and much of Central Asia in the late 1980s and early

1990s has barely reached the Arab States. This freedom deficit undermines human development and is one of the most painful manifestations of lagging political development.... Freedom is both the guarantor and the goal of both human development and human rights.[3]

But whatever academics said about authoritarian resilience, it seemed to me – working from 2001 to January 2009 in the National Security Council – that authoritarians were not all so confident themselves. When the news brought reports of a food riot in Egypt – even a relatively minor event in a relatively minor city – we would also receive reports of how the presumably all-powerful ruler, Hosni Mubarak, would react. He took such protests seriously, ordering increases in subsidies for various commodities and telling the organs of repression (police, army, intelligence agencies) to pay very close and energetic attention.

Mubarak appeared at those moments to see Egypt not as a sleepy land destined to remain unfree for decades or centuries, but as a tinderbox ready to explode at any moment. He viewed his own regime, it seemed to me, as the best that Arabs could tolerate: not democratic in the Western sense, to be sure, but as the only alternative to the only other possibility, which was chaos. In the face of American efforts to promote democracy and free elections in Iraq, he advised instead choosing a general: someone who could rule and keep order, avoiding the violence and disorder that overwhelmed that country after the U.S. invasion. Of course it was easy to dismiss and even to deride that recommendation: "what Iraq needs is a Mubarak!" But I thought, hearing him suggest it, that he was sincere in believing that he understood Arab politics far better than we Americans did. The choice, he was saying, was autocracy or chaos, and the argument that this is the only available choice continues to be made today.

THE LEGITIMACY DEFICIT

The problem with his recommendation was that it did not address a problem from which his own regime suffered and which most other Arab regimes shared to some degree: a lack of legitimacy. "Legitimacy involves the capacity of a political system to engender and maintain the belief that existing political institutions are the most appropriate or proper ones for the society," the great sociologist Seymour Martin Lipset wrote in 1959.[4] In Mubarak's eyes, his own regime and the one he was recommending for Iraq met that test, but in the eyes of the people of those countries they did not. As Bernard Lewis put it years before the Arab Spring, "These regimes have little or no claim to the loyalty of their people and depend for survival on diversion and repression . . . . In those Arab countries where the government depends on force rather than loyalty, there is clear evidence of deep and widespread discontent, directed primarily against the regime and then inevitably against those who are seen to support it."[5]

The Arab monarchies had, in differing degrees to be sure, the legitimacy that comes from time itself and in some cases from claimed descent of the royal family from the Prophet Mohammed. But the fake Arab republics – Iraq in the Saddam period, Tunisia, Libya, Syria, Egypt, Algeria, and Yemen – by definition entirely lacked this sort of legitimacy and sometimes worsened their own situation by seeking to adopt a form of family rule. There was a kind of sweepstakes over which of Qadhafi's sons might succeed him, just as Bashar al-Assad had followed his own father. In Egypt, Gamal Mubarak was appointed head of the ruling National Democratic Party (NDP) and was widely discussed – and as widely resisted – as his father's successor. Whatever legitimacy Qadhafi had gained from the Libyan revolution, or Mubarak himself had as a former general who had inherited power when Sadat was assassinated and Mubarak was vice president, their sons had none. In Ben Ali's case the corruption and rapacity of his family were legendary. It was increasingly difficult in all these cases to persuade the mass of citizens that, as Lipset put it, "existing political institutions are the most appropriate or proper ones for the society." Nonroyal family succession and growing corruption put paid to that possibility.

Nor could those Arab rulers attain legitimacy by their performance in office, as to some degree China's rulers have done. The 2016 survey of trust in government by the firm Edelman Worldwide put the United Arab Emirates (UAE), China, and Singapore in the top five globally, despite limits on political rights and free expression in all three countries.[6] The UAE and Singapore have effective governments; China is awash in corruption, but perhaps 700 million people have been lifted out of poverty there in the last thirty-five years.[7]

In contrast, the governments of those fake Arab republics were famous for their corruption, and if there was some economic progress, none produced an economic miracle remotely like China's. In no case did the population appear to attribute whatever progress was made to the regime's particular policies and to be grateful to those in power for it. (The best case can be made for Algeria, where a near civil war in the 1990s between the military regime and Islamist rebels may have cost 100,000 lives and left the populace with a high tolerance for stability at almost any price. And as I write, Algeria is that unique Arab non-monarchic dictatorship that has experienced little civil unrest.) Stagnation, both economic and political, was the order of the day in much of the Middle East, and it produced popular attitudes that were little understood but not surprising: "by the end of the 2000s, people in Egypt, Iraq, Syria, Tunisia, and Yemen were among the least happy people in the world," according to a World Bank study. And the cause was not poverty: "the low levels of life satisfaction . . . did not reflect dissatisfaction with the level of income inequality or the income growth of the bottom 40 percent. . . . The unhappiness was instead associated with low standards of living, widespread corruption, and the lack of fairness."[8]

The best source of legitimacy, the formal consent of the governed, was in all these cases absent. There were sometimes voting mechanisms, but elections were never fair or free. They were occasions, where they existed, to mobilize the masses in a ritualized show of support for the ruler, and dissent was allowed only to the minor extent that it was convenient for foreign policy purposes.

The legitimacy of the rulers of the Arab "republics" was, then, the Achilles heel of their regimes. And even had they been able to rule more efficiently and produce visible gains for their people, they would not have been fully legitimate for reasons so persuasively described by the China scholar Andrew Nathan:

> Like all contemporary nondemocratic systems, the Chinese system suffers from a birth defect that it cannot cure: the fact that an alternative form of government is by common consent more legitimate. Even though the regime claims to be a Chinese form of democracy on the grounds that it serves the people and rules in their interest, and even though a majority

of Chinese citizens today accept that claim, the regime admits, and every-one knows, that its authority has never been subject to popular review and is never intended to be. In that sense, the regime is branded as an expedient, something temporary and transitional needed to meet the exigencies of the time. Democratic regimes, by contrast, often elicit disappointment and frustration, but they confront no rival form that outshines them in prestige. Authoritarian regimes in this sense are not forever. For all their diversity and longevity, they live under the shadow of the future, vulnerable to existential challenges that mature democratic systems do not face.[9]

Like Bush's speeches, this analysis was inspiring and suggested that democracy could break out anywhere. But it does not explain why it took so long to appear in the Arab world or why the hopes died so quickly in most Arab lands. Why did academics, experts, area specialists, and states-men conclude that Arab dictatorships were eternal, when other dictatorships around the globe had been upended? Why do they continue to believe that democracy is so far away in the Arab Middle East?

THE DIVIDED OPPOSITION

To begin with, opposition to the entrenched Arab regimes was divided. While this had been true to some extent nearly everywhere, from the Philippines to Argentina, in many cases the divisions were relatively minor. Sometimes opposition leaders, such as Benigno Aquino, Nelson Mandela, or Lech Walesa, captured extremely wide support. In those cases, Western-style democracy was the accepted goal and religious divisions were not deep; Left–Right political divisions sometimes were, but in many cases really emerged only after the regime had been overthrown.

Nowhere were opponents so divided as in the Arab world – largely due to Sunni/Shia and other religious and ethnic divisions, and to Islamism and the fear of Islamism. (It is no accident that Tunisia, the most successful of the Arab Spring countries, is one of the most homogeneous ethnically and religiously.) As to those divisions, an adviser to the U.S. military effort in Iraq explained that when President Bush said, "do you not think Arabs want to be free?" he was asking the wrong question. The answer to that was very likely "yes, they do." The more telling question for Arabs, however, should not have been "do you want to be free," but "do you want your *neighbor* to be free?" If the answer is "no, my neighbor is a Shia, damn him" or "no, he is a Sunni and I don't trust him" or the like, the basis for building a democratic system is weak. Even individuals who may see democracy as a desirable goal in theory may elevate their group's need for power (or simply for safety) over free elections, free speech, free press, impartial justice, and other elements of a democratic system that might work to the advantage of rival or enemy groups. When a society is deeply divided along these lines, no group will agree to lose when losing may mean risking life, limb, and property without recourse. The fear of "winner take all" systems is great enough in any unstable democracy; in a political system that is newly opened and characterized by unbridgeable ethnic and religious divisions, that fear may overwhelm all other considerations.

The same fear characterizes even ethnically homogeneous societies where Islamist forces are powerful. Secular, liberal, Western-style democrats feared political Islam and wondered whether the Islamist groups were democrats at all. Regimes cleverly played on these fears, as Ellen Lust writes, "suggesting to secularist opponents that they were better off with the 'devil they knew' than the one they did not (i.e., the regime rather than Islamists)."[10] To the extent that Islamist and secular regime opponents mistrusted each other and failed to join forces, they were weakened and the regimes strengthened. Lust explains that her argument is not so much about whether there is an Islamist threat to democracy in the Middle East, "but whether or not democratically-minded opponents believe that there is a high probability that opposition groups exist that would potentially subvert a democratic opening." As she notes, this is analogous to the problem of Communist parties in post–World War II Europe: were they to be permitted or outlawed, and what would happen if they won an election?

Sometimes the regimes kept Islamists out of politics entirely, which had the effect of keeping their real intentions about democracy a mystery. This meant that there was no basis for secular forces to trust them. In other cases, such as Mubarak's Egypt, Islamists were permitted a political role. In the last parliament elected under Mubarak, in 2010, the Muslim Brotherhood was permitted to run, and it won eighty-eight seats – or more accurately, Mubarak decided that it would hold no more than eighty-eight seats. Mubarak was pursuing a different strategy: weaken the center, allow the Islamists some space, and then use the latter's comparative strength to argue to Egyptians and especially to the United States that he and his dictatorship were the only bulwark against political Islam. As an Egyptian analyst puts it, while Mubarak ruled "the secular opposition faced many more barriers. Those barriers ranged from intimidation to administrative obstruction. The regime would much rather demonstrate that the democratic opposition is insignificant than face a stronger pro-democracy opposition that would be accepted – both internally and externally – as a potential replacement for the NDP. The real danger for the regime is a strong pro-democracy opposition, not the Islamists. The Mubarak regime could rely on international support against the Islamists, but it could not count on support against a strong pro-democracy opposition."[11]

In 2007, the Egyptian human rights activist Saad Eddin Ibrahim drew the picture: "In Egypt . . . the Mubarak regime tries to decimate all liberal alternatives . . . Democrats are constricted and must think like guerrillas, while Islamists have more public space open to them."[12] This is the situation that led an Egyptian democracy activist to tell me, when she visited me in the White House in 2003, that she did not favor free elections in Egypt. "Not now," she said; "but in ten years, if we can be free to organize for the ten years." Because democrats are most often not very good at thinking and acting like guerrillas and conspiring in secret, they end up growing weaker and weaker while Islamists are able to organize – a matter to which we will return.

Of course, the appeal of Islamist groups was not a creation of the regimes, even if their actions sometimes aided the Islamists. What we can say here is that the strength of the Islamist groups, ranging from the then-peaceful Egyptian Muslim Brotherhood to al-Qaeda and the "Islamic State," added further strength to the defenses of authoritarian rule before – and since – the Arab Spring. The regimes had a clear argument to make: the status quo may not be ideal, but all the realistic alternatives are worse.

WHAT ARE THE GOALS?

On the other side of the barricades, the demonstrators had no clear common ideas of what they stood for. The Arab Spring revolts were not organized around democracy, or Islam, or any other single and central cause. "Revolt is generally spontaneous, reactionary, and short-lived, and its success hinges on the mobilization of broad segments of the population against the regime," Stephen R. Grand writes. "Democratization, on the other hand, requires a positive political vision, not of what was but of what could be."[13] But these Arab uprisings were *against* regimes and not *for* principles. Ben Ali had to go, and the rule of Assad, Qadhafi, and the corrupt Mubarak family had to end. Justice had to be implemented and dignity respected. The event that led Mohammed Bouazizi to immolate himself was not a stolen election or the closing of a newspaper. Rather, he was a street vendor who was slapped and humiliated by a female police officer, and the offense was to his dignity rather than his freedom. The lack of a unified purpose and set of goals among regime opponents was a powerful reason that analysts thought they would not succeed.

Nor could such goals be imported or be found by emulating successful patterns and practices from nearby nations. Studies of previous and more successful waves of democratization had found that a critical element was the existence of a model and magnet, such as the European Union. As Lucan Way writes about the "lessons of 1989" in the states freed from Soviet control, "the single most important factor facilitating democratization was the strength of ties to the West."[14] Some countries with stronger democratic histories and movements, like the Czech Republic, might have democratized successfully anyway, but in others the struggle would have been tougher (and still is). That nearby there existed successful and rich democracies, and a democratic club in which membership and its likely economic rewards required democratization, had a powerful pull. The influence of the United States in the Western Hemisphere played a similar role, as it did for countries whose most important foreign tie was to the United States – for example, South Korea, Taiwan, and the Philippines. No similar pull exists in the Middle East. Local aid donors in the Gulf are monarchies uninterested in or actively opposed to democratization. The Arab League is a weak organization compared to the EU and anyway exercises no influence toward democratization. And the Western democracies, including the United States, have rarely designated democracy as the goal that George W. Bush made it for a time.

It is not difficult, then, to conclude that the Arab revolts were doomed and to be surprised not by this result but by the way in which Tunisia has evaded it – so far, at least. In their essay, "Why the Modest Harvest?" Jason Brownlee, Tarek Masoud, and Andrew Reynolds argue that in the Arab Spring "there were no structural preconditions for the emergence of uprisings: The fundamentally random manner in which protests spread meant that a wide variety of regimes faced popular challenges."[15] Where they see a pattern, instead, is in the ability of regimes to resist those challenges. To do so, the regimes needed some combination of money, which is to say oil and gas wealth, and what they call "the precedent of hereditary succession." Regimes that lacked either, such as in Libya, Tunisia, and Egypt, were doomed. Money allows rulers to buy guns and loyalty; established hereditary succession appears to enhance the loyalty of the security forces and deepen over time the ties between them and the ruling family.

THE MONARCHIES SURVIVE

What is most interesting in that explanation for the longevity of monarchic rule is that the word "legitimacy" does not appear – neither in relation to their claimed descent from the Prophet Mohammed nor from sheer longevity over decades and centuries. But this argument is not fully persuasive. In Bahrain the royal family had some (though not enormous) oil revenues, had ruled since 1783, and had loyal security forces, but came to be viewed as illegitimate by the majority of the populace because the royals are Sunni while the majority of the people are Shia. The loyalty of the security forces is easily explained by the fact that they too are Sunni. Similarly, the army in Syria has been loyal to President Assad largely because its top leadership and many of its officers are Alawite, members of the same small (12 percent of the population) group as the Assad clan and likely to suffer various disadvantages and dangers if he fell. Syria had little oil wealth, but has had considerable Iranian aid to augment its small oil revenues. The point is that neither Bahrain nor Syria, which both had modest wealth and patterns of hereditary succession, has escaped tur-moil. Conversely, Jordan and Morocco have less available cash, but have escaped such troubles.

I would argue, then, that those scholars underestimate the power of monarchical legitimacy in explaining the success, to date, of monarchies (with the exception of Bahrain) in avoiding revolts. They also understate the ability of the monarchs to play a sophisticated game in which they are simultaneously above politics and deeply enmeshed in it. In any soci-ety, and especially in the Middle East today, there is constant political maneuvering. The political scientists Baghat Korany, Rex Brynen, and Paul Noble explain the situation of the monarchs best: "they appear to be in a position to establish many of these rules and to thereby act simul-taneously as both interested players and far-from-impartial umpires in the political reform process." Can it last? They are not sure:

> [I]t is not clear whether, in the long term, the monarchical institu-tions established within some Arab countries will ease future reform (by providing greater stability), delay it (by controlling its progress), or act as a serious obstacle (given the difficulty of reconciling monarchy and democracy). It is also not clear that monarchs can continue to be both umpire and player; they may be delegitimized by internal or external cri-sis, or present monarchs may be succeeded by future monarchs with less political skill or legitimacy.[16]

It may be, for example, that at the moment when a real shift toward a con-stitutional monarchy is required, the incumbent king is totally opposed to this outcome and will not bend. In that case, the monarchic system may break. The fact that Bahrain's royal family required outside military inter-vention to stay in power suggests that in Bahrain that break has already occurred.

For now, the other monarchs are able to maneuver not only around secular democrats but Islamists as well, and neither in Jordan nor Morocco are Islamist parties excluded from political life. They run in elections, and in Morocco they sometimes win. The fear noted earlier that the Islamists' entry into politics may lead ineluctably to an Islamist state is reduced in monarchies, because the king can act as guarantor of the existing order.

The slow introduction of electoral politics in a monarchic system has another advantage: it may blunt the lead Islamists hold when there is a sudden lurch into an open political system brought about by the toppling of a regime after a revolt. As noted earlier, when Mubarak fell he left behind a system in which he had crushed the liberal, secular, centrist parties, but had played games with the Muslim Brotherhood. The Brotherhood's leaders were not in exile or in prison; many were in business or in parliament and well prepared to expand their political activities.

THE ISLAMISTS AND THE OPEN DOOR

And when the Arab Spring materialized, Islamists jumped to take advantage. Most Islamists had long been extremely suspicious of democracy, which they opposed in principle. The outcome of elections, and with it changes in what was viewed as right and moral and acceptable, could not possibly be the proper guide to conduct; the guide was the Koran and the words of the Prophet. Moreover, Islamists were well aware of the repressive power of the state and had been careful not to provoke it by radical moves to seize power. The weakest element in Mubarak's repeated warnings about the Egyptian Muslim Brotherhood was that the group had abandoned violence decades before and hardly seemed the aggressive threat that he described. Brotherhood leaders had, after all, repeatedly decided to play the political game by the rules he set, agreeing to limits on where they would run candidates and on how many seats they could hold in parliament.

Now, after 2011, that changed. Shadi Hamid sums it up: "The care and caution that had characterized Islamist groups for decades was pushed to the side in the wake of the uprisings of 2011. There was little time for preparation. With striking speed, they widened their ambitions. There was a time when Islamists used to lose elections on purpose. Now they seemed intent on making the most of a moment they feared would pass them by."[17] The best example: after Mubarak fell, Brotherhood leaders stated clearly that they would not run a candidate for president of Egypt. On February 10, 2011, the day before Mubarak was forced out, a Brotherhood leader named Mohamed Morsi told CNN, "The Muslim Brotherhood are not seeking power. We want to participate, not to dominate.

We will not have a presidential candidate, we want to participate and help, we are not seeking power."[18] Sixteen months later he was president of Egypt. The best analogy here may be to the Russian Revolution, because before the collapse of the tsarist regime in World War I the Bolsheviks had no chance of seizing power. But once the regime collapsed the opportunity arose, and their organizational skills allowed them to seize it. Similarly, the Brotherhood had no chance of taking power while Mubarak ruled and no chance of overthrowing him. But once he was deposed by a widespread insurrection centered on Tahrir Square – an insurrection the Brotherhood did not start and in which it did not at first participate – it was the only group sufficiently well organized to grasp power, so it changed its objectives and did so.

The "care and caution" gone, these movements were liberated into politics. Once upon a time Islamists had viewed the state as a Western idea foreign to the world of Islam, whose proper organization required a pan-Islamic caliphate. Of course that idea has returned in the form of the "Islamic State" or ISIS, but the successes of ISIS in recruiting thousands of young Muslims from around the world do not prove that very many Muslims throughout the Middle East favor its proposals for the elimination of states and the end of all forms of nationalism. Most Islamist groups made their peace with nationalism, and the nation-state "became the framework in which politics took place." As Jocelyne Cesari describes it, "Islamist opposition movements gradually used Islam more as an alternative to secular nationalism promoted by state elites and less as a way to promote a pan-Islamic caliphate."[19] They did not oppose the existence of the state, but argued instead that it needed to be permeated by faith and justice, rather than corruption and repression. As Shadi Hamid puts it, "If following the sharia – for example, refraining from alcohol and adultery, observing the fast, and praying five times a day – is a precondition for salvation, then the state has a role in encouraging the good and forbidding evil."[20] To many, probably most, citizens of Arab states in the last century, the state has been less a provider of law and order and of common goods, such as security, education, and health services, than it has been a constant threat to their well-being. Its agents are abusive and erratic, its leaders corrupt and violent, its impact on them and their families rarely benign. So the Islamists looked to the Koran for guidance about the kind of state that was proper and just and to which loyalty would be owed, and explained to their fellow citizens how the reality of Arab states in the twentieth century contrasted with what the Koran required.

THE ARAB STATE

This was a powerful argument in any Arab country, because state institutions were everywhere weak and corrupt – with two exceptions. The security institutions were almost everywhere huge and immensely powerful; the phrase "mukhabarat state," named for the *mukhabarat* or intelligence service, came into use to describe who really held power in many Arab countries. And where there were monarchies the royal courts were potent as well. The civil institutions of the state, such as education ministries and courts of justice, regulatory agencies, and local governments, were most often very weak, performing poorly, and impervious to citizen pressure while elites and the "big men" of politics could get their way and protect their interests. Representative democratic institutions such as local assemblies and national parliaments were powerless in most Arab countries. There were exceptions: Kuwait's parliament could interpellate ministers and had forced several out of office, leading to political crises there. But in almost all Arab capitals before the Arab Spring, the parliaments were either nonexistent or were rubber stamps for the regime.

It is possible to view the establishment of these phony legislative assemblies as a step forward in the long-delayed arrival of representative democracy in the Arab Middle East. First they are created, then decades go by, but sooner or later the empty vessel is filled with political meaning. This happened briefly in Egypt after Mubarak fell – until parliament was suspended in 2012 and the executive began ruling by decree. And it has happened in Tunisia, which has a real parliament. Under the post–Arab Spring constitution adopted in Morocco, whoever heads the largest party in parliament is automatically named prime minister by the king – giving parliament and parliamentary elections some reality (though most power remains in the royal palace). In this view, progress is slow, but representative institutions are inevitable.

The Israeli scholar Amichai Magen describes that positive view this way:

> With the advent of the Arab Spring, freedom's long march had finally reached the southern shores of the Mediterranean and the Arab heartland.... Like water dripping on a rock, the forces of modernization and globalization have corroded and finally cracked open the last remaining region of the world that has long appeared – mistakenly, as it turned out – impregnable to the norms and institutions of political competition and accountability.... Urbanization, higher levels of literacy, and the internet produced social mobilization, attitudinal change, and expectations for a better life.[21]

Thus did "Freedom's March," as he described this theory, reach the Arab lands: "Viewed through this lens, the 2011 Arab revolts represent another important milestone in the centuries-long process by which modern political norms and institutions have traveled – by conquest, trade, and diffusion of ideas – from modest origins in eighteenth-century Europe to global dominance at the beginning of the twenty-first."[22] And as he explains, if this theory is correct, it must include an assertion that capitalist democracy has defeated or will defeat all its ideological rivals, from the old-fashioned Arab Socialism of Nasser to Communism to Salafi-jihadi ideology.

The "modest harvest" of the Arab Spring throws this theory into doubt. Perhaps what we are really seeing, as Magen also notes, is more simply widespread state failure. This is partly due to the lack of legitimacy, as we have discussed, but Magen takes the argument further: in many cases it is not the regime that is illegitimate but the state itself. States such as Syria and Iraq were colonialist creations, often held together by sheer brutality. They did not command the loyalty of their divided populations, whose key affiliations were to their tribe or religious sect. As Magen puts it,

> Rather than go through a slow, convoluted process of state formation culminating in the development of the rule of law, accountability, and national identity Arab states became states before they could truly become nations. But the experiment in instant state formation has basically failed,

and we are now witnessing the manifestation of this failure on a grand historical and regional scale. Arab states are mostly Potemkin-states; brittle entities increasingly unable to hold themselves together by commanding the loyalty of their populace and exercising an effective monopoly on the legitimate use of force within their borders.[23]

This is obviously not the case for an ancient nation like Egypt, which long predates the modern state, but there are few such examples.

THE MISSING DEMOCRATS

If loyalty to the modern Arab state is missing, and if the state itself does not function justly and efficiently, why do democrats not rise up to demand reform? The answer appears to be, "What democrats?"

This is not a new problem – to say the least. Gouverneur Morris reported to George Washington from Paris in the 1790s about the French Revolution that its leaders "want an American constitution, with the exception of a king instead of a president, without reflecting that they have not American citizens to support that constitution."[24] We will return later to the issue of "liberal" and "illiberal" democracy and the potential conflict between democracy and Islam or Islamism, but here it suffices to point out the paucity – though not the nonexistence – of support in the Arab world for Western-style reform. As Magen puts it, "Quite unlike in Central and Eastern Europe in the 1980s, there is no effective liberal opposition ready to succeed the old regimes – no Arab equivalent of the Polish Solidarity movement. Decades of modern autocracy in the Arab world have all but decimated the middle-class, liberal constituencies in most Arab countries."[25]

It might be better to say "decades of modern autocrats" have decimated liberal and non-Islamist opposition groups, and done so deliberately as we saw in the case of Mubarak. An example is the case of the Wasat Party in Egypt, a moderate Islamist group that was founded in 1996 and competed with the Muslim Brotherhood. Four times between 1996 and 2009 the state refused al-Wasat an official license, and it gained official recognition only after Mubarak was deposed. Those refusals were part of Mubarak's effort to weaken reformist and liberal groups that might attract a following – and might weaken his argument that the sole choice was between his own regime and Islamist extremism. The legalistic approach of al-Wasat was notable as well: its leaders made repeated efforts to gain legal recognition rather organizing their group underground.

But there is a deeper problem here, as the Egyptian American scholar Samuel Tadros explains:

> You cannot achieve a result if there is no one trying to achieve it. A liberal democracy is not born out of thin air. It requires the existence of liberal democrats. And if the term means something more than people who are simply not Islamists and not extreme leftists, then they are absent in Egyptian politics. There are very few liberals in Egypt, not because Egyptians are averse to liberalism or are different from any other people, but because there is no liberalism in Egypt. There is no liberal discourse in the public square. People cannot belong to an ideology that does not exist. With hardly any liberal books written in Arabic and no translations of the major works of Western liberalism, those liberals in Egypt are but a privileged few who are able and willing to read in a foreign language.[26]

What Tadros reports about Egypt is true more broadly in the Arab world, and Stephen R. Grand states the point sharply: "over the long term successful democratization requires the emergence of a political constituency that supports democracy.... At the end of the day, democracy requires democrats."[27]

We will revisit this question when we consider whether American support for democracy programs in Arab lands is actually a fool's errand – or worse, is likely to open the door only to Islamist takeovers. Tadros's pessimism raises the issue of why anyone should be even the least bit surprised about the outcome of the Arab Spring or the least bit optimistic about the prospects for Arab democracy.

There are both general and specific answers. At the global level, the question is whether in any society anywhere people actually prefer an abusive and corrupt regime. Who, after all, would prefer a situation where secret policemen come at midnight to arrest your spouse or parents or children? As the former Soviet dissident Natan Sharansky put it, "There is a universal desire among all peoples not to live in fear. Indeed, given a choice, the vast majority of people will always prefer a free society to a fear society."[28] Sharansky is not wrong, but each individual may have a different definition of his or her "society." A free society for my group, my "society," sure – but perhaps I view other groups not as potential participants in that free polity, but rather as threats to its freedom or its very existence.

In sustaining a democracy the question is not only whether the individual wishes to live freely – but also whether he or she wishes everyone else to live freely as well, in a truly democratic system. The divisions in Arab societies – Islamist and secular, Sunni and Shia, monarchist and republican – clearly weaken the chances for democracy, but societal divisions have not eliminated the acceptance of democracy as a goal. One need not accept only general, or philosophical, arguments that Arabs surely seek freedom because all men and women do. Studies of public opinion in Arab lands have produced plenty of evidence that a strong desire for freedom exists.

In a round of polls done in 2012–2014 – some of the latest surveys available as I wrote this – more than three-quarters of Arab respondents said they agreed or strongly agreed with the statement, "A democratic system may have problems, yet it is better than other political systems."[29] The conclusion drawn by the authors is that "Arab publics continue overwhelmingly to support democracy." Similarly, opinion surveys done in late 2016 found that Arabs saw "lack of representative government in some Arab countries" as the "greatest obstacle to peace and stability in the Middle East." The pollsters concluded, "Considering the choices made in each country for the two greatest obstacles to peace and stability, the lack of representative government . . . is the most frequent selection overall."[30]

An interesting and encouraging insight into the possibilities for Arab democracy is provided by what happened in parts of Syria when the hand of the repressive Syrian state was removed – even during Syria's bloody conflict. "Against all odds, village republics take hold in Syria" was the headline in an article in the UAE's English-language newspaper *The National* in July 2016. The bottom line: Syrians in many places reacted to the removal of the state by establishing democratic local government, chosen in free elections. Here are some excerpts from this article:

> You may think Syrians are condemned to an unpleasant choice between
> Bashar Al Assad and the jihadists. But the real choice being fought out by

Syrians is between violent authoritarianism on the one hand and grass-roots democracy on the other . . . . [W]e discovered the democratic option is real, even if beleaguered. To the extent that life continues in the liberated but heavily bombed areas – areas independent of both the Assad regime and ISIL – it continues because self-organised local councils are supplying services and aid . . . . [T]he Syrian desire for democracy burns as fiercely as ever. Where possible, the local councils are democratically elected – the first free elections in half a century . . . . As the US-led invasion of Iraq showed us, only the people themselves can build their democratic structures. And today Syrians are practising democracy, building their own institutions, in the most difficult of circumstances. Their efforts don't fit in with the easy Assad-or-ISIL narrative, however, and so we rarely deign to notice.[31]

Writing in 2015 in a *Journal of Democracy* article titled "People Still Want Democracy," the director of the Arab Barometer, Michael Robbins, asks whether after the Arab Spring "the uprisings' almost universal failure to produce democratic transitions [is] a signal that citizens in the region have given up on democracy?" He draws the opposite conclusion: "The uprisings and the events that followed did little to dampen the overall demand for democracy in the region as a whole. Citizens have continued to believe, as they did before the protests, that democracy is the best form of government and that the regimes in their countries have a long way to go to become fully democratic." Moreover, he concludes, "Not only do citizens hold favorable attitudes toward democracy, but vast majorities also agree that democracy, despite its problems, is the best political system." Nor do Arabs buy the usual arguments against democracy. "Few Arab citizens believe that democracy is harmful to the economy" and "few Arab publics blame democracy for the rise in regional instability that followed the uprisings."[32]

These findings are not anomalous. A slightly earlier analysis concluded, "According to Freedom House's annual 'Freedom in the World' report for 2010, no Arab country was a democracy at the time of either the first or the second wave of surveys, yet support for democracy is extremely high by a range of measures . . . . In fact, support for democracy in these countries is higher than in many longstanding democracies."[33]

Of course, what is meant by "democracy" can be debated: to some Arab participants, it may mean the end of poverty, or more economic equality, or more vaguely a just society, rather than the usual American political definition. Two political scientists who designed the Arab Barometer surveys note, "Respondents who support democracy are not necessarily democrats. They may support democracy, and sincerely, without necessarily possessing a democratic political culture orientation" – meaning such values as tolerance, interpersonal trust, or an interest in politics.[34] And even if the desire for democracy is strong, the ability to achieve and sustain it can be very limited for all the reasons we have seen, such as the lack of liberal democrats, the weakness of democratic parties, the underdevelopment or nonexistence of democratic institutions, the power of repressive security institutions, the lack of relevant democratic models, and religious and social divisions.

Moreover, democracy everywhere faces the challenge of individuals and groups who simply do not wish to give up the power they hold. This is a simple point but one whose power is often overlooked. As Stephen R. Grand summarizes it, "Left to their own devices, political leaders are unlikely to cede powers that they could otherwise exercise themselves.... What is striking in the country case studies in the preceding chapters is how often incumbents appeared to be the greatest obstacle to further democratization."[35]

The problem then becomes, who will take that power from them? A rival group of autocrats? An extremist group? Grand concludes,

> Democratization emerges out of a prolonged struggle between political leaders intent on maintaining their perquisites and citizens determined to circumscribe the power of those leaders in the name of creating more transparent, accountable, and participatory governance and protecting personal and political freedoms.... In the Arab world, it will take sustained engagement on the part of the people if they are to wrest control of government from the small circle of elites that have long dominated it and dismantle the "deep state" that successive authoritarian leaders have erected.[36]

For a brief moment the Arab Spring seemed to provide an answer to all these questions. The autocrats were being overthrown, the people were rising up and demanding democracy, free elections were being held – and then everywhere except Tunisia things fell apart. Once again scholars and political leaders wondered whether Arab or Muslim democracy, rather than being inevitable, was in fact closer to being impossible.

CHAPTER 2

Arab and Muslim Democracy

THE HIGH POINT OF DEMOCRATIC OPTIMISM WAS FRANK Fukuyama's book, *The End of History and the Last Man*, published in 1992. There he posited the nearly inevitable victory of liberal democracy, which was defeating all challengers:

> As mankind approaches the end of the millennium, the twin crises of authoritarianism and socialist central planning have left only one competitor standing in the ring as an ideology of potentially universal validity: liberal democracy, the doctrine of individual freedom and popular sovereignty.... [T]he fact that there will be setbacks and disappointments in the process of democratization, or that not every market economy will prosper, should not distract us from the larger pattern that is emerging in world history.... [T]he only form of government that has survived intact to the end of the twentieth century has been liberal democracy. What is emerging victorious, in other words, is not so much liberal practice, as the liberal idea.... [T]he remarkable worldwide character of the current liberal revolution takes on special significance. For it constitutes further evidence that there is a fundamental process at work that dictates a common evolutionary pattern for all human societies – in short, something like a Universal History of mankind in the direction of liberal democracy.[1]

Fukuyama in later works qualified these conclusions, but even in the original formulation one had to wonder about one missing element: there were not two challenges to democracy – authoritarianism and central planning – but three. Had Fukuyama left out Islam? He did discuss it, acknowledging its uniqueness, but suggesting that it would not last:

It is true that Islam constitutes a systematic and coherent ideology, just like liberalism and communism, with its own code of morality and doctrine of political and social justice.... And Islam has indeed defeated liberal democracy in many parts of the Islamic world, posing a grave threat to liberal practices even in countries where it has not achieved power directly.... Despite the power demonstrated by Islam in its current revival, however, it remains the case that this religion has virtually no appeal outside those areas that were culturally Islamic to begin with. The days of Islam's cultural conquests, it would seem, are over: it can win back lapsed adherents, but has no resonance for young people in Berlin, Tokyo, or Moscow.... Indeed, the Islamic world would seem more vulnerable to liberal ideas in the long run than the reverse, since such liberalism has attracted numerous and powerful Muslim adherents over the past century and a half. Part of the reason for the current, fundamentalist revival is the strength of the perceived threat from liberal, Western values to traditional Islamic societies.[2]

Fukuyama was right in suggesting that Islam would not win masses of converts from other religions, and perhaps over time he will be proven right about the vulnerability of Muslims to the attraction of liberal ideas. But we need to distinguish democracy and liberalism, for it is not only possible but likely that Muslims will adopt forms of democracy that do not seem sufficiently liberal to many in the West. We will discuss later what "illiberal democracy" might look like in Muslim and Arab lands.

The first question is whether Islam is compatible with democracy. The returns here are in, and the clear answer is yes. The problem with which we are dealing in the Middle East is not Islamic barriers to democracy but Arab barriers. As one study noted, in the thirty-year period from 1973 to 2003, "a non-Arab Muslim-majority country was almost 20 times more likely to be 'electorally competitive' than an Arab-majority Muslim country."[3] There are examples of Muslim democracies that Freedom House rates as free (Senegal) or partly free (including the most populous Muslim country in the world, Indonesia, as well as Kosovo, Bangladesh, Malaysia, Mali, Pakistan, and Turkey before the post-coup events of 2016). As the political scientist Alfred Stepan put it when he looked at this issue and summed up his findings, "We hope...that we have eliminated the basis for any theory of 'Islamic exceptionalism' when it comes to holding competitive elections. Some may say we have created 'Arab exceptionalism.'"[4]

Some of the Arabs' problems are not very rare. Arab states are what used to be called "underdeveloped." As Sanford Lakoff explains it, "All the usual Third World barriers to democracy are much in evidence: illiteracy and ignorance; tribalism and ethnic conflict; abysmal poverty for the masses coupled with privilege and luxury for the few; relatively high rates of population growth in low-growth economies where the numerous young are then sentenced to joblessness; the repression of women; and rule by corrupt, self-aggrandizing dynasts and dictators."[5]

What are the special characteristics of Arab societies that separate them from Muslim nations in Africa and Asia, and from other "underdeveloped" lands? Stepan and Graeme Robertson attribute the difference to history. A modern democratic state must first of all be a state, with borders, within which a genuine political community can develop and function. But many Arab states have arbitrary borders fixed by colonial powers when the Ottoman Empire fell apart, and the population inside the borders lacks "a strong affective attachment to, and identity with, the specific institutions and symbols of the political community within the country's boundaries." They are not nation-states, and that harms their ability to develop modern democratic politics.[6] These are the "Sykes-Picot states," created when Britain and France (represented by the diplomats Mark Sykes and François Georges-Picot) divided the region in 1916. To this Stepan and Robertson add another key, and no doubt related, factor: the outsized spending on security establishments and their outsized role. These "Sykes-Picot states" are also "*mukhabarat* states" – as we have seen, a reference to their internal intelligence and security services, called the *mukhabarat* in Arabic.

Other scholars such as Etel Solingen contrast the way East Asian leaders "watchfully steered states to macroeconomic stability and proper conditions for export-led growth," while in the Middle East, Arab leaders pursued heavy-handed state control that led to "rigid, exhausted and depleted state institutions presiding over current account and budget deficits; high inflation and unemployment; and scarce foreign exchange.... This Middle East pattern replaced and often decimated the private sector whereas East Asian growth models nurtured them. The former entrenched *mukhabarat* repressive states; the latter professionalized militaries with far more limited political control over the economy and polity." The result: the Arab states "became too weak to exert control over society except through force."

Though the end goal may not have been democracy, the East Asian model opened the door to it while the *mukhabarat* state kept it closed, as Solingen explains:

> Export-led models incepted by authoritarian leaders and ruling coalitions in East Asia were not precisely designed to advance democracy. However those models unintentionally encouraged democratic institutions via several causal mechanisms: fostering economic growth, stronger private sectors and civil societies, and more professionalized militaries attuned to outward-oriented growth. Over time several – though not all – authoritarian regimes in East Asia evolved into full-fledged democracies. By contrast, Middle East models engendered higher barriers to the development of democratic institutions: weaker private sectors and weakened civil societies less able to demand political reform and entrenched military industrial complexes better able to resist those demands.[7]

All states that are nondemocratic have powerful security forces, for the obvious reason: that is the only way those in power are likely to remain in power. But the mukhabarat state is different: "Middle Eastern and especially Arab exceptionalism was a reference not just to its authoritarianism but, at least for some analysts, also to the pervasiveness of subterranean networks of power emanating from coercive agencies."[8] The armed forces and the intelligence services, under centralized control, penetrate the entire state, and often the economy and society as well.

Egypt under President Sisi is a case in point: the military had intervened to remove President Morsi and the Muslim Brotherhood from power and then seized power over all aspects of the state. Robert Springborg sums it up well: the military was "visibly in charge of the state, the economy, public security, and indeed, everything" and by 2015 was "simultaneously trying to manage the economy, reconstruct the political system, conduct a counterinsurgency campaign, modernize its own forces, and devise a consistent foreign policy, all without substantial civilian input." The result is that the "relationship between the Egyptian military and state is turned on its head, with the latter reporting to the former rather than vice versa."[9] And there is no room in this model for progress toward democracy.

One must conclude, then, that whatever the barriers to democratic development in poor Muslim countries anywhere, the chips are stacked pretty high against Arab democracy. Indeed the only reason for optimism is the polls constantly showing, year after year, that the citizens appear to want something they call "democracy."

DEMOCRACY AND LIBERAL DEMOCRACY

We thus face the question of whether we are all talking about the same things and whether democracy would produce the liberal societies with which we are most familiar in the Anglosphere (Australia, New Zealand, Canada, the United Kingdom, and the United States), in Western Europe and the EU, and in most of the newer democracies of Asia and Latin America.

The simple answer is no, especially with respect to religious and sexual matters. For one thing, the liberal ideas that have been circulating in the West since Voltaire in the eighteenth century and John Stuart Mill in the nineteenth remain largely absent in the Arab world. Of course they are available now, due to the internet, but in English and French, and it is still fair to say that they do not circulate. Recall the words of Samuel Tadros quoted in Chapter 1: in Egypt, "[t]here is no liberal discourse in the public square . . . . With hardly any liberal books written in Arabic and no translations of the major works of Western liberalism, those liberals in Egypt are but a privileged few who are able and willing to read in a foreign language."[10] As one Kuwaiti liberal activist put it, "Kuwait has liberals, but there is no liberalism. There is a big difference between the two. You will find liberal individuals, but liberalism as a concept in society remains weak."[11]

Islamists are leading in a different direction, away from Western-style liberalism. If liberalism and liberal democracy depend on inalienable or constitutional rights, Islamists believe that there exist supra-legal and supra-constitutional principles that trump popular sovereignty. Those principles are God-given, and found in the Koran.

This does not mean an inevitable opposition to electoral democracy, because it may appear to Islamists that free elections are the most sensible route to power. Armed struggle favors those best prepared to wage it. In the mukhabarat state, which is typically both repressive and secular, there will usually be two such groups: first, the army and security services, and second, their enemies in the jihadi groups such as al-Qaeda or ISIS. Islamist political and religious groups like the Muslim Brotherhood and nonviolent Salafist parties and organizations will not be prepared for an armed fight.

So the Islamists may decide to seek power at the ballot box once that opportunity appears. The problem is what Islamists then do with the power gained democratically in free elections. The familiar phrase "one man, one vote, one time" sums up the fear that Islamists will use power legitimately gained to close off the possibility that they will ever lose it. In Egypt we saw just such a case in the conduct of Mohamed Morsi as president: his actions in power deliberately weakened rather than strengthened Egypt's new democratic system. Indeed he went so far so fast that a counter-reaction soon arose: a coalition that supported a military coup to remove him from power and that included most of Egypt's secular and liberal political leaders. They believed, at least then in 2013, that they and their principles would fare better during and after another period of military rule than after a few more years of Muslim Brotherhood dominance. But in Tunisia, the opposite happened: the Ennahda Party seemed chastened by power and sought out coalitions with secular parties. After its defeat in a free election, it agreed to relinquish power and to join a new government as the junior coalition partner.

One can attribute this discrepancy in conduct to unique historical factors or to the luck of good or bad leadership, but it does undermine the conclusion that always and everywhere an Islamist political victory spells the end of democracy. But again, what kind of democracy? Shadi Hamid asks this question in his book, *Temptations of Power: Islamists and Illiberal Democracy in a New Middle East*:

> At the end of history, Fukuyama wrote, "the state that emerges ... is liberal insofar as it recognizes and protects through a system of law man's universal right to freedom, and democratic insofar as it exists only with the consent of the governed." But what Fukuyama failed to grapple with is whether a state could claim the latter without enjoying the former. The question here is whether the democratic process, in the long run, will blunt the ideological pretensions of Islamist groups, forcing them to move to the center, back into the confines of the liberal democratic consensus.[12]

That "liberal democratic consensus" is multidimensional, and Islamists will have no trouble with certain aspects of it, such as equality before the law (at least for Muslims), independent courts of justice, or the fair counting of election ballots. But as noted, two aspects will give them the most trouble: sexuality and religion. As to the latter, Jocelyne Cesari has told us to expect what she calls "hegemonic Islam," rather than what we think of as freedom of religion. What does she mean?

> [M]ultiple initiatives to preserve the status of Islam as the religion of the nation through a discriminatory use of law, detrimental not only to religious minorities but also to Muslim citizens who wish to assert freedom of speech. Concretely, it means that places of worship, clerics, and institutions of the dominant religion are part of the state institutions and, in addition, that the central status of religion in public space is secured by blasphemy laws and limitations on conversion.[13]

This will produce, she tells us in another useful phrase, "unsecular democracy," which is "the limitation by law of the rights of the person on two levels: spiritual and sexual by criminalizing blasphemy, homosexuality, and indecency."[14] Indeed, the political goals of the Islamist blocs in Kuwait have included political liberalization but also cultural restrictions, such as gender segregation in schools, rejection of female suffrage, restriction of working hours for women, and laws punishing the expression of critical comments about Islam.[15]

So the Western principle that the state must regard and protect all religions and religious beliefs equally is discarded; traditional Islam has a special position. The state will likely pay the salaries for imams and the upkeep of mosques, and teach Islam in public schools. It will ban or severely limit prosyletizing by any other religion, while permitting it to Muslims. It will legislate traditional Muslim teachings and practices about the role of women and about family law (covering matters such as marriage and divorce, and women's legal rights to inheritance).[16]

The degree of "hegemony" in "hegemonic Islam" will vary from state to state, and Cesari herself points out that regimes of legal neutrality exist in Senegal, Indonesia, and Lebanon. And she was writing before Tunisia's Ennahda Party relinquished power and joined a secular-led coalition. Because these are among the freest Muslim and Arab lands, there appears to be an obvious link between the neutrality of the state on religious matters and the advance of political freedom.

But we should not expect that Arab societies will leap suddenly from "hegemonic Islam" to the kind of neutrality we idealize in the West, nor should we demand it. Democracy will not instantly produce liberalism on these questions, and secularization and democracy should not be confused as goals or as actual trends. The rise of democratic thinking mentioned in Chapter 1, seen for example in the Arab Human Development Reports, coincided with a "re-Islamization" and rise of both Islamist parties and Islamist practices in everyday life, as Olivier Roy pointed out.[17] A democrat need not be a liberal on these questions related to the role of religion. Certainly the converse is also true: a secularist need not be a democrat, and we have certainly seen many secular regimes that were brutally repressive, such as those of Assad in Syria and Ben Ali in Tunisia.

It was Fareed Zakaria who popularized the concept of "illiberal democracy" in his 1997 article in *Foreign Affairs*.[18] While historically democracy and liberalism have tended to arrive together, or liberalism has preceded the establishment of more democratic political systems, more recently we have been seeing democracy produce illiberal results that often reflected popular desires. Constitutional limits, equality before the law, separation of church and state, and other fundamental Western ideals were in some newly democratic systems being cast off or never adopted. Often ethnic, racial, or geographic rivalries or conflicts were reflected in the election returns.

In a sense this is normal. The adoption of a bicameral legislature in the United States, with one house selected to represent state and sectoral interests rather than population, and the continuing existence of the Electoral College, both reflect just this kind of conflict, and the outcome is less than purely "democratic." Democratic politics does not assume the absence of conflict; the American system in fact assumed its existence and sought ways to manage it. The many systems that provide for representation of ethnic or religious groups in positions of power (for example in Lebanon, where constitutionally the president must be Christian, the prime minister Sunni Muslim, and the parliament speaker Shia Muslim) are examples of other ways to address the need for conflict management.

But adverse interests that reflect the desire for land or money or jobs can be addressed by hard bargaining and political combat. Religion is a different matter, where compromise may appear impossible or even evil to many voters. This is not a phenomenon of Islam: our own practices of religious tolerance emerged less from the Enlightenment than from religious wars in Europe and "grudging truces in savage wars of religion" that lasted centuries.[19] Today the battlefield is within the Islamic world, and the problem is the same: compromise over religion is harder. Shadi Hamid explains,

> For Islamists, illiberal democracy is not an unfortunate fact of life but something to believe in and aspire to. Although they may struggle to define what it entails, Islamist parties have a distinctive intellectual and ideological "project." This is why they are *Islamist*... Illiberal democracies exist all over the world, but, whether of the leftist or right-wing varieties, their illiberalism is usually negotiable. Restricting personal rights or freedoms is a product of the desire to consolidate power, rather than stemming from any particular ideological conviction. Yet, illiberalism is central to the Islamist raison d'etre: they're supposed to be illiberal.[20]

Conflict is, then, inevitable, but we should recall that this is not a special weakness of Arab nations: every society needs to work through these very questions. Reaching the current set of solutions in the West took generations of bloody conflict, and some questions are not resolved to this day, especially those related to sexuality: witness the struggles over homosexual marriage and over abortion and the law in the United States over the last several decades. That Arab states and citizens should struggle, sometimes violently, to find compromises ought to be unsurprising. Moreover, that those compromises with respect to sexuality and to the role of the dominant religion in the region, Islam, will not look like the Western outcomes with which we are most familiar should also be unsurprising.

What may be most disturbing to Western observers is not that there will be political combat, but the sense that liberalism is doomed – that Islamists will win each engagement, such that democracy itself will inevitably produce terrible outcomes. If this is true, liberalism and democracy as we understand them are on a collision course that will leave liberalism dead and Islamism victorious in every Arab state. No doubt many Western observers would, faced with that choice, prefer a secular and authoritarian regime to a democratically elected Islamist state. Better Mubarak than Morsi; better the generals than the mullahs. But are the Islamists always going to win?

CHAPTER 3

Will the Islamists Always Win?

THE MOST DANGEROUS THING FOR THE ISLAMISTS IS TO BE loved by the people before they get to power and then hated afterward," said Rachid Ghannouchi, the leader of the Islamist party Ennahda in Tunisia.[1] This is to some degree what happened in Tunisia, where Ennahda won the first election but failed to maintain its popularity. What Ghannouchi understood was that the conditions that favor the Islamists under the *ancien régime* do not necessarily guarantee success once the political system opens up.

The critical point is that the repression Islamists suffer under military regimes and other Arab dictatorships does not typically crush them, but instead broadens their appeal and popularity – at least for a while. How does this happen?

THE ISLAMISTS' ADVANTAGE

First, those regimes are corrupt and the citizens know it. Wikileaks cables from the U.S. Embassy in Tunis that were made public in 2010 showed Tunisians that their suspicions and beliefs about their government were actually shared and confirmed by the United States. The *New York Times* reported that "the diplomats' disgusted and lurid accounts of the kleptocratic ways of the president's extended family helped tip the scales, according to many Tunisian commentators" and contributed to the January 2011 uprising.[2] But Islamist groups do not share in these riches, nor do they face any such temptations. Over time, this isolation from corruption means that they acquire a reputation for purity or integrity.

Second, ruling elites are mostly interested in remaining in and wielding power, and in their own further enrichment. While the state continues to provide a variety of social services, the quality and quantity of these services are typically poor – both because non-oil-producing Arab countries are poor and because the elites are largely uninterested in improving services for citizens who have no influence. The elites do not need to appeal to the masses for votes, so the complaints of poor citizens do not elicit government action. This opens a great opportunity for Islamist groups, which can offer social services (health care, education, food) as an act of charity that is greatly valued by recipients and establishes for the Islamists a reputation for humanism, energy, efficiency, and probity.

Third, while secular and liberal alternatives to the ruling elites do exist in most Arab states, they are very small and concentrated in upper middle class circles in the largest cities. Their outreach to the mass of poor and often rural citizens is weak. In part this weakness is the result of a deliberate strategy of the government, as we have seen in the case of Mubarak's Egypt: while the Muslim Brotherhood was allowed a significant minority presence in parliament (eighty-eight seats in Mubarak's last parliament, elected in 2010), liberal groups were treated far worse. The moderates and liberals were repressed more energetically than the Brotherhood, prevented, for example, from forming a more moderate Islamist political party.

In part the weakness of the more liberal forces is due to geography: it reflects the distance between urban upper middle classes and the rural poor. But even liberal and democratic NGOs located in the cities may have few contacts with the urban neighborhoods that are close to their offices: often, liberal NGOs have broad ties with Western capitals and funders but few internal links. Their budgets come from overseas. In a sense their constituencies are found in places like London and Washington, where in many cases their staff members were educated. Mubarak regime officials used to refer to such groups dismissively, when talking with us in the U.S. government in Washington, for those reasons. We were wasting our time working with those NGOs; they had no support; they did not understand Egypt. And the lack of competitive politics prevents such organizations and their staffs from learning how to campaign for their views and programs; repression further constrains their ability to learn. All this means that the more secular groups are weak competitors to the Islamists when the moment of open political competition does arrive.

Shadi Hamid points out as well that "most Arab countries lack strong, coherent party structures, yet, during democratic openings, citizens are asked to practice politics through political parties, which are weak or nonexistent. It can take years, if not decades, for new parties to build themselves up from scratch." Islamists did not have organized parties in many cases, but "as ideologically coherent movements, they could easily 'convert' themselves into parties.... Liberals didn't have the binding organizational structures of Islamists."[3] That gave the latter an immediate advantage.

So the Islamists emerge from long periods of repression with a political advantage, and it is this advantage that leads so many to fear a political opening. Will not democracy inevitably mean Islamist control?

Marwan Muasher, the Middle East analyst who is a former foreign minister of Jordan, argues precisely the opposite:

> Religious parties...found two voids to fill: one was the abandonment of the social terrain by ruling cliques increasingly interested in lining their own pockets, and the other was the political void created by the suppression of secular opposition. These groups benefited from the fact that most Arab states were social-authoritarian in their structure, meaning that at some point in the past they derived their legitimacy from social and welfare programs. As that function declined, Islamist parties managed to siphon off some of the governments' legitimacy by complementing or taking over the state's role in providing public services. Secular groups, meanwhile, were often either elitist, disengaged from effective constituent politics, or suppressed by governments and thus seen by the public as marginal. This experience suggests a counterargument bolstering calls for pluralistic reform in the Arab world: if the system is not opened up, only the Islamists can garner support.[4]

Muasher is arguing, then, that under the Arab dictatorships really only two groups are competing effectively: the regime and the Islamists. Opening up the political system is the only way that moderate and democratic voices can enter the debate.

And opportunities will arise. When Islamist groups enter government, they are subject to temptations for abuse of power and for corruption for the first time. The experience of Hamas in governing Gaza for the last decade is instructive: the group's popularity has declined as residents experienced abuses at the hands of new officials and heard stories about corruption at the top levels.

But there is more: the experiences of Islamists in private business or the social sector may not prepare them to govern at all. Obviously none will have experience running a government, and they may fail – fast. Promises of improvement will soon turn to ashes, and citizens – now allowed to vote freely – may punish malperformance. Given the poor resources that new governments will typically have at their disposal, it stands to reason that many promises will be unmet: the poor will remain poor, and it will take a very long time to build new hospitals, new schools, and new housing, even if money becomes available. "Islam is the answer" may be discredited as a slogan. Islamist politicians may appear to voters like all the other politicians – making promises they do not keep.

Of course, if voters have had a long and deep positive experience with Islamist groups they may be more loyal – but have they? For example, if they have been receiving social services from Islamist groups for many years, their commitment to people and groups they know well and that have performed for them and their families on very many occasions will presumably be deep. But many analysts now believe voters have far more limited exposure to such groups and their services than was widely assumed – and that what the Islamists have is mostly a *reputation* for the honest, efficient, and benevolent provision of services. The argument that groups such as the Muslim Brotherhood have touched the lives of most poor Egyptians was widely believed, but not proved with data. One study found that the Brotherhood's Islamic Medical Association was reaching about two million Egyptians annually during the Mubarak years. If true, that was only 2 percent of the population of roughly 90 million.[5] As Melanie Cammett and Pauline Jones Luong put it, "The causal link between social welfare provision and support for Islamists rests on a crucial assumption that has not been empirically substantiated – namely, that

Islamists supply social services both more effectively and extensively than other providers."[6]

The distinction between personal experience with social services provided by groups like the Brotherhood and the general awareness of their good reputation can have an enormous impact on the ability of Islamists to garner support. As Cammett and Luong argue, "It is this reputation for 'good governance' that enables Islamists to amass popular support and make electoral gains beyond those segments of the population with which they have come into direct contact or enjoy ideological affinity."[7] But that means the support, though wide, may also be thin:

> [R]eputation is a tenuous basis for popular support. Cultivated under authoritarian rule, Islamists' reputation for being uniquely competent, trustworthy, and pure does not automatically transfer to the democratic context and can easily be dispelled once Islamists compete for and hold the reins of power. Thus, voters tend to punish Islamist parties more severely than their secular rivals for being ineffectual, dishonest, and especially corrupt because they have failed to live up to these expectations.[8]

Others have commented on the same issue and reached similar conclusions; for example, Harvard's Tarek Masoud, in his paper, "Why Do Islamists Provide Services, and What Do Those Services Do?" finds that "fewer recipients of Islamic services trusted the Brotherhood than non-recipients ... and the same is true of the Salafis."[9] This finding again suggests that the social services supplied by Islamist groups do not buy strong loyalties. The Islamists' reach under the repressive state is not broad enough to rival that of the state and does not reach the mass of the populace. But they hear about the Islamists' efforts and form an opinion about them. The Islamists are also using "the vocabulary and values of Islam" in the struggle against a state that is entirely corrupt and repressive. This allows them to reach beyond those who are very poor or entirely committed to political Islam, to broader groups within the society that oppose the state and wish to see its power curtailed.[10]

The result is an enormous advantage for the Islamists at the moment when the regime falls – under certain conditions. Cammett and Luong summarize:

[I]t is precisely because Islamist movements are not only popular but also dominate the oppositional space under authoritarian rule, that they are poised to sweep democratic elections. The nature of this advantage, then, is that Islamists are better positioned to exploit revolutionary moments and win founding elections than their challengers.... Having a reputation for purity reinforces the credibility of the Islamists' message and promotes its appeal beyond those who come in direct contact with Islamists or their institutions. It is this reputation for "good governance" that enables Islamists to distinguish themselves in the streets and at the ballot box. Where Islamists can build and sustain such a reputation vis-a-vis their competitors – including the party of the incumbent regime – we expect them to gain mass appeal under political repression and perform well in founding elections. Where they face competitors that can legitimately claim to be competent, trustworthy, or pure, or where issues such as regime incompetence, rampant corruption, and immorality are not valence issues, Islamists will be less likely to generate broad popular support.[11]

WHY ISLAMISTS CAN BE BEATEN

These arguments suggest that the grip of the Islamists is less firm than might be feared. But when politics appears, and elections impend, the question becomes which political movements can quickly organize and win masses of votes. Free national elections require parties and candidates to mobilize to attract mass followings. Who has the means and organization to do this, besides the Islamists? As we have seen, moderate and liberal parties often arrive at this juncture weakened by years of repression – and inexperienced and unskilled at reaching out to the poor masses and especially to those living outside the largest cities.[12]

At the ideological level, the Islamists will present some version of their view that the main organizing principle of the state and the society should be Islam. More moderate groups will present their own ideas, either that the state should be secular or that it should reflect some mix of Islam and Western-style democracy. The issue is not really whether such a mixture is plausible in principle, but whether it will persuade voters. Unschooled in the ideals of Western democracy, why would they vote against Islamist forces that may emerge from the dictatorship period looking heroic, honest, and principled?

Here let me add a vital detail: the question is not only whom the majority of voters will support in the first free election, the "founding election," but also whom they will support in the second and the third. As mentioned, Islamist parties do not have the record of success that reports of their strength might sometimes suggest. This has certainly been the case in non-Arab Muslim states such as Malaysia and Indonesia, neither of which as I write is ruled by an Islamist party. In the 2014 parliamentary elections in Indonesia, secular nationalist parties won 68 percent of the vote and Islamists got 32 percent, a poor showing attributed to "a lack of ideological distinction from secular nationalist parties, competition from the state in the provision of social welfare, and lost claims to moral superiority in the wake of damaging corruption and sex scandals."[13] The more explicitly Islamist a party was, the worse it fared – and one such group won too few votes to get into parliament at all. In the 2014 presidential elections, there was no Islamist candidate. Nor did the Islamists emerge triumphant after the fall of the Suharto dictatorship in 1998, because they were then, and remain, divided. Divisions among Islamist groups have also prevented them from ruling in Malaysia, though their influence in politics there is greater. What has not happened in either case is what some studies might have predicted: an Islamist victory as soon as Islamist parties were free to seek support openly, followed by permanent Islamist dominance.

But even if we stick to the Arab nations, Egypt provides a good example of the mixed success of the Islamists. The first post-Mubarak election there brought Mohammed Morsi of the Muslim Brotherhood to power, but the story is more complex than that. In the first round of the 2012 presidential elections, in May, Islamist candidates (Morsi and another Brotherhood figure, Abdel Moneim Aboul Fotouh) got a combined 42 percent of the vote compared to 56 percent for secular candidates. In the runoff, Morsi faced former Gen. Ahmed Shafik, who had been a minister in Mubarak's government. Shafik was in many ways the weakest candidate the secular side could have produced, tainted as he was by closeness to Mubarak and derided as a "*felloul*" or "relic" of the previous regime.

But the election result was almost a tie: in the June run-off Morsi got 51.7 percent of the vote and Shafik 48.3 percent.

In Tunisia, freedom brought a rush of support to the Islamist party Ennahda. The October 2011 elections gave Ennahda 41.47 percent of the vote and 90 of 217 seats in the National Constituent Assembly, the body that was to write a new constitution. But by the 2014 parliamentary elections Ennahda's share fell to 26 percent of the vote, and it had to relinquish power.

So Islamists can lose, even in situations where non-Islamist parties are weak and divided. They can lose because the Islamist camp too is divided; because they have not proved successful while holding power; and because large segments of the population, while devoutly Muslim, are able to discern the difference between supporting the moral urgings of their religious leaders and believing them to have the talents needed to run a country in the twenty-first century. The Islamists can lose because their very organizational power has a flip side: as Eric Trager put it in writing about Egypt, "none of the Brotherhood's competitors could count on a similarly committed membership or possessed the Brotherhood's well-oiled, nationwide chain of command. But, at the same time, the Brotherhood's organizational characteristics meant that it was deeply insular – and this became a tremendous liability once it achieved power."[14]

The deciding factors might best be termed political – the changing elements of the political situation facing voters in a given year and on a given day. Samuel Tadros's analysis of the Islamist victory in Egypt in 2012 explains how the electoral system itself helped magnify the influence of small, rural areas over that of Cairo. He discusses the attractiveness of the individual candidates presented by each party and the ways in which the Brotherhood and Salafist groups used their most popular figures in certain districts to attract the most votes. The Islamists were more united than the secular opposition – the opposite of the Indonesia situation – and therefore able to present a persuasive platform that the other side lacked. The secular bloc was "an amalgam of Christians, the business-oriented middle class, socialists, human rights activists, leftists, and Arab nationalists, [that] had nothing in common except their hatred and fear of the Islamists. Having no common ideology, they lacked the ability to offer the Egyptian people any clear alternative to the Islamists."

He then sums up the situation:

> The non-Islamists' electoral campaign was also chaotic and disorganized.
> While the Islamists announced their candidates' names early and reached
> out to voters well before the elections, non-Islamist voters were still try-
> ing to discover who the Egyptian Bloc's candidates for the individual seats
> were the day before the election. Outside of the Coptic Church's efforts,
> no voter mobilization campaigns were conducted. Non-Islamist parties did
> not bother with the groundwork of gathering information and data on
> the districts, their voters, and their specific issues and problems. The gen-
> eral assumption seemed to be that you can win an election campaign by
> bombarding television audiences with ads. Furthermore, the quality of the
> candidates chosen was weak.[15]

Ideology certainly played a role, and Tadros also writes of "a deeper failure to take Islamism seriously." The problem, he says, was that "[t]he
non-Islamists viewed the Islamists as clowns. Since the Islamist argument
did not make sense to them, they assumed it wouldn't make sense to the
average Egyptian either.... What they ignored was that Islamism offers
a coherent worldview presenting its followers an explanation of the past,
present, and future – and of the world itself. Islamism encompasses a
moral structure that is the only available one for Egyptians. When an individual in Egypt might not be particularly religious, there is no alternative
ethical compass to guide one's life other than Islamism." It is, of course,
impossible to assess how much of the Islamists' victory was attributable to
this ideological or religious factor and how much to the "political" factors
Tadros enumerates. But the 72 percent of the seats in parliament won by
the Islamists in 2011 appears to have been their high-water mark, and as
noted in the 2012 presidential election their candidate barely nosed out
the secular "*felloul*" General Shafik.

ONE MAN, ONE VOTE, ONE TIME

The ability or inability of political forces (whether Islamist or secular)
to organize for success in subsequent elections will not matter if there
are no such elections or if they are not fair and free. This is the suspicion
that non-Islamist groups harbor about Islamists, and there is good reason

for it. Turkey's Islamist leader Recep Tayyip Erdoğan won several free elections, but then began to close off political space for any opposition, attacking opposition parties as well as the independence of the judiciary and freedom of the press. Egypt's Mohammed Morsi followed a similar path. To take one example, he instigated prosecutions for the crime of "insulting the president" to silence critics. In his one year in power, his government used this law far more than it had been used by King Farouk (when the crime was "insulting the king") in his sixteen years in power or by Hosni Mubarak in his thirty years in power.[16]

It was this feeling that Islamist forces were seeking to remain in power permanently that led to Erdogan's temporary setback in Turkey's June 2015 parliamentary election, which denied him the majority he needed to amend the constitution. Having failed at the ballot boxes, Erdogan took advantage of the coup attempt against him in July 2016 to crush all opposition, purging the bureaucracy, security services, and courts and seizing all the power of the state in his own hands. It was the fear that Islamist forces sought to eliminate all opposition and seize the state entirely that led to the military coup in Egypt in 2013. That coup appeared to have very widespread support in Egypt when it occurred, because Morsi's rule had united just about every political force outside the Brotherhood itself against him and millions took to the streets to demand his ouster in the days prior to the coup. In my own experience watching political development around the world, military coups are rarely tried or successfully completed without very substantial popular support, and so it was in Egypt – where the coup succeeded – and in Turkey – where for *lack* of public support, it failed.

The basic point remains: the initial Islamist advantage will be permanent if politics is frozen once they reach power. Turkey's Erdogan has been widely quoted as saying that democracy is like a train: once you get to your station, you get off.[17] Democrats, and their supporters in democratic governments around the world, must struggle to denounce and defeat any such moves, and as I will argue in later chapters this is a key suggestion for U.S. foreign policy: to target efforts at preventing backsliding when democratic gains have already been won. International indifference to encroachments on newly established or restored democratic rights and practices will make them far more likely to succeed, and the United States should be a leader in protecting fledgling democracies.

But the advent of additional elections after Islamists win the first one is only an opportunity to defeat the Islamists, not a guarantee that it is possible or likely. Is it? Why be optimistic?

To begin with, there are the polls, noted in Chapter 1, that suggest that there is substantial support for democracy on which to build. Here is one summary of the Arab Barometer survey of late 2014:

> Comparing results from three waves of survey data over the past decade, the Arab Barometer finds that support for democracy remains high but support for political Islam has decreased.... Support for political Islam is substantially lower. In no country do more than half of respondents say religious leaders should have influence over government decisions. It is often far less support, including just 34 percent in Algeria, 27 percent in Tunisia, 20 percent in Egypt and 9 percent in Lebanon. Moreover, support for political Islam declined over the past decade. Algeria has witnessed the most dramatic decline, with support for political Islam falling from 60 percent in 2006 to just 34 percent in 2013. A similar decline has occurred in Egypt, where 37 percent supported political Islam in June 2011 compared to 18 percent in April 2013, a 19-point decrease. Most other countries witnessed a similar decline, including Palestine (-15 points), Iraq (-11), Lebanon (-9) and Yemen (-7).[18]

Of course even if these numbers are right they provide only the opportunity, not an assurance of success; other factors such as organization, funding, and political skills will also have a great impact on political outcomes. But the numbers no doubt reflect a phenomenon mentioned earlier: that once in power, the shine comes off the Islamists' reputation for integrity and competence. Marwan Muasher puts it best: "Islamists began losing their aura of holiness the moment they entered the political arena. Whether religious or secular, conservative or radical, in or out of government, all those who enter the political fray can no longer invoke some unique higher wisdom. Electorates across the Arab world will now view all who aspire to lead them on an equal footing, as politicians."[19]

And the people will quickly be proved right: once confronted with temptation in the form of corruption, bribery, and opportunities to crush their opponents, many Islamists will yield – thereby eroding their popularity outside their own ranks. If it is correct that they have enjoyed a positive reputation among citizens who had little direct contact with them, the new, more direct contact with an oppressive and corrupt government run by Islamists will soon overwhelm that old reputation.

The old authoritarian state the Islamists are replacing did not produce democratic or economic reforms. Neither are the new Islamist officials likely to produce quick economic progress, in part because they may have little or no relevant experience and in part because the needed reforms may be very controversial. What is needed is a quick and potentially painful turn toward the free market, but even in Europe new (post-Communist) governments have often been unable or unwilling to undertake sufficiently radical change. And even if ultimately successful, such change may take years to produce widespread economic gains.

Moreover, Islamist groups are likely to arrive in power without any real plans for how to use it – other than having vague slogans like "Islam is the answer" or a desire to populate the government with their fellow Islamists. But what of actual policies for the economy or education or housing or transportation? Eric Trager describes the Egyptian Muslim Brotherhood's "lack of a specific policy agenda" and argues that none of the organization's leaders "seemed to know what specific policies an Islamic state would actually implement, other than banning certain vices."[20]

In the shorter run, Islamists in power may face the choice between implementing too few economic reforms, which means that voters will find their campaign promises of change to be hollow, or a thorough reform, which could lead to voter backlash from those who initially lose ground. And voter dissatisfaction leads to the temptation to shut down or limit debate, to their using the power of the state as their authoritarian predecessors did.

Doubling down on "identity" politics – stressing religion instead of performance – will be another temptation for the Islamists in that situation, but will be more likely to narrow than to widen their base of support once they are in power and show themselves incompetent to rule. Meanwhile any failure to use its newly won power to "Islamicize" the state and society will lose the ruling group some of its support base, which imagined that such steps would quickly be imposed. As Shadi Hamid writes, "For Islamist groups, there is considerable pressure from their own rank-and-file to stay faithful to the cause. Given high levels of political fragmentation and polarization during transitions, they cannot afford to alienate their most committed supporters."[21]

Simply put, it is easier to complain than to govern, and Islamists will inevitably start losing support once they confront the difficult choices that being in opposition allowed them to escape. The political scientist Quinn Mecham offers this analysis:

[A]s Islamist groups develop opportunities to govern, they will be required to use new skills and make a wide range of political choices, which they have historically been able to avoid making while in the opposition.... Finally, as transitioning Arab states inevitably struggle with poor performance and as tensions across identity groups become heightened through government repression or the discriminatory policies of emerging organizations, sectarian conflict and Islamist militancy by marginal groups has the potential to become much more prominent.... As Islamists participate in governance, the process of governing will force elected Islamist parties to make difficult decisions that have the potential to complicate their Islamic identity and lead to dissatisfaction among the parties' traditional constituents. Ambiguities in political platforms, in which specific policy-based solutions to social and political problems are often glossed over in favor of religious values or slogans, may both compromise the quality of governance and make it difficult to manage the diverse set of expectations held by supporters. Likewise, many members of Islamist groups with no practical experience in governing have been elevated to positions of authority for which their previous professional and political experiences leave them essentially unqualified. This raises the risk of the Islamist parties being unable to meet the high expectations for their behavior in office as well as for their ability to remedy political, economic, and social ills in their respective countries.[22]

Others emphasize that the Islamists' old-fashioned political advantages are being eroded by technology: "mobilization for collective action through social media has aged their mobilization style."[23] The huge protests in Tahrir Square that helped bring down Hosni Mubarak were not organized by the Muslim Brotherhood, nor did Ennahda lead the protests that forced Ben Ali to flee Tunis. Under the old regimes in past decades, and before the internet, emails, and texting, the Islamists' networks – including especially the mosques – were often the sole means of communication outside regime control. That advantage too is now gone.

THE NEED FOR POLITICS

The political fate of Arab countries that emerge from authoritarian regimes is not set in stone and the victory of Islamists is not inevitable. Certainly, Islamist groups do enjoy numerous advantages when the opportunity for competitive politics arises, the flip side of the conditions under which they suffer during the period of authoritarian rule. But many of those advantages are eroded or disappear once politics opens up, and they are forced to make difficult choices: choices about economic policy and, above all, choices about how quickly and radically to try to move toward the religiously guided state and society that they have held out as the ideal. Compromise erodes their own base and its enthusiasm and support; refusal to compromise can offend the majority of voters. Efforts to impose their religious views and practices can evoke wide protest; efforts to suppress the protests can create more of them and alienate broad sectors of society, including the security forces.

If these points are right, it seems obvious that Islamist groups should be permitted to become part of the new political scene when authoritarian regimes are deposed. But this is in fact an extremely controversial issue, and many in the region cite the example of Egypt to demonstrate why Islamists should never be permitted to engage in politics. They do not accept the rules of the game, the argument goes, and if they gain power once, then politics is in effect over. They will never leave power and will undermine and pervert the political system to avoid ever relinquishing their dominance.

We can see from Tunisia that this generalization is overly broad. There, Ennahda relinquished power peacefully, as party leader Rachid Ghannouchi explained several months later:

After Ennahda participated in the first elections of October 23, 2011, we had the opportunity to form a government made up of Islamists ... but we chose to install a coalition government of moderate Islamists and moderate secularists to prove that coexistence between these two trends in our country is possible and that democracy can be implanted in the Arab world. Democracy can flourish in the Arab world; Tunisia is not an exception.

We faced difficulties when some terrorist groups tried to disturb the country, and impede our progress toward democracy. So Ennahda participated in a national dialogue with all Tunisian parties, 22 parties from all sides of the political spectrum.

Finally, we decided to step down from our governing position without losing an election, facing a counterrevolution or coup d'état. We realized that although we had the right to retain power because of our electoral victory, the Tunisian people would not get a constitution without our stepping down .... The opposition had withdrawn from the constitutional assembly and refused to continue drafting the constitution. We could have continued without them. But we would have produced a constitution for the Ennahda party, not the Tunisian people as a whole. So we took a difficult path towards general consensus.

After five difficult months of dialog, we reached consensus with other parties and Ennahda relinquished power in favor of a neutral government. We were not obliged to leave power. We had the full right to retain it. We are not angels. We would like to have power. But we fervently believe that a democratic constitution is more important for Tunisia than Ennahda retaining power.[24]

Soon after Tunisia's turn toward democracy, I hosted a lunch meeting for Ghannouchi, in November, 2011, at the Council on Foreign Relations' office in Washington. We had never met before, and having the meeting was a risk: was he a Muslim democrat or a Muslim Brother in disguise? I received several calls and emails from friends in think tanks and from former colleagues in the government telling me that Ghannouchi was a Brother, that he was taking me in, and that he had simply learned in his years in exile how to use a discourse that would fool Westerners – especially those who wanted to be fooled. It was a reasonable argument at the time. But in the years since then we have seen that it was wrong: Ghan-nouchi has led his party toward offering genuine support for democracy.

The Tunisian case would be of limited interest were it entirely isolated and were Ennahda the only Islamist group that had ever behaved respon-sibly or had refrained from undermining the political system, but that is not the case. Islamist parties in other Arab countries, including Jordan and Kuwait, have worked within their systems, and Morocco's governing party, the Justice and Development Party, has led a democratic govern-ment since 2011. The term "Islamist" is used to cover terrorist groups like Boko Haram, the "Islamic State," and al-Qaeda; the Islamist parties in Jordan, Kuwait, and Morocco, as well as Tunisia; and many more parties in Asian Muslim countries. Clearly the exclusion of terrorist and nihilist groups like ISIS and Boko Haram is one thing and that of Ennahda is quite another: some groups want to kill infidels and disbelieving Muslims, while others aim at cultural conservatism and the promotion of Islam within democratic or near-democratic systems.

A 2015 analysis of Ennahda by Monica Marks makes the point that while in government the party "underwent a process of deep political learning" that would not have been possible had it been excluded from any share of power or even from contesting for power.[25] A year later, that process continued at Ennahda's Tenth Party Congress, held in May 2016. Marks observes, "For this 10th congress to adopt a broadening, proactive vision, Ennahda members and leaders also needed first to feel confident that democracy had become the only game in town," and she quotes Ennahda leader Said Ferjani as saying, "Islamism is not an ide-ology for governing. It's a language of opposition."[26] Certainly Ennahda has not abandoned Islam, but has come to believe that its role is above all Tunisian rather than transnational – "bringing pragmatic, Islam-inspired good governance to the Tunisian polity" – and that by supporting a democratic system and a constitution that "upheld freedom, justice, and human dignity – higher principles and objectives of Shariah" it was ful-filling its religious role.[27]

In fact, at that party congress Ennahda further separated its religious and political roles; for example, deciding that party leaders could not simultaneously hold leadership positions in religious associations and in the party and were prohibited from preaching in mosques. Such decisions were an extension of previous thinking in Ennahda and by Ghannouchi, but were nevertheless striking and indeed historic. It remains a movement inspired by Islam, but not Islamist in character; it is becoming a political party and movement increasingly reminiscent of the Christian Democratic movements in Europe. As Marks puts it,

> This narrative recasts Islamism as a kind of situation-contingent liber-ation theology – an oppositional framework developed during decades when dictators banned Ennahda from usual forms of political engage-ment. Although suitable for that time, many Ennahda leaders now argue that Islamism is ill-adapted to a context in which liberation (i.e., a seat at the democratic table) has been achieved, and in which religiously oriented parties must govern pragmatically.[28]

In an extraordinary speech, Ghannouchi told the delegates to the party congress that "Ennahda has changed from an ideological movement engaged in the struggle for identity to a protest movement against the authoritarian regime and now to a national democratic party. We must keep religion far from political struggles."[29] That evolution was the product of democratization and could not have occurred had Tunisia remained a dictatorship and had Ennahda remained a persecuted move-ment. An Ennahda member of parliament in Tunisia, Sayida Ounissi, summarizes this point: "being able to experiment with four years of actual political governance has had more impact on its identity and political dis-course than decades of underground activity."[30]

Similar processes, though far less evolved to this point, can be observed elsewhere. In Jordan, the Muslim Brotherhood "has never been driven underground; its leaders were never systematically jailed." This experience, combined with that of watching Mohammed Morsi fall from power in Egypt, has led to a moderation of demands: "further reforms but not maximalist ones." Most Salafis in Jordan are political quietists, co-opted by the regime and "incorporated into state institutions." More-over, "electoral contestation transformed Islamic politics in Jordan into a form of ethnic politics" because the Brotherhood began to rely increas-ingly on the votes of Palestinian Jordanians.[31] In Kuwait, the local Broth-erhood branch has a "well-established place in the country's history," and its agenda "is shaped by local realities more than a desire to take over rule." There, Islamist groups promote political liberalization, cooperating with non-Islamists to that end, and oppose cultural liberalization – in areas such as the role of women or speech about Islam.[32] In Morocco, Islamist groups have participated in elections and accepted "the religious foundations of the state – not to challenge the king's role as 'Commander of the Faithful,'" which is obviously an exceptional compromise for them to make. They have stressed bread-and-butter issues, and competition among Islamists has largely replaced challenges to the existing order. The Islamists "play by the rules of the political game: dictates laid down by the state and realities presented by domestic and regional political circumstances." The result is that "the particular structural contours of Moroccan state policy – specifically in relation to religious activism – have significantly shaped Islamist behavior and ultimately beliefs," leading to an "accommodationist approach."[33]

What these cases of Islamist groups have in common is not only the outbreak of realism among some in reaction to events such as the ouster of Mohammed Morsi but also their reaction to imposed local limits on their activity. The Egyptian case may come to prove both that the absence of any limits is dangerous and that the bluntest and most violent forms of repression will themselves produce violence. But the other Arab cases suggest that, when clear limits are set, many Islamist groups can engage in political participation in ways that reduce violence, enhance the nation's political stability, and may even change their own outlook on some issues.

More broadly, there are other reasons to believe that Islamists will not always be able to hijack the political system even if they win power fairly in it. The first is that the security forces are likely to prevent such an outcome – precisely as happened in Egypt. In 2012, Jamie O'Connell of the University of California-Berkeley School of Law argued that

> It is unlikely that democratically elected Islamists governments in Arab countries would overthrow democracy in order to entrench permanent Islamist rule, because their mostly secular military forces might well stage a countercoup, backed by Western countries, and then purge the Islamists from power.[34]

His analysis proved prescient, for the following year the Egyptian Army did just what he predicted. (O'Connell was wrong in suggesting that all

"Western countries" would "back" the coup in the sense of promoting and celebrating it, but certainly none opposed it with any vigor.) But military intervention is in any event no panacea, for several reasons. It is hardly a reliable path toward stable democracy, as can be seen in Egypt and in Algeria – where having seized power the military seems intent on retaining it permanently. Moreover, it will not always work, as the failure of the coup in Turkey in 2016 demonstrated. But O'Connell is correct in suggesting that fear of the military can be a restraining factor on Islamists.

The United States need not applaud such interventions any more than it must applaud Islamist victories. This point is worth stressing: to argue that Islamists will not always oppose or prevent democracy is not to argue that we favor their victory, any more than explaining that the military may restrain Islamist ambitions is arguing for coups. The question I am asking is whether democratic politics is too dangerous to try because Islamists will hijack it, everywhere and always. In those democratic contests, the United States will never favor Islamist victories because the Islamists' goal is to create a society antithetical to many of our own fundamental beliefs: for example, about the role of religion in politics and about women's rights. To admire Ghannouchi for embracing democratic politics is not to say we hope he wins elections or that we ourselves embrace the kind of society he wishes, in the long run and presumably through electoral victories, to create.

HOW TO DEFEAT ISLAMISTS

There is another very powerful reason to believe that, while military power may restrain Islamist ambitions, the exercise of that power is problematic. For the security forces may remove the Islamists – but that is not the same as defeating them. Their ideas will not be defeated, nor will opposing democratic ideas be strengthened, by military interventions. That can only happen through an open political debate, and Turkey illustrates the point. Islamist groups were removed from power by the military repeatedly and their parties outlawed. After the 1997 coup that forced out Islamist prime minister Necmettin Erbakan, for example, his Welfare Party was closed down by the Constitutional Court. But it resurfaced as the Virtue Party in 1998, and that was in turn closed down in 2001 by the Constitutional Court. The same movement resurfaced soon after as the Justice and Development Party (AKP), founded in 2001, and by 2003 the party's leader, Recep Tayyip Erdogan, was prime minister; he was elected president of Turkey in 2014. But as noted, in June 2015 he and his party suffered a setback in parliamentary elections that denied him the supermajority he needed to change Turkey's constitution (even though the party remained the largest single one in parliament). In the November 2015 elections Erdogan regained his majority – but not the supermajority he sought. Only after the failed coup of 2016 could he seize the powers he coveted and that he could not win at the ballot box.

Secularist groups in Turkey repeatedly relied on the army and the judiciary to defeat Islamist opponents, instead of organizing effectively to defeat them politically. They were "saved" by the army, but "saved" as well from developing needed political skills. Finally, in 2015, with Erdogan himself having reduced the power of the army during his years in power, the secularist groups were forced to rely solely on their ability to persuade voters – with mixed results, due in part to the AKP's superior organization (and in large part, of course, to its control of the state). And the effort by a portion of the military to "save" Turkey's secularist/Kemalist tradition produced exactly the opposite outcome in 2016.

The contrast between Tunisia and Egypt in 2013 is striking. In Egypt the Brotherhood was not defeated at the polls but by the army. Given the extremely broad opposition that developed to the Brotherhood and to Mohammed Morsi in just one year in power, one can rightly lament that they and he were not crushed by the voters in the next election rather than being removed by the army. It is, of course, easy for a foreigner to believe that Egypt might have been better off had Morsi's critics been willing to wait for the next election: we do not live in Egypt and were not suffering under oppressive Brotherhood rule. Nor is it possible to prove that there would ever have been another free election, given the autocratic tendencies Morsi clearly exhibited.

For while the army's intervention saved Egypt from Morsi, it also brought with it a wave of repression of all political activity – Islamist, secular, democratic, liberal – and of freedom of expression. An election defeat for the Brotherhood would not have had that impact. Nor did the coup strengthen democratic and liberal forces, as might have happened in an election campaign where they were forced to learn how to win votes. The army suppressed the Brotherhood, at least for now, but may also have radicalized it in a way that a "mere" electoral defeat would not have. It seems obvious that involvement in politics, as in Tunisia, can moderate Islamist conduct; in Egypt, with electoral politics foreclosed, would it be surprising to see the most radical and indeed violent and terrorist sectors growing in influence?

Jamie O'Connell's conclusion is that

> when it comes to defusing the power of political Islam, democracy may be the worst form of government – except all the others. Arab autocrats' repression of opposition is widely considered to have been among the most important contributors to Islamists' popularity.... Supporting Arab autocrats is therefore likely to strengthen Islamists in the long run, unless they are repressed with a thoroughness that would require extreme brutality.[35]

That brutal repression may be happening in Egypt, where the jails are full of political dissenters including Islamists, and where mass death sentences were in 2014 and 2015 routinely handed down by the courts. But would a period of extreme brutality likely lay the foundation for a period of democratic politics or simply for a continued and extensive period of autocratic rule?

There is certainly a real danger that Islamist parties will try to impose a political outcome, and indeed a political system, that most Westerners and more importantly many Arabs will view as unacceptable. As Shadi Hamid asks, "What happens when Islamists become more secure in power and the fear of being destroyed subsides? Islamists are Islamists for a reason."[36] Answering his own question, he writes that "a strictly liberal democracy would violate their freedom of religion and freedom of belief. Liberalism cannot hold within it Islamism."[37]

How can the Islamists be prevented from trying to remake their society? Hamid concludes that repression works – in that it can sometimes "force" (Hamid's word) moderation: "increasing levels of repression, rather than resulting in radicalization, can have a moderating effect on

Islamist groups, pushing them to reconsider and redefine their policy priorities."[38] Why? In part, because the Islamists often operate a variety of institutions (such as schools or medical clinics, and, of course, mosques) that can be easily damaged or shut down and that the movements will wish to protect. Moreover, Islamists may respond politically, hoping that a show of moderation will beget official moderation and less repression. Or, they may hope that a show of moderation may allow them to portray the crackdowns as unjustifiable or excessive and thereby get them decreased – or at least generate more sympathy for their own plight under repression. Showing moderation is a smart tactic, as Hamid explains: "The fear of repression leads Islamists to deemphasize Islamic law and underscore their democratic *bona fides*, in the hope that this will give paranoid governments less reason to attack them. Doing so also attracts liberal and leftist support – as well as international sympathy – all of which can serve as a layer of protection."[39]

So repression can work sometimes – but not always. There is always the danger that repression will lead not to moderation but to its opposite. This is what happened in Algeria in the 1990s. When Islamists appeared likely to win the scheduled 1992 elections, the military removed the president, took power, and canceled the polling. The leading Islamist party was banned and thousands of activists arrested. An insurgency quickly began, leading to a civil war that left 150,000 to 200,000 dead. Twenty-five years later, the military still rules. In Egypt, the military's candidate, Gen. Abdel Fattah el-Sisi, won the presidency in 2014, but instead of returning the country to normal political life undertook a broad campaign to destroy the Muslim Brotherhood. Repression, mass jailings, and official violence (including killings) grew, and the targets quickly expanded far beyond the Brotherhood. If Islamists are excluded from civic and social activity, politics, and the media and from religious and social activism and simultaneously subjected to brutal repression, what are left as areas for activism are violence and the kind of street protests likely to end in violence. Given the upsurge in terrorism that began in 2015, Egypt's trajectory may come to resemble that of Algeria. As Stephen Brooke argued in 2015, the Muslim Brotherhood's strategy of organizing protests is unlikely to bear fruit or to continue forever:

The longer this strategy drags on without bearing fruit, the more likely it becomes that disaffected and frustrated activists drift into violence ... particularly for those on the front lines of the protests bearing the brunt of police crackdowns and confrontations with security forces, the leap between passive protest and active violence becomes shorter and shorter. It is likely that a number have already taken that step, but as alternative avenues for popular activism are crimped off, more may follow them.[40]

By 2016, both the United Kingdom and Canada were warning their citizens against traveling to Egypt: the United Kingdom warned travelers of "a high threat from terrorism,"[41] and Canada was advising citizens "against non-essential travel to Egypt due to the unpredictable security situation."[42] Similarly, the U.S. Department of State "warns U.S. citizens of threats from terrorist groups in Egypt and to consider the risks of travel to the country,"[43] while the U.S. Embassy "restricts its employees and their family members from traveling outside of greater Cairo and Alexandria without prior approval and advises all U.S. citizens to carefully consider the security implications of travel outside of greater Cairo, Alexandria, and major tourist destinations."[44]

Hamid's assessment (of how repression can "force" Islamist groups to moderate) may be correct when the goal of government policy is repression – but not when it is elimination. Then, a move toward moderation will obviously bring the Islamists no benefits; they are in a war for survival against a regime that wants them dead or away in prison rather than being reformed. Egypt may be a test case, where over the decades of Mubarak's rule the Muslim Brotherhood moved away from the use of violence – but may now move back.[45] Similarly, it seemed that in the Mubarak years the Brotherhood moderated its doctrines on matters like the role of women and the place of Christians in Egyptian society. But Mohammed Morsi's year in office suggested that the Brothers had not given up their thirst for absolute power or their desire to remake Egyptian society. As Olivier Roy explains it, the Brothers and their Islamist rivals "are not known for their attachment to democracy. Even if they have given up talk of the 'Islamic revolution,' they still put religion at the heart of their agenda ... why should Islamists, with no democratic culture to speak of, behave like good democrats who believe in pluralism?"[46]

Roy's optimistic answer is that "the constraints and dynamics characteristic of the social, religious, political, and geostrategic fields in which these parties must operate" will force the Islamists to change. This is possible, but often the real competition the Islamists face will come from other Islamists. The rivalry between Salafist parties and the Muslim Brotherhood in Egypt provides a good example. It may seem more sensible to Islamists leaders – and indeed, it may *be* more sensible as a political strategy, at least initially – to try to maximize their support among fundamentally sympathetic Islamist-oriented voters than to "moderate" and seek voters elsewhere in the electorate.

In trying to explain why the Egyptian Brotherhood failed to moderate after winning the 2013 election, Eric Trager notes that "the Brotherhood faced its most serious political challenge from hardline Salafists, and this compelled it to embrace a far more theocratic constitution than it otherwise might have." But he adds that the Brotherhood was organized as a revolutionary vanguard party and not a democratic political movement. The group's "rank-and-file . . . wanted the Brotherhood to consolidate power quickly, rather than governing inclusively," so moderation would have threatened "the internal cohesion on which vanguards depend." And Trager notes that the Brotherhood tried to govern Egypt as it had governed itself internally: with "unchecked executive authority," intolerance toward outsiders, and a complete lack of transparency and democratic structures. Trager is right, and other analysts have reported that "political decision-making . . . remains extremely centralized" in the Brotherhood.[47] So Trager sensibly advises that when trying to predict how Islamists will govern if they win power, we should "look beyond Islamist groups' stated aims and examine how they actually function internally. . . . As the Brotherhood's brief rule in Egypt illustrates, Islamists' organizational culture frequently determines their political behavior far more than their ideological pronouncements."[48]

The history of the twentieth century suggests the wisdom of this analysis, for vanguard groups such as Communist parties often spout manifestos designed to appeal to broad audiences and filled with words like "freedom" and "democracy." But when their internal structures are essentially Leninist, one can be reasonably sure that is how they will rule if they get the chance. Conversely, groups that espouse Islamist philosophies but allow for debate and contestation in their own ranks are far more likely to adapt successfully to democratic politics.

Taken together these analyses suggest that Islamists, when they gain power, may sometimes become more moderate and sometimes not, as they respond to varying internal and external pressures. And this in turn suggests that opening the door for such debates among Islamists, in their movements and parties, is a fruitful path for governments to take. That door may have to be forced open when Islamists' internal party structures are centralized and Leninist in character. That is a difficult task, especially for governments whose own parties are centralized and undemocratic in organization; for example, the ruling parties in Egypt under Mubarak and Algeria under Bouteflika. Egypt's National Democratic Party was no more open and democratic in its own structures than was the Muslim Brotherhood.

But this is another argument for more open and democratic political systems, and more open and democratic political parties. The ruling parties in the "fake republics" were not political parties in the Western sense, but tools of the dictatorship. That is the key reason they could not compete with the Islamists, who presented ideas, and described a state where justice and law prevailed and where the government did not humiliate its subjects. The "party" of the government mobilized votes and handed out favors, but it had no ideas that could combat Islamism. It could not describe a better life. In a battle of ideas, freedom and democracy (in the Western sense) may win more support than Islamist proposals, but in fake republics and military dictatorships there is no battle of ideas: Islamists win by default. It is sensible, then, for pragmatic and not just idealistic reasons for the United States to urge an opening in such political systems, for doing so means urging the regimes actually to try and defeat Islamist ideas and proposals. "Mere" repression cannot achieve this. Political party laws that force democratic internal structures, including party meetings where votes determine outcomes and where party leaders are democratically elected, are one step that can help change the nature of the political activities of Islamist movements and that of sitting regimes.

But this raises the broader question: why should Islamists be permitted to engage in political activity at all?

ISLAMISTS IN OR OUT?

In most Arab countries substantial minorities can accurately be called Islamist, depending on how pollsters ask the question. Can these countries evolve toward democracy if Islamists are allowed into the political system – or conversely if they are excluded entirely from politics? Which is more dangerous, including them or excluding them?

The answer depends in part of definitions of Islamism and Islamists. Individuals whose views are founded in their religion, or who seek parties that represent the virtues they see in Islam, should not be excluded from political activity any more than should devout Christians. But clearly those who would use violence to achieve power – those whom Trager describes as more revolutionary vanguard groups than religious organizations – or would use any power they won in a free election to undermine the democratic system present a different challenge. Daniel Pipes describes the problem this way: "Islamism offers a way of approaching and controlling state power. It openly relies on state power for coercive purposes."[49] This is precisely what we saw in Egypt under Morsi, and the Egyptian Muslim Brotherhood is hardly the only Islamist group whose commitment to democracy is at least questionable. A generation ago the great scholar Elie Kedourie saw Islamism as an absolute bar to democracy: "the desire for democracy and the desire for rule by the Sharia are utterly incompatible and irreconcilable."[50]

The problem with excluding Islamist political forces is in part that while some "Islamists" will fully match Pipes's and Trager's warnings, others – like Ghannouchi – will not. And if all parties and individuals called "Islamist" are excluded, progress toward democracy is a great deal harder. As Larry Diamond explains,

> To isolate Islamist parties and organizations means, in essence, to endorse the status quo of political stagnation in the Arab world – for there is no way that democratization can proceed in any Arab country today without finding some measure of accommodation with at least some substantial

segment of political Islam. The goal must be to draw these parties into a process of democratic elections, democratic governance, opposition responsibilities, and pluralistic coexistence so that they are forced to respond to demands from their constituencies for real achievements in governance as opposed to mere ideology and rhetoric. When political parties have to assume responsibility for passing legislation, crafting compromises, creating jobs, and picking up the trash, it has a leavening effect.[51]

Well, it may or it may not. It does not appear to have had that effect on Mohamed Morsi and his brethren, nor (in very different circumstances) on Hamas. But the new democratic experiment in any Arab (and for that matter, Muslim non-Arab) country is badly weakened if it excludes a substantial group of citizens. They will quickly come to see "democracy" as a sham, a system designed to bar them forever from any role in determining the future of their country. The possibility of broadening and deepening support for democracy over time is substantially weakened if a large minority (and more so if a possible majority) of citizens is told they will have no role now or ever. Also weighing on any decision to exclude "Islamist" groups is the history of their failures in electoral contests, which suggests that they can be and often are beaten (especially in Muslim-majority countries in Asia).

The operative question is then whether it might be possible to allow some Islamist participation while mitigating the risks of an Islamist takeover. The best approach may be to allow for the Islamist role under certain preconditions. As Stephen R. Grand suggests,

[S]ome basic conditions should be stipulated, either through legislation or within a constitution, that all political parties must adhere to if they wish to participate in the political process. They should include requirements to take an oath of allegiance to the state, to respect the outcome of democratic elections, to abide by the rules of the constitution, and to forswear violence. The approach toward Islamist parties should be based on the principle of "innocent until proven guilty." Political parties and movements that agree to the minimum standards should be permitted to participate until their behavior contravenes those standards.[52]

To Grand's stipulated conditions I would add the one discussed a few pages earlier: the requirement for internal party democracy. And that requirement, as I argued, cannot be applied only to Islamist parties: it must apply as well to the secular parties and those backing the regime in power.

A version of this issue of Islamists in politics was confronted, unsuccessfully, when Palestinian parliamentary elections were held in 2006. The question then was whether Hamas, a terrorist group that is part of the Muslim Brotherhood, would be permitted to run despite its refusal to meet international demands for renunciation of violence, adherence to previous negotiated agreements with Israel, and acknowledgment of Israel's right to exist. Pressured, Hamas still refused to meet all three counts. Nevertheless it was allowed to participate, with this explanation given by then-United Nations Secretary-General Kofi Annan: "Ultimately, those who want to be part of the political process should not engage in armed group or militia activities." The key word was "ultimately." Secretary of State Rice defended the position this way: "There are periods of time of transition in which one has to give some space to the participants, in this case the Palestinians, to begin to come to a new national compact."[53]

Why was Hamas permitted to run? Because the ruling party, Fatah, saw the elections as a means to gain legitimacy through electoral victory – a victory it saw as certain. Barring Hamas's participation would taint the election and undermine rather than reinforce Fatah's legitimacy, Palestinian officials argued, reducing the election to the farces seen in Syria, Egypt, and elsewhere in the Arab world. The most important error the Bush administration made was to permit a terrorist group to engage in politics without first laying down its arms and indeed without even pledging to do so. It thereby gained the advantage of fighting with both "ballots and bullets" simultaneously. But we also erred in failing to understand that in the event of a Hamas victory our conditions (and those of the EU and United Nations) on Hamas participation in government (meet international demands for renunciation of violence, adhere to previous negotiated agreements with Israel, and acknowledge Israel's right to exist) would be seen as undemocratic and hypocritical barriers to democracy, rather than as safeguards of peace.

The circumstances of that case are different from that of most Arab polities, because Palestine is not a country and its political system coexists with the Israeli presence in the West Bank. In the end, Hamas won a majority of seats in the Palestinian legislature, but was not permitted to govern because it did not – after the election – make any move or even any gesture toward eliminating its armed elements or bringing them under state control, or meeting the other international demands. One might say the "innocent until proven guilty" approach was applied here so that Hamas was allowed to run in the elections. But when Hamas failed to move after the elections it was judged "guilty," leaving many Palestinians and other Arabs crying foul.

Both Ennahda in Tunisia and the Muslim Brotherhood in Egypt would have passed the "innocent until proven guilty" test, but the results in those two cases were quite different. Ennahda in Tunisia was indeed not guilty, but the Brotherhood moved quickly in ways that seemed to augur the end of Egypt's brief democratic moment.

What is to be done when, as in Egypt, the Islamist group wins an election and then proceeds to undermine democracy? First, the chances of that happening may be reduced by the insistence that those pledges mentioned by Grand be made, very publicly, as a condition of participation. (This is precisely what was not done in the Hamas case.) Second, several of the pledges might be controversial within the group, splitting and weakening it. Third, if the pledges are broken by an Islamist group that gains power or a share of power, the basis will clearly and justly have been laid for removing them from power later, as happened in Egypt. My own view of the 2013 Egypt coup is that it was defensible, and that the United States would have been far better off acknowledging that it was a coup – and saying that sometimes coups were inevitable and/or beneficial when democratic systems were being subverted by a government in power. This would have focused the ensuing debate on what the Brotherhood had done when in power in the previous year, rather than on what the army had done by removing it from power in the previous days.

This issue – what to do about groups or individuals who use a political opening to achieve power and then subvert democracy – is not an Islamist or an Arab problem alone. We have seen it in cases as far afield as that of

Hugo Chavez in Venezuela, Jean-Bertrand Aristide in Haiti, and Robert Mugabe in Zimbabwe. All of them won power in free elections and then abused that power to destroy opposition parties, crush dissent, jail opposition leaders, and bring their country's fragile democracy to an end. U.S. policy in all these cases has been weak, failing to react quickly or effectively to the compromise of democracy. The difference in the Egyptian case is that there was a domestic actor, the army, which was not under the Brotherhood's control and responded to the widespread public protests by removing the regime.

When Islamist groups act to subvert democracy, they should earn the same treatment any such group should elicit: wide public opposition and resistance and, in extreme cases, the forcible removal from power. But because it is obvious that coups and violent revolutions are hardly the best basis for building democratic politics, they should be supported only when there is truly no other alternative. When the problem is the Islamist parties' *policies*, the best approach is to concentrate not on trying to get the group to abandon those policies or on crushing the group, but on *defeating* it. Whatever the impact of repression, once a political system begins to democratize it will seem increasingly illegitimate to repress normal and peaceful political efforts by the Islamists. Nor will repression by the security forces persuade the majority of citizens that Islamist answers to public policy questions are simply inadequate and wrong. Only non-Islamist and anti-Islamist leaders, parties, and movements can do that.

Allowing Islamists the freedom to engage in politics clearly carries risks, but so does excluding them. The issue may hinge less on how Islamists react to exclusion than on how the polity as a whole evaluates their role and conduct. If Islamists are repressed, and especially if that repression is brutal, they may continue to win public sympathy. An antidemocratic (and even, in extreme cases, a violent) reaction on their part may be excused if they are seen to be treated with violence and brutality by the government in power. But if they are permitted to compete, what happens when they lose – as may well happen, and indeed has often happened in Asia and then in Tunisia? They may adjust, as Rachid Ghannouchi appears to have done in Tunisia, and hope that responsible conduct and continued preaching will ultimately win them a larger share of power again. Given the problems the new (non-Islamist) democratic government will face, this is a reasonable prospect. In other words, they may develop into and act as Islamic democrats, winning power fairly, using it to advance their agenda, and relinquishing power when they lose elections.

Or they may conclude that democracy does not work for them and that Islamism must be imposed. They may reach this conclusion either because they believe they will never be able to win a majority, or because they may think they will never be given a fair chance to govern even if they do win, and will be removed from power as Mohammed Morsi was in Egypt. There is some evidence that this is happening, and that the number of Islamist democrats is declining.[54] But if *this* is why they abandon democracy, how likely is it that they will take a majority of their fellow citizens with them? How sympathetic are groups that cannot persuade a majority of citizens of their case and their cause, and then seek power despite their rejection? Obviously there is a risk here that they may prove sufficiently powerful and well organized to seize power, but how great is that risk? Majorities who have tasted democracy and voted against the Islamists will oppose them, as will the security forces and most outside influences, from the Arab League to aid donors to neighboring governments.

We will return to some of these issues when considering in Chapter 5 what policy the United States should adopt in the Arab world. But the conclusion is clear that Islamist groups should not be excluded on a wholesale basis from participation in democratic politics unless and until their own conduct has made it evident that they will not abide by the rules of the game and they have refused even to pledge to do so. Placing preconditions on their participation, in the context of establishing rules of the game for all parties, is a reasonable step. Given that some parties (perhaps with a name change) are likely to have supported the previous repressive regime, or even been key parts part of it, such pledges to the new, democratic rules of the game should be required of all participants, not only the Islamist groups. As noted, that step may help produce more democratic conduct, may divide and weaken groups that are not actually committed to democracy, and may provide stronger grounds to remove a party that while in government subverts the new democratic system. But this is a far better path than exclusion, because exclusion will not persuade citizens that their ideas are wrong and dangerous. Only an open debate, led by other parties, can do that.

CHAPTER 4

The Trouble with U.S. Policy

A MERICAN POLICY TOWARD DEMOCRACY IN THE ARAB states has wavered over the decades from uninterested and skeptical (usually) to supportive (occasionally), but even when it has been supportive, it has often been ineffective. As the political scientist Sarah Bush of Temple University writes, one of the reasons why democratization has been so slow in the Arab world compared to all other regions is that international pressure, including U.S. pressure,

> in the Middle East is different than is that international pressure in other parts of the world. Specifically, international efforts to promote political liberalization in most of the countries in the Middle East have been half-hearted at best and often combined with forceful international efforts to promote the authoritarian status quo .... The United States and European states claim to support democratic principles in the Middle East. Their actual commitment to promoting democracy in the region is ambivalent, at best, and is often combined with considerable support for regime maintenance.[1]

SUPPORTING DEMOCRACY: THE BUSH YEARS

This lack of interest or enthusiasm is not very difficult to explain. One ingredient is fear that political openings will lead to Islamist takeovers that would change friendly countries and allies into enemies. (During the Cold War, the fear was that political openings were likely to give opportunities for the Soviets and their allies to gain ground in the Arab world.) Another ingredient is pessimism about the chances for democracy to succeed. Political openings are thought very unlikely to produce democracy, and the fear is that instead their result would be Islamist rule or sheer chaos – with state failure opening opportunities for jihadi groups. Further, the ineffectiveness of American support for democracy is in part related to our failure over many decades to support political groups and parties, concentrating instead on NGOs and "civil society."

In the immediate aftermath of the 9/11 attacks, the Bush administration struggled to understand why Arab terrorism had been aimed at the United States. Many in the State Department proffered the predictable "Arabist" view: Arabs hated the United States because of its warm support for Israel. Change that and the hatred would be drained away. Others proffered another traditional view: that terrorism was the product of economic deprivation – of want and poverty.

President Bush rejected all this advice and came to a different conclusion. He believed that the hatred that led to terrorism against the United States emerged from a "freedom deficit" and from regimes and dictators that left "a legacy of torture, oppression, misery, and ruin." And there was scholarship to back that conclusion. A 2003 review of terrorism globally by Alan Krueger of Princeton and Jitka Maleckova of Charles University in Prague found,

> Apart from population – larger countries tend to have more terrorists – the only variable that was consistently associated with the number of terrorists was the Freedom House index of political rights and civil liberties. Countries with more freedom were less likely to be the birthplace of international terrorists. Poverty and literacy were unrelated to the number of terrorists from a country. . . . Instead of viewing terrorism as a response – either direct or indirect – to poverty or ignorance, we suggest that it is more accurately viewed as a response to political conditions and longstanding feelings of indignity and frustration that have little to do with economic circumstances.[2]

Supporting democracy as part of the struggle against terror has been criticized as "instrumentalizing" and "tainting" democracy promotion, subordinating it to other foreign policy goals.[3] The danger is that in some circumstances democratization may empower radicals or be thought to run the risk of doing so, and in those cases the terrorism argument will under-mine rather than strengthen the argument for supporting democracy. No doubt such circumstances may arise, but if the link between repres-sion and terrorism exists, as Krueger and Maleckova suggest, it consti-tutes a powerful argument for a general policy of supporting democracy. And this is not because democracy will appeal to hard-core jihadis and lead them to become peaceful democratic politicians. As Shadi Hamid explains,

> Democracy, whether in its liberal or Islamist manifestations, will not con-vince al Qaeda to give up arms or channel its efforts into the political pro-cess. Those in the jihadist hardcore can only be defeated through military and law enforcement means. For them, it is too late. What democracy can do, though, is prevent those most susceptible to extremist recruitment – tens of millions of frustrated Arabs and Muslims throughout the Middle East – from turning to political violence, by giving them alternative outlets for peaceful political expression.[4]

And what is the alternative? Further support for repression in the hope that it will produce peace and stability? In his 2003 speech to the National Endowment for Democracy, President Bush argued that backing friendly dictatorships had not worked:

> Sixty years of Western nations excusing and accommodating the lack of freedom in the Middle East did nothing to make us safe – because in the long run, stability cannot be purchased at the expense of liberty. As long as the Middle East remains a place where freedom does not flourish, it will remain a place of stagnation, resentment, and violence ready for export.[5]

He urged instead support for "successful societies." These he described as societies that "limit the power of the state and the power of the mil-itary," "protect freedom with the consistent and impartial rule of law," "allow room for healthy civic institutions – for political parties and labor unions and independent newspapers and broadcast media," "guarantee religious liberty," "privatize their economies, and secure the rights of property," "prohibit and punish official corruption," and "recognize the rights of women."

In his Second Inaugural Address in early 2005, Bush took these views further:

> We have seen our vulnerability – and we have seen its deepest source. For as long as whole regions of the world simmer in resentment and tyranny – prone to ideologies that feed hatred and excuse murder – violence will gather, and multiply in destructive power, and cross the most defended borders, and raise a mortal threat. There is only one force of history that can break the reign of hatred and resentment, and expose the pretensions of tyrants, and reward the hopes of the decent and tolerant, and that is the force of human freedom.
>
> We are led, by events and common sense, to one conclusion: The survival of liberty in our land increasingly depends on the success of liberty in other lands. The best hope for peace in our world is the expansion of freedom in all the world.

What did this mean for U.S. foreign policy? Bush stated, "It is the policy of the United States to seek and support the growth of democratic movements and institutions in every nation and culture, with the ultimate goal of ending tyranny in our world." This was the "work of generations," but we would commence the change. And we understood that we in the United States had merely a supporting role, because "Freedom, by its nature, must be chosen and defended by citizens."[6]

SAUDI ARABIA

No country in the Arab Middle East at that time passed the tests Bush mentioned. That did not mean we would break relations with old friends, so translating his belief into policy was a difficult task. What exactly did Bush's words mean for relations with allies such as Saudi Arabia or Egypt? Perhaps the best answer is to say they meant something – some change in policy. But in my view they did not mean enough. In the case of Saudi Arabia, for example, it was obvious that lectures to the royal family about democracy would not get us very far. A serious dialogue with the Saudis did commence on the subjects of religious freedom for non-Muslims living in the kingdom and on Saudi dissemination of hate-filled literature about other religions. These subjects were raised directly with King

Abdullah, and pledges were made.[7] What became clear to the Saudis was that the president wished them well, but was also a religious Christian who cared about religious freedom. American officials were not raising these subjects to destabilize the kingdom, nor did our pressure emerge from hostility. Instead it was the product of American principles held deeply at the highest levels. (Similarly, the American official who raised religious freedom most often with the Chinese government was in fact President Bush, who repeatedly urged Jiang Zemin and Hu Jintao to consider a loosening of tight restrictions.)

Yet if one looked at Saudi policies and practices from 2001 to 2009, during Bush's terms as president, it cannot be argued that there was serious American pressure or impact, except when it came to the religious police and the suppression of religious practice other than Islam.

I visited Saudi Arabia in January 2001 as chairman of the U.S. Commission on International Religious Freedom and part of a small Commission delegation. In a meeting with U.S. Embassy staff, top officers there told us that there were some limits on practicing Christianity that affected embassy staff members, but nothing too harsh. When those officials left the room and I could chat informally with lower-level staff, they told a different story – of very tough limits and of real fear of the religious police. Though Saudi law said private religious devotions were permitted, in fact when a few cars were parked at the private home of an embassy staff member on a Sunday morning, they were likely to be harassed because a Christian worship service was suspected – and was not going to be permitted. For Catholics it was worse, because they needed a priest to perform the sacraments, and priests were not permitted in the kingdom.

The top embassy officers' refusal to acknowledge these facts was revealing of a broader unwillingness to challenge the Saudis on any internal issue. During that visit I met with the ambassador of the Philippines, who represented most of the Christians then living in the kingdom: Roman Catholic Filipinos living there as engineers, nurses, doctors, drivers, and other workers. There were at least a million of them in Saudi Arabia in 2001, as there are now, and they could not practice their religion. I asked the ambassador whether he had confronted the Saudi government on this issue. His quiet answer was frank: "Have I? You know,

I am the ambassador of the Philippines. You people represent the United States of America. Have you?"

We had not, at that point, though in the Bush years we did – to a degree. And over time the religious police were reined in, though this may have been because of their harassment of family members of the Saudi elites rather than because of the way they treated Western Christians. On political matters, we did not challenge the Saudis. I recall no conversations that went beyond religious issues (which did include freedom of religious practice for non-Muslims living in Saudi Arabia and terrorism-related matters, such as what Wahhabi imams were preaching and which groups Saudi government funds were supporting around the world). On the possible role of Saudi citizens in their own government, for example through municipal elections, I recall no conversations.

EGYPT

The case of Egypt was different, no doubt because it was a republic rather than a monarchy and, unlike Saudi Arabia, was in theory pledged to the democratic principles we were espousing. Considerable pressure was put on the Mubarak regime in 2004–2006 for some movement toward a more open political system. It began to work: for example, previously Mubarak had been selected by the rubber-stamp parliament and had never actually run for president. In 2005 the constitution was changed to provide for direct election of the president. Someone would actually run against Mubarak for the first time. This would not be a fair election, but the principle would be established – or so the Bush administration hoped – that might lead to truly fair and contested elections some time in the future, perhaps once Mubarak (then seventy-seven years old) was gone.

Michele Dunne of the Brookings Institution wrote in 2006 that "the political opening that began in late 2004 in Egypt has been unlike any seen in the country in at least twenty years. It has resulted so far in Egypt holding its first-ever presidential elections as well as parliamentary elections that were significantly fairer and more transparent than in the past, although marred by violence. Political dissidents are making bolder demands, most of the taboos on criticizing the regime have been swept away, and there is now more opposition representation in

Parliament than at any time since the 1952 Free Officers' coup."[8] The immediate impact was to change the nature of the 2005 elections. Khairi Abaza reported, "In an unprecedented step in post-1952 politics, the Egyptian opposition enjoyed some access to state-controlled media... opposition candidates had a real opportunity to address the Egyptian public on a relatively large scale.... The 2005 presidential elections gave a new momentum to political life."[9] This was only a beginning, of course, which the Bush administration acknowledged: a White House spokesman said, "We expect it will be part of a process of continuing political reforms and that the flaws that were visible in this election will be corrected" in the parliamentary elections that were to come later in 2005.[10]

There was no doubt in anyone's mind what produced these reforms: as James Traub writes in *The Freedom Agenda*, they were all undertaken "under pressure from the Bush administration."[11] Traub quotes an Egyptian human rights lawyer describing the background to the reforms and finding that "the most important part was Bush," and Traub himself concludes, "The Bush administration succeeded in pushing Hosni Mubarak further than anyone might have guessed."[12]

How was Mubarak pushed? Spending on democracy assistance for Egypt was increased from roughly $5 to nearly $50 million during the Bush years. About $30 million in military aid (out of a total military aid program of nearly $1.3 billion) was suspended in reaction to the imprisonment of a leading human rights advocate. But pressure from the top was far more important: after all, even that increase in "democracy funding" of $45 million over eight years, roughly $5 million a year in a nation of 90 million people, was more significant symbolically than practically. So was the small and temporary suspension of a part of our military aid.

What pressure from the top? Secretary of State Condoleezza Rice canceled a visit to Egypt to protest the imprisonment of opposition leader Ayman Nour, and in 2006 free trade talks with Egypt were frozen over Nour's imprisonment. As James Traub writes, "The regime was stunned. Washington had never before exacted any price for acts of domestic repression."[13]

And top officials of the administration – starting with the president – pointedly discussed human rights issues. Traub notes, "In private, Bush urged Mubarak to loosen the iron grip on political debate and assembly. Mubarak began ever so delicately opening the pressure valves that governed political expression . . . . The Bush administration was determined to push hard on this half-open door. Several weeks after the [2005] inaugural speech, Bush called Mubarak to urge him to open up the political playing field, and to permit independent figures to monitor the election."[14]

Rice spoke out in Cairo when she visited there in June 2005. Speaking at the American University there, she said this:

> For 60 years, my country, the United States, pursued stability at the expense of democracy in this region here in the Middle East – and we achieved neither. Now, we are taking a different course. We are supporting the democratic aspirations of all people.
>
> President Mubarak's decision to amend the country's constitution and hold multiparty elections is encouraging. President Mubarak has unlocked the door for change. Now, the Egyptian Government must put its faith in its own people. We are all concerned for the future of Egypt's reforms when peaceful supporters of democracy – men and women – are not free from violence. The day must come when the rule of law replaces emergency decrees – and when the independent judiciary replaces arbitrary justice.
>
> The Egyptian Government must fulfill the promise it has made to its people – and to the entire world – by giving its citizens the freedom to choose. Egypt's elections, including the Parliamentary elections, must meet objective standards that define every free election.
>
> Opposition groups must be free to assemble, and to participate, and to speak to the media. Voting should occur without violence or intimidation. And international election monitors and observers must have unrestricted access to do their jobs.
>
> Throughout the Middle East, the fear of free choices can no longer justify the denial of liberty. It is time to abandon the excuses that are made to avoid the hard work of democracy. There are those who say that democracy is being imposed. In fact, the opposite is true: Democracy is never imposed. It is tyranny that must be imposed.[15]

Middle Eastern rulers reacted to American pressure in varying ways. Mubarak did, in 2004–2006, bend under it, though he never claimed in conversations with American officials to be moving toward democracy or a more open political system. During his visit to Bush's Texas ranch in 2004, we choreographed an opportunity for the president to speak with Mubarak and his son Gamal about these issues. The thought was that perhaps in an off-the-record conversation and without his entourage present, he and his son would be willing to discuss his political legacy and the direction in which Egypt should move in his waning years (he was then seventy-six) – and afterward.

This plan failed: when President Bush asked Mubarak to tell us how, given that the average age of the population was so low and it was really a young country, he viewed Egypt's political future, Mubarak immediately changed the subject from political reform to educational reform and asked Gamal to respond.

But at least in 2004–2006 there was real pressure on Egypt for political reform, and it was sufficiently strong to produce change. That pressure was reduced in the administration's final years, as I discuss later.

LIBYA

Libya was a very different case, where it is fair to say that other priorities had by the end pushed human rights issues aside. When Bush entered office, Libya had long been a pariah state under UN sanctions (though those were suspended in 1999). Qadhafi's repressive rule and his support for and practice of terrorism had destroyed relations with the United States. Muammar Qadhafi ruled with an iron hand, and there was not even a pretense of democracy. Human rights conditions were poor, and the United States said so repeatedly, which was all we could do – lacking diplomatic relations with Libya and any presence there.

But as the United States prepared for its invasion of Iraq, Qadhafi apparently feared he was next and sought to change his relations with the world and especially the United States. In 2002 Libya reached agreement with the families of the Lockerbie victims, leading to the cancellation of UN sanctions in September 2003. More strikingly, in March 2003 Qadhafi's representatives approached the British government with an offer to negotiate the end of Libya's nuclear and missile programs in exchange for normalization of ties with the United Kingdom and the United States.

This led to months of negotiations, and finally in December 2003, Prime Minister Blair and President Bush announced that agreement had been reached for the dismantling of all nuclear, chemical, and biological programs and the limitation of missiles to a striking distance of less than 300 kilometers – with all this to be guaranteed by a new inspection regime.

Over the following year, Libya's nuclear and missile programs were eliminated, with most of the nuclear operation shipped to the United States. In 2006 the United States removed Libya from the list of states supporting terrorism and restored diplomatic relations. By October 2008, shortly before Bush left office, compensation payments to the victims of Libyan terrorism and their survivors were completed, and Bush himself spoke with Qadhafi by phone to express satisfaction that this had been accomplished. The administration issued a statement stating, "Libya has taken important steps on the road to normalizing its relations with the international community, beginning with its renunciation in 2003 of terrorism and weapons of mass destruction. The United States will continue to work on the bilateral relationship with Libya, with the aim of establishing a dialogue that encompasses all subjects, including human rights reform and the fight against terrorism."[16]

Thus the use of force in Iraq, Qadhafi's fear that force would be used against him, and skillful diplomacy achieved results that had been thought impossible. Blair and French president Jacques Chirac visited Libya in 2004, the United States began to encourage American investment there, and Secretary Rice ultimately visited there in September 2008. The achievements – getting Qadhafi to abandon and denounce support for terror, compensate Libya's victims, and abandon his missile, chemical and biological warfare, and nuclear weapons programs – were extraordinary. But it has to be admitted that the administration did nothing to promote a political opening or more respect for human rights in Libya. The rhetoric even softened: the State Department's 2003 *Country Reports on Human Rights Practices* covering Libya, released in February 2004, began this way: "The Socialist People's Libyan Arab Jamahiriya is a dictatorship." The following year it began, "The Great Socialist People's Libyan Arab Jamahiriya is an authoritarian regime." Administration officials said that during Rice's visit she would raise human rights issues, but she did not do so at all in public.[17]

Qadhafi or at least his son Saif al-Islam played the game on the subject of democracy and human rights. Saif was educated in Europe and knew what we wanted to hear. In September 2008 Saif said he was abandoning public life to devote himself to promoting political and economic reform. During his visit to Washington in November 2008, he told CNN that it was time for Libya to "embrace democracy and establish a parliament and a constitution."[18] Because Saif was seen as a likely successor to his father, his statement was taken seriously and seen as the key to Libya's future; in the press, Saif was for years widely hailed as a democrat and reformer. The *Washington Post* reported on "his commitment to political freedoms,"[19] and CNN called him "an open advocate of democracy."[20] During his 2008 visit to Washington, I met with him in the Executive Office Building because he wanted, it was said, to discuss how his foundation might most effectively promote change in Libya. He was, as advertised, soft-spoken and fluent in English. His travels and statements helped persuade Western governments that Libya might be on the right track.

But there was no change in Muammar Qadhafi's ideology nor in the way he ruled Libya during the Bush years, so one must acknowledge that we simply elevated national security goals over the promotion of human rights and democracy there. There were plenty of justifications for doing so. While we had never promised Qadhafi we would lay off, there was concern that going after him in the aftermath of the nuclear deal would be seen as bad faith, a kind of "bait and switch" tactic aiming at removing his weapons of mass destruction and then overthrowing his regime. Given Qadhafi's history and personality, there appeared to be little reason to think that pressure for internal change would work. Especially at a time when Qadhafi had given up a good deal to the West, he would likely be even more reluctant than usual to give any sign that the regime's hold was weakening.

Even if one grants that such arguments are plausible, the bottom line is that we did not pressure him for political reform in the aftermath of the change in our relations after 2004. We acted as if we had achieved all that could reasonably be done, leaving to a successor administration the next steps. It does seem to me unlikely that our pressure would in fact have had much impact in Libya, but we clearly should have done more than we did.

Libya's collapse and civil war after the uprising in 2011 that overthrew Qadhafi show why: the country's institutions were destroyed during his decades in power. They will have to be rebuilt. If outside pressure could have started that process earlier, perhaps marginally under Qadhafi, it would have helped.

TUNISIA

There was human rights pressure on the Ben Ali regime in Tunisia, though it was limited by the low level of attention Tunisia attracted in those years due to its very small size and minimal strategic significance. When Ben Ali visited Washington in 2004, both Bush and Secretary of State Powell raised political reform and human rights with him privately and publicly, and the public mention was seen as a rebuke or even a humiliation.[21] But Ben Ali's appearance was in February 2004, and he was the first Arab leader to visit the White House after Bush's powerful November 2003 address on the twentieth anniversary of the National Endowment for Democracy. One can argue that the visit itself (Ben Ali's first invitation to Washington in fourteen years) demonstrated that in the view of Washington cooperation in the "war on terror" outweighed domestic repression – or Ben Ali would never have been given this honor. After all, he had most recently been "elected" president for a five-year term in 1999 with what he claimed was 99.94 percent of the vote. Under the Tunisian constitution, that would have been his third and last term, so he staged a referendum in May 2002 and claimed he had won approval by 99.52 percent of the vote to amend the constitution and remove term limits, numbers that would have made Stalin proud. (He then had himself reelected president in October 2004, claiming that he had won 94.49 percent of the vote.)

The U.S. Embassy maintained contacts with Tunisia's beleaguered human rights community. I can recall an incident when embassy officers went to meet with officials of the Tunisian League for Human Rights. The meeting had been arranged in advance, and the Tunisians were awaiting their guests. But Ben Ali's police blocked access to the building and told the Americans the human rights activists were not available. Meanwhile, those activists opened the windows of their office and shouted down that they were indeed present and waiting for the meeting. The effort by the Americans to see them would have helped their morale, but the success of the regime in blocking the meeting, without repercussions from the United States, had the opposite effect.

So American pressure on Ben Ali was limited and consisted mostly of calls for greater respect for human rights, rather than real pressure for movement toward democracy. The State Department *Country Report* on human rights in Tunisia for 2004, for example, stated, "The Government's human rights record remained poor, and the Government continued to commit serious abuses."[22] But reporting on systematic human rights abuses and pushing for changes are two different things. As one analyst put it, "Tunisia's poor record on political democratization, especially the respect for human rights, is a source of embarrassment for the United States. Hence, on occasions the Bush administration has criticized Tunisia for its human rights record.... In essence, the United States has recurrently expressed concerns about the poor state of democratization on the one hand, but praised Tunisia for its role in 'stabilizing the region and combating terror.'"[23]

The best defense of American policy would be that, unlike the case of Egypt, Tunisia was considered insufficiently important to be worthy of real pressure. None of us thought of Tunisia as an influential country, and even progress there was not felt to be likely to have any impact on the rest of the Arab world – again, unlike Egypt. And we believed that, unlike Mubarak, Ben Ali would not be moved by our pressure, given the limited American role in Tunisia when compared to that of France and the EU. Indeed, though our criticism of Tunisia's human rights violations was not accompanied by much pressure, that criticism and our support for human rights groups there made our policy more defensible than that of the Europeans. Still, any judgment of U.S. policy in that period would have to acknowledge that it fell far short of Bush's inspiring rhetoric.

YEMEN

Yemen presented a different story: we considered Yemen under Ali Abdullah Saleh to be a case of democratic progress. Perhaps we were fooled, or we fooled ourselves. Saleh, a former military officer, had ruled North Yemen since 1978 and been president since the country's unification in 1990. Unlike Tunisia, Yemen was not a case of vast repression where a strong state ruled every square inch of the territory. As a Congressional Research Service analysis put it, "the country's rugged terrain and geographic isolation, strong tribal social structure, and sparsely settled population have historically made it difficult to centrally govern (or conquer). This has promoted a relatively pluralistic political environment."[24] The central government's hold on the country was weak, and Saleh ruled more by a system of patronage and vast corruption (and by giving key posts to his family members) than by establishing a police state.

Saleh held his first presidential "election" in 1999 and claimed 96 percent of the vote. (The opposition leader had not been permitted to run, and Saleh's only opponent stated that he himself would vote for Saleh.) When Saleh visited President Bush in November 2001, shortly after 9/11, talk was of counterterrorist assistance and not democracy. This was the first of Saleh's four visits during the Bush years (2001, 2004 as a guest at a G-8 summit, 2005, and 2007).

Saleh was sly and remarkably attuned to the changing rhetoric in Washington. In July 2005 he announced that he would not run for reelection. In June 2006 he reversed himself (bowing to what he claimed was popular demand) and ran in the September 2006 presidential election. This time he allowed opposition and claimed only 77 percent of the vote, so when he visited in 2007 President Bush congratulated him on his election victory – and indeed that election was "judged mostly fair by foreign observers."[25] The BBC reported that the 2006 election was "the first time President Saleh has faced a serious challenge,"[26] and the EU Observer Mission claimed that despite its shortcomings this election saw for the first time "an openly-contested electoral process take place that represented a milestone in the democratic development in Yemen. The elections benefited from the full engagement of all major political parties and were notable for the degree of freedom enjoyed by all candidates to assemble and to express their views so that, for the first time in the political history of both Yemen and the region, an incumbent faced a real challenge at the polls."[27]

Saleh and his ambassador now turned the tables on us when it came to rhetoric, demanding more aid in view of Yemen's new democratic achievements. How were we to see Saleh's maneuverings and this 2006 election? Was it a real competition or an extension of Saleh's endless years in power? Gregory Johnsen, a student of Yemen, sums it up well:

> The dissonance between these two expectations – that there would be a genuinely competitive contest that was nonetheless certain to renew the mandate of President 'Ali 'Abdallah Salih – allowed observers to see what they wanted to see in the election results. If they wanted to see progress, they saw it in the huge increase from past campaigns in the tallies of opposition candidates. If they wanted to see a stalled democracy slipping back into dictatorship, they saw it in the ineluctable fact that Salih won another seven years in power. Yemen's presidential election was both the election it was supposed to be and the election the government wanted it to be.
>
> The September 20 balloting provided Salih with a resounding victory, while at the same time demonstrating that Yemen had a strong and independent opposition. In many ways, this was the best-case scenario, both for the government and for its Western counterparts. The outcome solidified Salih's position domestically and internationally, while giving foreign governments and institutions the political cover they need – a "democratically elected" leader – to proceed undisturbed in their dealings with the Yemeni regime.[28]

Yemen's desperate poverty (it was the poorest country in the Arab world) and al-Qaeda's presence there (made manifest in the 2000 attack on the *USS Cole*) no doubt helped induce us to celebrate the election and see in Yemen the makings of a democracy, rather than the growing disaster that emerged fully after 2011. But looking back now even with full knowledge of its tragic path, Yemen is not a case like Libya or Tunisia where the administration simply placed other goals ahead of human rights or did not follow up human rights pronouncements with firm pressure. For his own reasons as well as to curry favor in Washington and gain increased aid, Saleh took a significant step toward opening the political system and permitting opposition to his rule to crystallize and organize. Recognition of this in American policy was no mistake, even if the rhetoric was sometimes excessive.

EGYPT, BUSH, AND THE FREEDOM AGENDA

Throughout his years in power, Bush continued to display his own passion for human rights and democracy. In June 2007 he attended a meeting of dissidents in Prague where he met democratic activists from seventeen nations (including Egypt's Saad Eddin Ibrahim). He continued to argue that the lack of freedom was the underlying cause of terrorism: "In dark and repressive corners of the world, whole generations grew up with no voice in their government and no hope in their future. This life of oppression bred deep resentment. And for many, resentment boiled over into radicalism and violence." He proposed the antidote: "The most powerful weapon in the struggle against extremism is not bullets or bombs – it is the universal appeal of freedom." Accordingly "the United States is committed to the advance of freedom and democracy as the great alternatives to repression and radicalism."

This commitment would be expressed in several ways, Bush said at the conference. Meeting with dissidents very publicly was one way. Bush also proposed a "Human Rights Defenders Fund to "provide grants for the legal defense and medical expenses of activists arrested or beaten by repressive governments." He said he had "asked Secretary Rice to send a directive to every U.S. ambassador in an un-free nation: Seek out and meet with activists for democracy and human rights."

Bush then mentioned several Muslim nations and the argument that, because they were friends, they would presumably be immune from pressure. Not so:

> The United States is also using our influence to urge valued partners like Egypt, Saudi Arabia, and Pakistan to move toward freedom. These nations have taken brave stands and strong action to confront extremists, along with some steps to expand liberty and transparency. Yet they have a great distance still to travel. The United States will continue to press nations like these to open up their political systems, and give a greater voice to their people. Inevitably, this creates tension. But our relationships with these countries are broad enough and deep enough to bear it. As our relationships with South Korea and Taiwan during the Cold War prove, America can maintain a friendship and push a nation toward democracy at the same time.

Of course, maintaining that balance would be a neat trick, requiring great skill and great determination. But Bush argued that there was no alternative to a pro-democracy policy: he noted the argument that "ending tyranny will unleash chaos" and that "a safer goal would be stability – especially in the Middle East," but then voiced his disagreement with it: "The problem is that pursuing stability at the expense of liberty does not lead to peace – it leads to September the 11th, 2001." As to the argument that "democracy will bring dangerous forces to power," he agreed that individual elections can turn out badly but in the long run "people will not vote for a life of perpetual violence."[29] So Bush's personal passion for this cause never flagged, and in late September 2008 – just months before the presidential election and the end of his second term – he met with another group of dissidents while in New York for his last address to the UN General Assembly.

But by 2006, his passion was less often reflected in American foreign policy. In some cases, individual U.S. ambassadors blocked or simply ignored initiatives from an administration with which they did not sympathize and that was moving toward its close. In other cases, and despite the president's claim that "America can maintain a friendship and push a nation toward democracy at the same time," other diplomatic or security goals were allowed to push support for democracy aside. One White House official is quoted as telling Saad Eddin Ibrahim, the Egyptian human rights activist, in September 2006 that "I'm sorry, professor . . . we need every ally we have in the region."[30] As several analysts wrote in 2007 about Egypt,

> After pushing fairly assertively (and with some success) for reform in Egypt in 2003–5, the United States dropped the issue just as suddenly in 2006 because its priorities shifted from transformation back to traditional diplomacy to contain regional crises . . . . Islamist gains in elections in Palestine, Egypt, and elsewhere created doubts within the administration about the wisdom of pressing forward assertively on electoral democracy.[31]

I would dispute this interpretation, though the net effect – dropping the issue – remains the same. In my view, the administration (led in this case by Secretary Rice) decided to push energetically for Israeli-Palestinian peace talks. Efforts began as early as the summer of 2006, after the Israeli-Hezbollah war in Lebanon, and led in November 2007 to the Annapolis Conference and the ensuing negotiations. As had long been the case, Egypt's relations with Israel and its influence on the Palestinians were thought to play an important part in any such peace effort. Mubarak and his foreign minister were viewed as key players, so antagonizing them was seen as undesirable: priorities had changed.[32]

It is worth noting again, however, that programming did not change, nor was spending on democracy programs slashed. What changed was the message from the top: the pressure was reduced. Rice's Cairo speech of June 2005 was the high-water mark, and by the time Bush spoke in Prague almost exactly two years later, Egyptian officials would have considered his words to be mere talk. By the end of the Bush administration, the "Freedom Agenda" was to be found largely in the president's own rhetoric and his meetings with dissidents and activists. In the Middle East, the sharp edge of the policy had been blunted.

AND THEN CAME OBAMA

The incoming Obama administration did not seem to realize this, and reacted to what it viewed as an unrealistic and aggressive policy of promoting democracy by largely dropping the subject. As Joel Brinkley of the *New York Times* noted in April 2009, "neither President Obama nor Secretary of State Hillary Rodham Clinton has even uttered the word democracy in a manner related to democracy promotion since taking office more than two months ago.... Democracy, it seems, is banished from the Obama administration's public vocabulary."[33] And as James Traub describes, "Secretary of State Hillary Clinton was the first leading official to indicate an open break with the language of democracy promotion. In an address to her new colleagues at Foggy Bottom, Clinton spoke of the 'three Ds' underlying effective foreign policy – defense, diplomacy and development. Democracy apparently didn't merit a mention."[34] In her early 2009 visit to China, Clinton made clear the new policy of pushing human rights and democracy goals aside: "our pressing on those issues can't interfere with the global economic crisis, the global climate change crisis, and the security crisis."[35]

Fawaz Gerges in his book, *Obama and the Middle East*, summarizes the new policy:

> Until the fall of Tunisian president Zine El Abidine Ben Ali in early 2011, Obama and his advisers preferred to bolster local autocrats and refrain from saying or doing anything in public that weakened them. During its first two years in office, the Obama administration did not take risks on oppositional forces; its hard-core material interests could not be sacrificed on the altar of human rights and the rule of law. The Obama foreign policy team, led by Secretary of State Clinton, pursued a quiet, gradual, low-risk approach toward the promotion of human rights.... [T]he foreign policy team did not push Middle Eastern dictators to reform.
>
> Obama came closer to the dominant realist approach to American foreign policy toward the region, an approach that aimed at retaining the status quo through backing pro-Western rulers and eschewing moral imperatives, such as the promotion of the rule of law and human rights. Prior to his 2009 trip to Cairo, he was asked whether he considered Mubarak an authoritarian leader. He responded directly, "No, I tend not to use labels for folks."
>
> Obama embraced Mubarak as a wise old statesman of the Arab Middle East, a trustworthy ally.... Whatever reservations Obama had about Mubarak's oppressive and corrupt rule – if any – he did not make them public. In fact, when asked if the US government considered Mubarak a dictator, Obama and Vice President Biden separately said that the Egyptian leader was not a dictator, simply because he was an ally.[36]

The president's famous 2009 speech to the Muslim world was given in Cairo, home to a dictatorship when there were capitals of Muslim democracies to choose from.

The Obama team did not anticipate the "Arab Spring" revolts that displaced first Ben Ali in Tunisia and then Mubarak in Egypt, but neither did academic experts, intelligence agencies, or diplomats assigned to the region. How did the administration respond to the uprisings?

Not nimbly. The U.S. response, writes Jason Brownlee, was that first the administration "would urge calm – and by implication a return to the undemocratic status quo – but if opposition forces forced the ruler out, U.S. officials would extol the victory as if they had been seeking democratic change all along. Until events broke in one direction or the other, Washington sought to demobilize protesters and restabilize allied regimes."[37] Secretary of State Clinton famously said, "[O]ur assessment is that the Egyptian Government is stable," just two weeks before Mubarak fell. In March 2011 she was still talking about Bashar al-Assad, the brutal dictator of Syria, as a "possible reformer."[38]

Far more important was the overall policy reaction to the Arab Spring and its failure (except in Tunisia): instead of more democracy promotion and efforts to protect human rights, there was less. The administration deepened its belief that promoting democracy was a low priority, both because of its (perceived) small chance of success and because our friends in the region chafed against it. In Egypt, just as there had been little criticism of Mubarak in what turned out to be President Obama's first two years and Hosni Mubarak's last two, so there was little criticism of human rights violations during Mohammed Morsi's rule as president from July 2012 to July 2013. As Eric Trager describes it, "The Brotherhood's behavior came at no cost." The Obama administration was perceived by Egyptians as endorsing the Brotherhood in Egypt's ongoing political struggle "without compelling Morsi to do anything in return," because "the administration largely avoided criticizing him, even as his behavior worsened."[39] Then the administration refused to label the military coup that ousted Morsi a coup, nor did it complain much about human rights violations during the period of military rule after Morsi's ouster. The head of the military junta, Gen. Abdel Fattah al-Sisi, was elected president in 2014 and human rights conditions worsened terribly in 2014 -2016, but again the Obama administration's criticism and pressures for more freedom of expression and assembly were very limited.

And this was the general pattern of policy, not just toward Egypt but also generally. Tom Carothers of the Brookings Institution, often viewed as the leading scholar of American policy to promote democracy and human rights, described the phenomenon at the end of 2014:

> U.S. assistance to advance democracy worldwide is in decline. Such spending has shrunk by 28 percent during Barack Obama's presidency and is now less than $2 billion per year. The decline has been especially severe at

the U.S. Agency for International Development, which traditionally funds the bulk of U.S. democracy assistance and established itself in the 1990s as the largest source of such aid worldwide.... Why this striking reduction in democracy aid? It is not a product of a broader contraction of U.S. foreign aid spending, which remains robust overall. Rather, it is a policy choice, reflecting both skepticism about the relative importance of democracy work by senior U.S. aid officials and, more generally, the muted emphasis on democracy-building by the Obama foreign policy team.[40]

Elsewhere Carothers refers to the Obama administration's "highly uncertain commitment" to democracy and the "U.S. hesitation to push hard for democratization in many places."[41] (This problem was not exclusive to the Arab world: in July 2015 President Obama chose to visit Ethiopia and while there twice called its repressive government "democratically elected."[42] But in its sham elections the ruling party won every seat in parliament, and the government was especially repressive of civil society organizations.) Other analysts, at the Atlantic Council, noted, "Since 2013, the US administration has downgraded its regional policy initiative on Arab reform, eliminated a special coordinator post for Arab transitions, and scaled back democracy assistance."[43] This pattern was also visible when it came to the terrible human rights situation in southern Sudan: "Key administration posts, including the special envoy to Sudan and South Sudan, ambassador to South Sudan, and assistant secretary of state for African affairs, have remained vacant for extended periods during his presidency."[44] Whatever more general problems within the administration these vacancies showed, they certainly revealed a lack of energy and attention when it came to dealing with this human rights crisis.

So what was left? Again here is Carothers' assessment: "a policy apparatus frequently behind the curve of events, soft on old, backward-leaning friends in the region and unable to connect well to the new currents of political thinking and action among young Arabs," and "pursuing the line that has defined its response so far: a divided policy marked by sincere but reactive support for Arab political progress when it does occur but no real proactive support for democracy where dictatorship persists."[45]

REMEMBERING THE COLD WAR

Every new administration tends to view its predecessor's policies with deep skepticism, especially if there has been a change in the party holding the White House. This was certainly true in the Obama case, where the Bush "Freedom Agenda" was written off as rhetorically excessive and simply unrealistic – and as a feature of the Iraq war. Democracy promotion was tarred, in the eyes of many officials, as just another flawed Bush policy when it was in fact a bipartisan approach that had been institutionalized under Presidents Carter and Reagan and grew out of far deeper historical roots.

From presidential rhetoric and the speeches of the secretary of state to slashed budgets, the Obama administration revealed its skepticism of democracy promotion from the very beginning. Then came the upheavals called the "Arab Spring," and the reaction was to turn further from the issue. This is not surprising, for several reasons. First, the many barriers to democracy that led to the belief in "Arab exceptionalism" seemed no weaker after the Arab Spring: religious, ethnic, and social divisions and the lack of powerful models and magnets for democratic reform, for example. Moreover, the chaos in Iraq, Syria, and Libya contributed to a desire for order, regardless of human rights conditions and even if they were worsening. And this was magnified greatly because of the growth of the Islamic State or ISIS, whose tentacles were visible not only where the group rose to power, in parts of Syria and Iraq, but also in North Africa. American policy saw President Sisi, for example, as a key ally against jihadis more than as an increasingly repressive ruler.

Déjà vu all over again, one might say. As the scholars at the Atlantic Council put it, "After the terrorist attacks of September 11, 2001, the United States and its European allies were quick to work with now-overthrown autocratic leaders in Tunisia, Egypt, Yemen and even Libya to combat terrorism and keep a tight lid on political dissent and religious expression in the name of internal security. Nearly fourteen years later, the rise of ISIS and the threat of jihadists with Western passports are resuscitating that same short-term thinking."[46]

This policy line was hardly limited to the Obama administration and the Middle East, and has a long history: it was followed often during the

Cold War in backing anti-Communist dictators. Their repressive policies, and the internal situations those created, were too often overlooked as long as they remained on the American side against the USSR. Thus did the United States back the Batista regime in Cuba and the Somoza regime in Nicaragua in the name of anti-Communism, only to see those regimes fall and be replaced by Fidel Castro and the Sandinistas, respectively. But what was the lesson? That the United States should have backed the dictatorships more aggressively and prevented Communist takeovers? That a power vacuum allows the most violent and extreme elements to seize power? Or that repressive regimes elicit deep popular opposition and thus pave the way for their own doom, so that the United States should oppose them and promote human rights and democracy?

As I discussed in the introduction to this volume, in the Reagan years these questions were answered with a policy of democracy promotion symbolized and to some degree institutionalized in the National Endowment for Democracy (NED). The NED was established with a central grant-making program and four institutes: those linked to the Democratic and Republican parties, the AFL-CIO, and the U.S. Chamber of Commerce. But in the 1980s these institutions were new and small; the main action remained in the White House and Department of State. The United States acted directly and at the highest levels to replace the junta in South Korea through free elections and to end the Marcos dictatorship in the Philippines. U.S. policy pushed to replace the generals running governments throughout Latin America – in El Salvador and Guatemala, Chile and Brazil, Paraguay and Uruguay – through free elections that reestablished democracy in countries where it had prevailed at times in the past.

These actions were taken not because the dangers of chaos, and of extremist and Communist-backed takeovers, were not understood, but precisely because they were. Repressive regimes were seen as likely to be overthrown sooner or later: recall John F. Kennedy's 1962 view, quoted in the introduction, that "[t]hose who make peaceful revolution impossible will make violent revolution inevitable." Better to try to promote a transition to democratic, pro-Western forces than wait for chaos to overtake the regime in power. Moreover, American alliances with such repressive regimes were thought likely to leave lasting negative views of the United

States among the populace. So the threat of extremist violence and Communist victory became, in the end, a spur to act against such regimes, rather than a justification for supporting them indefinitely.

Of course, there were *realpolitik* calculations, as well as principled support for democracy, in this American policy: officials concluded that the regimes would ultimately be unstable, that more years of repression might radicalize the opposition and be more likely to lead to Communist gains, *and* that there was a strong possibility of establishing stable and democratic governments to replace the rulers in power.

The analogy to today's Middle East is partial. As in the older cases, a dangerous threat exists that chaos will replace order. As I write, the governments of Iraq and Syria no longer rule throughout those countries, having lost that key ingredient of statehood: a government monopoly on the use of force. Al-Qaeda and ISIS exist throughout the region and can gain territory and power if governments are unable to fight them successfully. We have learned in Tunisia and Egypt that regimes that appeared stable were, in fact, brittle and overthrown after only weeks of protests. We have also seen that even decades in power will not win a regime legitimacy when it is viewed by the people as incompetent, corrupt, and abusive.

We can also see in Egypt as I write that repression can radicalize the opposition. By 2012, when it won a national election, the Muslim Brotherhood had long abandoned violence and terrorism – for perhaps thirty-five or forty years. But after the Brotherhood was thrown out of power, the eliminationist policy of the Sisi government – not only suppressing the Brotherhood as Mubarak had done but also killing its members and officers – led to a debate over violence within the organization, and many younger leaders now espouse a return to violence.

Where the analogy to the 1980s fails is in our belief in the likelihood of establishing stable democratic states. In Latin America, and in other countries where U.S. influence was enormous, such as South Korea and the Philippines, those chances were believed to be high. Previous experience with democracy, the cultural influence of Europe and the United States, and dependence on U.S. assistance combined to foster optimism that was in the event borne out. For all the reasons we have been discussing, that optimism does not exist in the case of the Arab Middle East.

FROM DEMOCRACY PROMOTION TO "CIVIL SOCIETY"

One key result has been the shift to supporting "civil society" organizations. These are groups that are expressly apolitical, in the sense that they do not contest for power – for the right to govern. Instead they work for particular goals that are related to improving society, some of them closely related to politics and some not: protecting the environment, increased rates of literacy, women's rights, protection of children, elimination of racism and protection of minorities, free elections, and advancing and protecting freedom of the press and of speech are examples.

More generally these organizations fight for human rights, not for systemic change and a share in power: they are not political parties. But these groups do help lay a foundation for the building of a democracy, and if a democratic opening is attained they can play a key role in sustaining it. Civil society organizations can be the nucleus of protests: As Stephen R. Grand puts it, "while civil society may make many contributions to the democratization process – educating citizens about democracy and teaching them new skills, training new leaders, and serving as mini-laboratories for democracy – its most important contribution is often the sheer force of its numbers." These organizations, if large enough, contain what he calls "the latent threat of citizens flooding the streets in protest."[47]

And civil society can do more than protest: it "has a crucial role to play not just in bringing down dictators but also in the messy and unending business of ensuring that even the most well-intentioned democratic political system does not become dictatorial.... The civic sector can play an equally valuable role in helping keep democracy on track long after a dictator has fallen. It can prod, petition, protest, and persuade newly elected leaders to respect new democratic institutions and procedures."[48]

There are other advantages that make support for civil society organizations so attractive to Western political leaders, diplomats, democracy and human rights activists, and donors. Tom Carothers explains their appeal:

> In many societies moving away from authoritarian rule, emergent political parties lacked institutional coherence and public credibility. Political ideologies and the very idea of political parties suffered a persistent legitimacy

deficit. In such contexts, the fresh concept of civil society was appealing both to local citizens and international policymakers and activists hoping to assist these transitions. It had a pleasing, nonideological quality, several steps removed from the dirty give-and-take of partisan politics, while also suggesting an alternative route to citizen engagement.[49]

Just so: politics was often dirty, full of unattractive power seekers and self-promoters, and forcing choices over divisive issues. The civil society NGOs were so much more appealing than many political groups to both indigenous actors, who were often young activists, and Western supporters. Moreover, there was a concern about the legitimacy of support for one political group or another – a concern that did not exist when it came to supporting NGOs dedicated to matters of principle like freedom of expression. Aid donors accused of intervening in the internal political affairs of foreign countries might worry about support for a political group that was vying for power. But the Arab nations were all signatories of the Universal Declaration of Human Rights and most had also signed the International Covenant on Civil and Political Rights, so donors to NGOs could explain that all they were doing was holding these governments to their word.

Often political groups and parties were led by people from the old regime, or extremists of one variety or another, or populists, or rabble-rousers. Sometimes parties that appealed to Western observers because they were secular either shared some of the NGOs' characteristic weaknesses (such as appealing only to small, educated elites in the capital) or were attached to (and sometimes created by) repressive regimes. The fact that a party was "secular" rather than Islamist was no guarantee that it would be a reliable steward of democracy and human rights, and "secular" parties often "have roots in authoritarian regimes and close ties to the security state."[50]

Contrast the individuals who led and populated the civil society organizations: very often they were middle class in background and Western educated, speaking good English and sharing with the Westerners a commitment to idealistic causes. They lived in the capital city and were easily reachable by Western embassies and the offices of Western NGOs. They were secular, as were so many of the Westerners with whom they interacted. They knew not only our language but also our methods: accountability, bookkeeping, using reason rather than bombast. And if such attributes did not always, of course, characterize our own domestic politics, they did characterize the goals and methods of the aid programs for human rights and democracy that we ran.

It would be a great mistake to overlook the substantial contributions that civil society groups made in very many cases. They were able to draw people into the political life of the nation (even if indirectly), give some young leaders a chance to emerge, and create communications networks that in emergencies like the Tahrir Square demonstrations proved critical. Their mastery of new methods of communications such as Facebook and Twitter allowed them to outsmart or at least outrun the police and other organs of repression. They highlighted some key issues related to democratic development. They were able to attract and maintain Western donor financial and political support, even when the donor governments were friendly with the repressive regimes that would have preferred all these programs to be shut down. They kept a candle burning.

THE NEED FOR POLITICS

So this pattern was entirely understandable – this favoring of "civil society" organizations rather than involvement in supporting political groups. But it did not work – and could not.

The best explanation of why not is offered by Princeton Lyman, the long-time American diplomat who served as Assistant Secretary of State for Africa and as ambassador to South Africa, in a discussion of the historic contributions of Nelson Mandela. It is worth quoting at length. Mandela had been asked by Nigerian activists to support an oil embargo meant to pressure their own government. He declined to give it, arguing that international sanctions would be helpful only if there was a "strong indigenous democratic movement" that could take advantage of them, which in his view Nigeria did not have. Here is Lyman's analysis:

Mandela provided one more lesson about the promotion of democracy, and perhaps it is the most important of all . . . . Without the equivalent of an

ANC – without a strong indigenous democratic political movement – neither international pressure nor domestic advocacy would assure a democratic outcome.

The ANC was not a civil society organization. It was a political movement dedicated to coming to power and to governing according to the principles by which it had lived. It was therefore different from the United Democratic Front, the nonracial antiapartheid coalition which spearheaded the "ungovernability campaign" that undermined the apartheid regime in its final days. The ANC was also different from the many civil associations that mobilized people at the grassroots level against apartheid. These movements played a major role in bringing down the apartheid regime, but they were not in a position to govern when apartheid fell. They were not structured for that, and they had not been deeply immersed in the principles of governing over a period of many years. They were not political movements in that sense.

What Mandela was saying to the Nigerian activists is that, in the absence of political movements dedicated not just to democracy but also to governing when the opportunity arises, social, civic, and economic pressures against tyranny will not suffice. International democracy-promotion efforts, if they do not address this political factor, ultimately will fail. Mandela never abandoned his commitment to democracy, nor have his successors in South Africa. But they learned from hard experiences that democracy cannot be imposed from outside, and that it cannot be brought to fruition without indigenous political leadership committed to it.

It is safer to focus on civil society. But Nelson Mandela's legacy tells us something else. Not even a leader as extraordinary as Mandela, at the helm of a new and almost miraculous democracy in South Africa, could bring democracy to a country where there was no indigenous democratic political movement. The Arab Spring too tells us that civil society is not enough. The question, then, is whether outsiders can contribute to the development of serious, dedicated, democratic political movements.[51]

Lyman here identifies several of the problems inherent in "civil society" NGOs. As we have noted, their location in the capital and the middle-class (and often secular) background of their leaders very often mean that they have little reach into the rest of the country. Marina Ottaway writes, "Advocates of democracy move in a small world, somewhat isolated from their own societies. They congregate in their NGOs and progressive think tanks, and write commentaries for domestic and pan-Arab newspapers. They reach across borders to like-minded people in other Arab states, but do not attempt to reach down into their own countries."[52] Their leaders know each other, but not much about the rural masses or the workers in the industrial sector. Their means of communication in social media work well in the capital to bring people to demonstrations and protests, but are not effective in mobilizing groups with which they had no previous contact.

In part this is because "civil society" has often been too narrow a concept, leading to a focus on what Carothers calls "the rather specialized set of policy-related nongovernment organizations that carry out advocacy work and civic education directly relating to what aid providers consider to be core democracy issues, such as election monitoring, government transparency, and political and civil rights."[53] These are "advocacy groups devoted to public interest causes – the environment, human rights, women's issues, election monitoring, anticorruption, and other 'good things.'" What are missing are the groups with far deeper roots in society: "religious organizations, labor unions, and other groups [that] often have a genuine base in the population." Too often civil society organizations with Western backing "have only tenuous ties to the citizens on whose behalf they claim to act, and they depend on international funders for budgets they cannot nourish from domestic sources."[54]

Especially noteworthy is the frequent lack of ties to labor: "In many transitional countries, unions are potentially among the most important civil society actors. Unlike many of the groups reached by aid programs expressly aimed at civil society development, labor unions have genuine ties to large numbers of citizens, are able to mobilize people for forceful civic action, and have the ability to come up with domestic funding. Yet when U.S. aid providers talk about aiding civil society and developing programs, labor unions are not part of the picture."[55] Several studies of democratic progress in sub-Saharan Africa found that worker or union protests were "central to democratization" in a significant number of cases,[56] as they were in Tunisia – where the entire democratic experiment might have collapsed were it not for the intervention of the trade union movement.[57] So ignoring (or failing to appreciate fully) trade unions can be a fatal flaw. They are the one civil society organization that least reflects the liabilities and weaknesses of most others and has the broadest social reach.

The second problem with the "civil society" approach is that the networks of protesters and civil society activists were unorganized and lacked identifiable leaders. As Marc Lynch writes, "The leaderless network structures which can hold together a disparate coalition of millions of protesters around a single, simple demand – 'Mubarak must go' – are typically far less effective at articulating specific, nuanced demands in the negotiation process that follows."[58] The NGO sector did not produce individuals with the political skills needed at key moments: the ability to express political demands, to develop a program, to negotiate successfully with other civic groups and with those holding power (the army, the intelligence agencies, the most powerful economic actors), and above all to win mass support.

Third, by their very nature, groups of civil society organizations – each dedicated to protests and activism on behalf of one cause or another – could not produce a political program. Their purpose is, after all, not to change the government, but to achieve specific and often narrow goals. They could not move "From Protest to Politics," as the great American civil rights leader Bayard Rustin explained in a seminal 1965 article about the civil rights movement in the United States. There he wrote of the many challenges facing the black population and concluded that "all these interrelated problems, by their very nature, are not soluble by private, voluntary efforts but require government action – or politics."[59] That meant political organization and strategy to elect officials who would hold and wield power, a process that soon spread throughout the American South. Larry Diamond calls this process, in the current Arab context, "the skillful aggregation of interests and national coalition building. These are the things political leaders – not least, political party leaders – build and do, but a notable feature of the Arab Spring, especially in Egypt and Libya, is the way that protests and resistance have leveled old political parties and organizational hierarchies without establishing broadly supported and effective new ones in their place."[60]

To put it differently, "democracy ultimately arises out of stalemate"[61] or "a prolonged and inconclusive political struggle."[62] Such a stalemate is the product of political battles, not civil society and NGO activity. Civil society groups can provide the basis for political action; as Brownlee, Masoud, and Roberts write about Tunisia, "a relatively strong civil society with a mixture of religious, non-religious, and labor-based groups meant that political contestants from across the political spectrum possessed significant resources for mobilizing voters into the country's first democratic elections."[63] But those resources had to be translated by political parties into the search for votes.

ELECTIONS WITHOUT PARTIES

These problems are compounded because of the central role of elections in American and European democracy programs. As scholars have noted, "Western democracy-promotion strategies...were markedly "electoralist," in that they focused on holding multiparty elections."[64] When there is such an emphasis, it is inescapable that the role of parties is magnified.

This emphasis on elections is not surprising. Elections are attractive because they are events that can be seen and in some ways measured; for example, how many people voted and how many parties competed. They are also organizing events, leading political actors to seek publicity, partners, and support. They are of course an indispensable element of any movement toward democracy, because they provide the only way to measure public support for rival candidates and parties and the only way to assert popular sovereignty over the government.

Yet the argument against elections has also been powerfully made in essence on the ground that many countries are not "ready" for these events. They lack the necessary preconditions: a level playing field where rivals can compete fairly, equal access to mass media, equal opportunities to speak to the voting population, fair mechanisms for counting the votes, and a political and party system that presents well-articulated alternatives to voters. Moreover, if nondemocratic parties are permitted to run, the proper rules of the game are undermined. In all those circumstances,

THE TROUBLE WITH U.S. POLICY

it is argued, political contestation through elections can be distortive: it can set back rather than advance democracy.

These are powerful arguments. Fake elections have often been part of nondemocratic systems, used by regimes like those of Ben Ali and Mubarak as a means of political organization and control. The Arab Human Development Report for 2004 noted,

> Totally or partially elected parliaments now exist in all Arab countries except Saudi Arabia and the United Arab Emirates. However, the right to political participation has often been little more than a [constitutional] ritual.... In most cases, elections have resulted in misrepresenting the will of the electorate and in low levels of representation for the opposition. Hence, elections have not played their designated role as a participatory tool for the peaceful alternation of power. These elections have generally reproduced the same ruling elites.[65]

The Tunisian political scientist Larbi Sadiki refers to "electoral fetishism" where elections are "badges of democratic pretense worn by traditional monarchs and secular presidents." His indictment is rough:

> The Arab Gulf rulers, like fellow Arab rulers, look upon electoralism as being a resource to contain pressure from within and without to reform. It adds to them; but it does not take away from their power. They confer it upon their societies; and they see it more or less as a 'gift'. More importantly, there should be no illusion as to where the locus of power resides – not in the partially elected assemblies and councils.... [T]hese elections are not designed to challenge the status quo. The vote is thus added to the other 'goods' distributed by the state: health, education, welfare handouts, employment and consumer bargaining power.[66]

U.S. policy has generally supported, and indeed pressed for, elections, and that is the right choice in most circumstances. For one thing, few people are fooled by the sort of phony elections to which Sadiki refers. When a ruler announces that he has been reelected with 90 or 95 percent of the vote, can there be any citizens who really believe him? When Bashar al-Assad claimed victory in his 2014 election with 88.7 percent of the vote, or Zine al-Abidine Ben Ali claimed 90 percent in his 2009 election, no one was fooled, and the election result did not add to the ruler's legitimacy.

But elections sometimes have a far more positive effect. Stephen R. Grand notes their impact in Africa: "elections, however imperfect, have over a relatively short period of time become the focal point for political life.... They remain far from free and fair, but the fact that they are happening at all, in Uganda and so many other places on the continent, represents important progress. As flawed as the elections may be, they provide a mechanism for the beginning of competitive politics and open up the possibility for even more profound changes over time."[67] That was the hope when the United States pressed Hosni Mubarak to hold elections in 2005 for the presidency and for parliament. Even if the first election is not free and fair, it may be the precursor to later elections that are better. Or arguments about the elections may become a focus of political protests, so that a "bad" election actually moves the country forward toward democracy by mobilizing support for free elections. On occasion, a "bad" election has mobilized enough opposition to bring down a government, as happened in Kyrgyzstan in 2005. Stealing an election can sometimes be dangerous for a regime in power.

As Isobel Coleman and Terra Lawson-Remer write in *Pathways to Freedom,*

[T]he evidence suggests that the process of holding elections, even very flawed ones, creates a voting muscle memory that proves important when real elections finally occur. Elections also sow the seeds of public expectations that over time can blossom into democratic demands that cannot be ignored – and, contrary to the expectations of elites, cannot always be controlled. In short, countries with some experience with elections tend to realize greater success in their transitions to substantive democracy.... It is thus worthwhile to promote elections in autocracies, even if flawed and fraudulent, as long as they permit some competition.[68]

The last words are important – "some competition." Degrees of repression vary, and there will be occasions when participation in an election is a mistake. For aid donors like the United States, the best path is usually to allow local democrats to decide. They know the system better and what opportunities may exist – and know the risks they face if they challenge the powers that be.

The argument against elections is part of the argument for what is often called "sequencing." Fareed Zakaria, among others, has argued for going slow on elections, developing first the institutional bases for them: the rule of law, electoral systems and laws that work fairly, and freedom of expression. There are several problems with this argument, the first of which is that those conditions may never come into existence – except after a change of government that elections may help bring about. Rulers rarely give up power voluntarily; it must be seized from them, and the peaceful way to do it is through elections. If elections are ruled out because conditions are not ideal, rulers have a simple tool for staying in power: make sure those conditions never come into existence. In other words, elections are not the final product *of* a democratic transition but a critical element *in* it. Without them, improving state institutions runs the risk of improving the means of repression and helping tyrannies stay in place. As Steven Levitsky and Lucan Way put it in their book about "competitive authoritarianism,"

> [S]tate-building is critical to stable democratization, but it may also provide the bases for stable authoritarianism. This observation has important implications for recent debates about sequencing and democratization. Advocates of sequencing – in which state building occurs prior to (and thus facilitates) democratization – assume that sequencing postpones rather than precludes democratization. Democracy is simply pushed back to a subsequent stage. However, effective state-building in a transitional or weak authoritarian regime may not be (except in the very long term) an initial step in a sequence that ends in democracy. Rather, it may push regimes down an entirely different path – that of authoritarian consolidation. In other words, instead of postponing democratization, state-building may effectively preclude it.[69]

The second problem with the sequentialism argument is that the United States cannot set the timetable by which people living under dictatorships seek to end those dictatorships. Is the United States really supposed to argue against elections when the people of a country want them? As Tom Carothers asks, while it may be better to build up the rule of law and other essential elements of democracy before going further, "what to do if the people of the society are pressing for democracy? Should the U.S. government tell them not to?" To push back against citizens asking for a greater role in their own country's governance would be an astonishing role for the United States. As Carothers rightly concludes, "For better or worse (and I think much for the better), people all around the world have democratic aspirations. Unprepared though their societies may be for democracy, they yearn for a voice and a vote, not several preparatory generations of mild dictatorship."[70]

Democracies around the world have become committed now to promoting elections, and an elaborate international structure of election monitoring groups has developed. This is in part because, among the many difficult, amorphous, ambiguous activities that can be called "democracy promotion," monitoring elections is tangible, finite in time and effort (and cost), visible, and mostly measurable. All this is to the good, especially if (as is increasingly common) monitors extend their coverage from Election Day itself to the weeks and months before. That way they are reporting not only on the casting of votes and the vote-counting mechanisms on Election Day but also on the fairness of the entire process – access to voters, ability to campaign, and the like.

Civil society groups are often usefully involved in election monitoring, but the importance of elections returns us to the issue of parties. Elections require parties; if elections are to advance democracy, they must involve democratic parties presenting both candidates and platforms – arguments, policies, and theories – to the voters.

CIVIL SOCIETY AND PARTIES

In fact, political parties perform functions that civil society organizations simply cannot. Ken Wollack, president of the National Democratic Institute for International Affairs, describes them well. They aggregate and represent social interests and thereby give political participation a structure. Work in a party structure provides excellent and practical training for future politicians and government officials. In parliament, parties "translate policy preferences into public policies." When there are no democratic political parties, there is no hope of maintaining a democratic political system. Civil society activism without political parties "creates a vacuum" that "sows opportunities for populists and demagogues who seek to emasculate parties and legislatures, which are the cornerstones of representative democracy." Thus Wollack concludes, "The international community must respond to the need to build, sustain, and renew political parties."[71]

It can even be argued that Western support for civil society NGOs not only failed to help such political parties and actors emerge but even made things worse. Samuel Tadros, the Egyptian American activist-turned-scholar, has described how this can happen:

> With abundant funding, civil society organizations were becoming more attractive to young Egyptians than political parties.... A new generation of activists was trained to approach Egypt's democratic deficit from a rights perspective, not politics. People were trained how to protest and challenge autocracy; no one was trained on how to politically organize, formulate programs, and compromise. The depletion of talent from political parties would be a problem that would have a profound effect on the future of the Egyptian revolution....
>
> The generation that had left politics for human rights advocacy could not be suddenly expected to make the transition back. Human rights defenders are fighting for a noble cause. They do not negotiate; they never compromise. There is no negotiation between the abused and the abuser, no compromise between the tortured and the torturer.... Pragmatism is not a virtue in the world of human rights advocacy...
>
> Politics was not only a game the revolutionaries refused to play; it was also one they completely disdained. Looking back, that was hardly surprising. The cause of their success in toppling Mubarak was the reason for their failure thereafter. The appeal to abstract principles and empty slogans was instrumental in uniting people against a dictator but was meaningless as a program of elections and governance; the training on the latest technology was ill-suited for developing policy programs; the mobilization of outside parties was necessary for a revolution but incapable of winning elections.[72]

Here Tadros is agreeing with the analysis first made a decade and a half ago by Quintan Wiktorowicz that civil society organizations "are more an instrument of state social control than a mechanism of collective empowerment." Wiktorowicz does note "the possible, though still limited, role of civil society in the mobilization of opposition, dissent, and alternative voices." Nevertheless he writes that civil society organizations are "embedded in a web of bureaucratic policies and legal codes which allow those in power to monitor and regulate collective activities ... rendering much of collective action visible to the administrative apparatus" and reducing "the possibility of a challenge to the state from civil society." In the end, "civil society is never autonomous from the state" and has "only varying degrees of independence." Thus he concludes that optimism about the role of civil society should be "tempered by the reality of the political context. In much of the Middle East, civil society does not act as a conduit for freedom; instead, it further extends the state's social control over its citizens."[73]

A key question facing Western nations, including the United States, is thus whether to move from promoting civil society NGOs to helping support the organization and/or strengthening of political parties. This question should in one key sense actually be less difficult in this decade than in previous ones. The partial success of the "color revolutions" in Central and Eastern Europe and then of the "Arab Spring" – in both cases, success at least in bringing down regimes if not in establishing stable democracies – has led regimes to treat civil society organizations as repressively as they do expressly political ones. Regimes and dictators are closing the space for all civil action of all types. As Tom Carothers explains,

As NGO sectors grew in size and visibility in many developing and post-communist countries, they lost their innocence in the eyes of power holders. Human rights and advocacy NGOs increasingly came to be seen as nimble, influential challengers to established state authority. Not just the color revolutions in Georgia and Ukraine and the Tulip and Cedar revolutions in Kyrgyzstan and Lebanon, but numerous other instances of public mobilization against stagnant regimes fundamentally changed how political elites viewed the potential power of civil society.[74]

In that context, the advantages of supporting civil society groups while eschewing the more "confrontational" political ones begin to disappear.

The support for civil society groups rather than political activities is part of a broader problem in democracy assistance that Sarah Bush has called "tameness." She shifts the focus from donors and target countries to what she calls "the democracy establishment" of implementer organizations. Her 2015 book, *The Taming of Democracy Assistance: Why Democracy Promotion Does Not Confront Dictators*,[75] focuses on the grantee organizations implementing the democracy programs devised by government agencies in Washington. Democracy assistance has become bureaucratized and has in a sense become a business. Bush's book is a needed reminder that most "democracy assistance" or "human rights" programs are not implemented by the U.S. government but by intermediaries: sometimes American or other NGOs, and very often profit-making companies staffed largely by former government employees. They seek to keep government contracts rolling by producing measurable gains – for example, an increase in the number of women elected to parliament. This is a good example, because what is measurable in quantitative terms – the number – may overshadow the more important underlying factors, such as whether in the country in question the parliamentary elections are free and whether the parliament actually has any role in governing. Similarly, election monitors may find that Election Day polling was professional and accurate and may tote up the number of votes counted – without giving sufficient emphasis to an electoral context that may make truly fair elections impossible.

How do you quantify gains in democracy? When the USAID inspector general audited the organization's "democracy and governance" activities in Egypt, the report contained phrases like "the mission did not achieve 28 percent of its planned results" and "the mission has had limited success in strengthening democracy and governance in Egypt. On average, projects met 65 percent of their planned activities for 2008." Given the way government bureaucracies work, it is not surprising that USAID has put in place careful rules about its grants to implementing organizations. There must be some way to follow up, evaluate, and account for funds spent. But consider these sentences in the inspector general's report:

> USAID has developed extensive guidelines on the management of assistance awards and requirements for implementers... USAID's Automated Directives System (ADS) 303, *Grants and Cooperative Agreements to Nongovernmental Organizations*, states that technical representatives should review and analyze reports, monitor reporting requirements, and ensure the recipient's compliance with numerous terms and conditions of the award.[76]

Such bureaucratic rules almost ensure that money will flow to organizations set up and run precisely to meet those quantifiable requirements, rather than to confront tyranny and build democratic political challenges to it.

The need for quantifiable gains and the need to maintain access to target countries – because if they are barred, their business opportunities disappear – lead contractors to seek activities that are more "tame" and less confrontational. As Sarah Bush summarizes the issue in a 2013 article, "Such programs help organization win future grants and work in many countries in the world, but there is no clear evidence that they bring about genuine democratic development in host countries."[77] This is not accidental: the implementing groups "gain access to target states suspicious of American or foreign interference by implementing programs that do not directly confront autocrats, such as programs geared towards improving local governance." The problem is that "tamer programs can also play into the hands of autocrats seeking a veneer of democracy while consolidating power."

As Bush puts it in her book, "Aiding democracy abroad is a good thing, but democracy aid in its current form is not always."[78] Bush studied 10,000 programs funded by the NED, because as she noted "most observers rightly regard the NED as the most confrontational, most nimble, and least measurement-obsessed American democracy donor." Yet she found that "measurable projects increased from about 20% of the NED's projects in the 1980s to more than half today.... Confrontational programs decreased from about 80 percent of the NED's projects to less than half today."

This problem extends as well to donors, both nonprofit funders and government aid agencies. As Tom Carothers puts it,

[M]any organizations have scaled back work they believe might be politically sensitive... Often... scaling back is hard to see from the outside because it consists of quiet, subtle changes in what funders sponsor and the kinds of partners they are willing to work with, changes that funding organizations prefer not to talk openly about.[79]

In sum, donors and implementers may sometimes have different goals: the donors to advance democracy; the implementers to survive, expand, and thrive. Programs whose goal is democracy will not attain their stated goals if they are increasingly characterized by a desire to avoid trouble and keep the government contracts rolling in. Programs whose goal is democracy will necessarily fall short if instead of working to advance democratic politics they choose to work with civil society organizations that cannot – or deliberately choose not to – engage in democratic politics. And programs will fall short if donors become reluctant to support any politically sensitive activity at all.

THE DEMOCRACY BUDGET

As Princeton Lyman recounted, Nelson Mandela understood all of this. The issue is whether we do. Today, American support for democracy and human rights remains too often focused on civil society NGOs and uncontroversial projects.

It is surprisingly difficult to determine how the U.S. government spends its "democracy assistance" or "human rights" money. One problem is that many agencies, even the Department of Defense, have a piece of this pie – or bake a pie of their own. The government has tried to bring it all together at the website, www.foreignassistance.gov.

According to that website, the total foreign aid budget planned for FY 2017 (the last available when I write this) was $34 billion. This included activities and grants by the State Department, USAID, and all other elements of the U.S. government. Of that total amount, the category called "Democracy, Human Rights, and Governance" accounted for $2.7 billion or less than 8 percent. And under that heading come several subheadings: Democracy, Human Rights, and Governance-General; Rule of Law and Human Rights; Good Governance; Political Competition and

Consensus-Building; and Civil Society. It gives some sense of what programs are actually undertaken that there are nearly 700 programs under "Civil Society" and more than 500 under "Good Governance," while "Political Competition" comes in at 336 (and even those often have little to do with political party activity). To take one example of what "good governance" can mean, one USAID program in Egypt tried to improve the efficiency of tax collections. That is an important part of the modernization of any government, but it has nothing to do with democracy or human rights. And should it be an American goal to help a dictatorship improve its efficiency at taking money from the population?

How much support for political party activity is there, really, in all the U.S. government spending on "democracy?" It is hard to tell exactly, but the answer is clearly "surprisingly little." The bulk (85 percent by some accounts) of the budget dedicated to democracy and human rights is spent by USAID's Bureau of Democracy, Human Rights, and Governance. For FY 2017, its budget request was $2.3 billion. USAID's Bureau of Democracy, Human Rights, and Governance says on its website that its programs cover aid to civil society NGOs, training of election observers, assistance to survivors of abuse and torture, and opposition to trafficking in persons. The rubrics under which all its programs are listed are "Supporting Free and Fair Elections," "Supporting Vibrant Civil Society and Independent Media," "Protecting Human Rights," "Promoting Accountability and Transparency," "Importance of Democracy, Human Rights, & Governance to Development," and "Countering Trafficking in Persons." Unsurprisingly, USAID stays away from political parties, leaving that work to the NED and its party institutes – but sometimes funding their work in those areas.

For the State Department's Bureau of Democracy, Human Rights, and Labor (known as DRL) the budget request was a much smaller $78.5 million. What does it do with these funds? Its own description is that it wants to "minimize human rights abuses, support democracy activists worldwide, open political space in struggling or nascent democracies and authoritarian regimes, and bring positive transnational change." Its programs support human rights defenders and human rights NGOs, which are extremely worthy goals but traditional in the sense of backing civil society NGOs and not political parties. Its Middle East programs, according to the Bureau's website, focus on goals such as training journalists, promoting religious tolerance and women's rights, election monitoring, and legal services.

The Obama administration's budget request for DRL for 2016 described its activities this way:

> Through the implementation of innovative programs and use of new technologies, the FY 2016 request for the Human Rights and Democracy Fund will address human rights abuses globally, wherever fundamental rights are threatened; open political space in struggling or nascent democracies and authoritarian regimes; support civil society activists worldwide; and protect populations that are at risk, including women, religious and ethnic minorities, indigenous populations, and lesbian, gay, bisexual, and transgender peoples.[80]

Something was glaringly missing in this list that extended to "transgender peoples" in the struggle for human rights and democracy: political parties.

The National Endowment for Democracy, whose budget is just under $190 million for all its activities, also undertakes almost no work directly with parties. Instead that activity is left to two NED affiliates that are party institutes, the National Democratic Institute (NDI) for International Affairs and the International Republican Institute (IRI), which are not formally affiliated with the Democratic and Republican Parties but are staffed by people aligned with one or the other.

The NDI total annual budget is $120 million, and the IRI budget is roughly $55 million. But much of the work they do is also targeted at civil society programs, like so much of the USAID and NED activity. IRI breaks down its activities into categories such as "youth leadership," "women's empowerment," "civil society initiatives," and "strengthening electoral processes." Work on "multi-party political systems" is only one of these focuses, where the target is "strengthening the ability of parties to develop and present issue-based platforms and represent citizens" and strengthening internal party democracy. Similarly, NDI lists its activities under several rubrics, including "gender, women, and democracy," "elections," "citizen participation," "debates," "democracy and technology," "democratic governance," "political inclusion of marginalized groups," and, finally, "political parties."

Under that rubric NDI explains its approach:

> Political parties are a central feature of any democracy. They are the vehicles by which citizens come together freely to campaign for public office, express their interests and needs, and define their aspirations for their society. While there are parties without democracy, there can be no democracy without political parties. Parties in many countries may be flawed, but they are also indispensable in democratic governance.... The Institute's political party programs fall into five general areas: comparative research, party systems, internal organization and structure, elections and campaigning, and legislative performance. NDI's work in each of these areas enables parties to foster closer connections to the public and develop policies that more effectively address citizens' needs.[81]

IRI spends about $23 million on "strengthening political institutions" and "multi-party political systems," but as noted these are very broad categories. So how much is actually spent on political party work? The best estimates I could get from the NED were about $5 million per year for IRI and about $4 million a year for NDI. Some party work may be included in other budgets, which would increase these amounts, but on the other hand the numbers include related NDI and IRI staff salaries, travel, and indirect costs.

These numbers give us an order of magnitude. As the Project on Middle East Democracy summarized, "[T]he share of democracy and governance funding [in U.S. assistance to the Middle East] was highest in the Obama administration's first budget request (for FY10) at 7.4 percent, but has averaged only 4.8 percent annual from FY11 through his final budget for FY17."[82]

Another way of judging at least the trajectory of U.S. government spending on democracy and human rights is to look at budgets for the Millennium Challenge Corporation (MCC). The MCC was established in 2004 to provide "economic assistance through a competitive selection process to developing nations that demonstrate positive performance in three areas: ruling justly, investing in people, and fostering economic freedom." "Ruling justly" means "promoting good governance, fighting corruption, respecting human rights, and adhering to the rule of law," and countries that might otherwise qualify for assistance (such as Vietnam) have been rejected due to their human rights abuses. In FY2006 and FY2007 about $1.75 billion was appropriated for the MCC, but the amounts began to fall during the Obama years: to $1.1 billion in FY2010 and then staying around $900 billion thereafter – in other words, half the amount from the previous decade. The Bush administration actually requested $3 billion from Congress in FY2006 and 2007, but the Obama administration never requested more than $1 billion.[83]

The United States spends upward of $2.7 billion a year on the general activity it calls supporting democracy and human rights. Of that amount, it appears that about one-third of 1 percent is spent directly helping develop democratic political parties. If this estimate is wrong and we multiply the numbers arbitrarily by three, we would be able to say that 1 percent of all funding for the support of human rights and democracy is for party work. While there is no magic number that is the "right" amount or percentage to spend, surely 1 percent or less is far too low. NDI was correct to state, "While there are parties without democracy, there can be no democracy without political parties. Parties in many countries may be flawed, but they are also indispensable in democratic governance." That being the case, the failure to do more to help them is a signal flaw in American efforts.

A HUMAN RIGHTS POLICY MEANS TROUBLE

When the Reagan administration came to office, many officials saw human rights policy as a mistake, a Carter-era obsession, and a left-wing goal. As I explained in the introduction, over time those views were corrected, and they were no longer the policies of President Reagan and Secretary of State Shultz. But formulating a human rights policy was difficult, especially in the early days.

Perhaps the major critique that we lodged against the Carter policy was that it was focused on human rights rather than democracy, or on incidents rather than systemic change. In today's context, we would add that too much emphasis on civil society and NGOs rather than on politics might mean never mounting a serious challenge to tyrannical regimes. In the medium and longer run, we believed that the way to prevent human rights abuses was to support democratic systems and the men and women building them – and not just protest when such people were imprisoned or abused. As we used to say, "They can arrest them faster than we can get them out." The better approach if it was possible was, to use this example, to seek a system that did not jail political prisoners, rather than trying to free political prisoners one by one, year after year.

This approach became quite clear in South Korea, as David Adesnik and Sunhyuk Kim explain, noting

> the contrast in how the Carter administration and the Reagan adminis-
> tration approached both US-ROK diplomacy and the challenge of democ-
> racy promotion. Although strongly committed to human rights, the Carter
> administration hesitated to challenge the legitimacy of authoritarian gov-
> ernments, preferring to focus on preventing specific actions, such as tor-
> ture and unjust imprisonment. Thus, while the Carter administration wel-
> comed the democratic opening of 1979, it remained passive when Chun
> wrested power back from the civilians. Initially, the Reagan administration
> rejected democracy promotion, preferring to focus on the solidarity of
> anticommunist governments, both authoritarian and democratic. Yet over
> time, the administration reversed its course. Thus, at a critical moment in
> 1987, President Reagan sent a personal letter to Chun Doo Hwan, insist-
> ing that Chun find a peaceful solution to the prevailing crisis. Ironically,
> Reagan's word carried considerable weight precisely because Reagan had
> embraced Chun without hesitation during the early and uncertain days of
> his regime.[84]

This insight remains valid today: we need not only a human rights policy focusing on "specific actions" but also a policy of promoting democracy. That policy must include the promotion of democratic political parties, without which democracy is impossible, and it must include an element of confrontation of oppression. "Tameness" is always an attractive option to most diplomats and to the State Department, and its virtues in smooth-ing bilateral relations are clear. But that means our support for democ-racy is verbal and minimal, rather than robust.

If we are serious about human rights and democracy we must still accept that "a human rights policy means trouble," as I wrote in that 1981 memo reprinted in the introduction. The question is whether we are willing to face that trouble and embrace it as the price of an energetic policy. In the next chapter, I describe what a more energetic American policy in support of democracy might look like.

CHAPTER 5

What Is to Be Done?

WHY SHOULD THE UNITED STATES SUPPORT THE CAUSE of democracy, and the people struggling for more open and democratic political systems, in Arab countries? We should review the answers to that question before looking at ways to make such a pro-democracy policy more effective.

REALPOLITIK AND *UNREALPOLITIK*

At bottom, the answer is that indifference to democracy and human rights – to the rule of law, freedom of speech and press, regular and free elections, and, above all, to legitimate governments – is an *unrealistic* policy. Whether we approach the subject from a moral or a pragmatic viewpoint, and while acknowledging the claims of legitimate monarchies, Arab governments that close off all political space will become less stable over time. In addition to associating the United States with repression and abandoning individuals and groups that, peacefully, seek the political rights in which we believe, we would in the long run – and most likely the medium run – be helping lay the foundation for instability. Moreover, democracy is likely to be a stronger barrier to terror and to extremist Islamist groups than repression, for all the reasons noted in earlier chapters.

During and after the Arab Spring, the monarchies did not collapse, while most of the "mukhabarat states" did. One way of describing this is that a viable state structure other than monarchy has yet to be found in the Arab world (as always with the exception of Tunisia). Arab political culture, this argument might continue, makes it impossible to overcome ethnic, tribal, and religious divisions except under a hereditary sovereign.[1] Democracy is therefore impossible – except as the long-term result of movement toward a constitutional monarchy, because democracy cannot be built in a situation of state failure.

But there is an alternative possibility: that the collapse of these regimes instead reflects at least in part the lack of democracy because it reflects their lack of legitimacy. Being nonmonarchic states, the only available sources of such legitimacy other than democracy would be economic performance, which is not realistically available outside the oil-producing states, or religion, as in the Islamic State's caliphate. Otherwise, legitimacy must include an element of democracy – an element, that is, of popular sovereignty and public participation in the government of the country.

The *realpolitik* argument has been that existing repressive Arab regimes are at least stable and in many cases are friendly to the United States. Support for democratic activists will damage existing friendly relationships, the argument goes, and may open the door to chaos or to Islamist rule. The problems with this argument are legion, beginning with the fact that the United States cannot choose when reform should begin and how far it should go, how much repression should be used to protect an incumbent regime, or how strongly a population will demand protection of human rights and a role in governing their own country. The United States did not create the Arab Spring revolts; it did not dispatch a million Egyptians to Tahrir Square or decide in 2011 that Ben Ali had to flee Tunis. Arabs rejected the regimes that ruled them, and had ruled them so poorly. Would we have been better or worse off, in 2011 and 2012 and in the years before, had we been pushing harder in Arab countries for democracy and human rights? Would popular opinion of the United States have been more positive or less had it been widely understood that we were distancing ourselves from regimes we thought brutal, unpopular, and ultimately doomed?

When it comes to friendly monarchies, we do not wish to see them overthrown and see disorder replace them – along with the many opportunities that disorder provides to the worst elements in any society. But when we express concern about long-run legitimacy, when we say that some real role must be found for the people of the country in the monarchical system, we are not sowing chaos: we are seeking long-term stability. Surely the case of Iran is proof of this, for it was only in the chaos that occurred after the shah fell that the Islamic Republic could have been created. The fall of dictatorships in Cuba in 1959 and Nicaragua in 1979 teaches the same lesson, as indeed does the story of Russia in 1917. The lesson is not that any existing regime must be supported lest something worse arrive, but that without reform something worse eventually will, filling the space that regime collapse has created. So one important way of understanding American support for democratic reform is that we are seeking to avoid dangerous regime collapse in friendly Arab states.

This means that the "mere" difficulty of building Arab democracies is not per se a reason to abandon the effort. Failure endangers the United States only in two cases: when it leads to vast chaos or Islamist rule, or when it badly damages U.S. relations with an incumbent repressive regime whose good will or cooperation we need for our own reasons. As to the latter, the management of such relations obviously calls for skillful diplomacy. Justice Holmes once said that even a dog can distinguish between being tripped over and being kicked, and Arab regimes and the people who run them can surely distinguish between efforts to overthrow them and efforts to persuade them to open their political systems, slowly, to a wider aperture with the goal of their long-term stability. American pressure for free and fair local elections, to take one example, will very often not be appreciated by Arab rulers, but if we explain our methods and goals competently, they will understand that we see our long-term interests as fully aligned and that we seek to stabilize, not destabilize, their countries. Our objective like theirs is a system in which the populace sees the current monarchical system as the best bet for long-term progress for the country. We and those royal families may well disagree on the safest paths to stability, but our calls for greater respect for the rights of citizens will not destroy bilateral relations when our ultimate goals and theirs are shared – and when they see us acting to protect regional security.

This last point is critical. We will not be able to persuade ruling families that we are acting to preserve stability when they see the United States taking a posture of apparent indifference to regional security or appearing to favor their enemies. American policy toward Arab monarchies exists within a context, and that context includes Iran and its policies toward its neighbors. The argument that "we are concerned about your security and stability" will seem little more than a joke when the American policy maker advancing it is simultaneously pursuing a policy of accommodation with rising Iranian hegemony and a steady decrease in American influence in the Middle East. The converse is also true, and American actions that reassure our Arab allies about our commitment to regional security provide an opportunity to discuss internal security.

BAHRAIN

Bahrain is a useful case study. The majority of the populace is Shia while the royal family is Sunni, a situation that has produced friction. But it has not always produced violence or a growing distance between the Shia majority and the royals: for decades there was a modus vivendi that allowed Shia citizens to live, practice their religion, and partake of the country's economic progress. During the Bush years Bahrain was seen as a stable and reasonably enlightened place, and it attracted a good deal of foreign economic activity – not only investment but also the use of Manama, the capital, as a Middle East headquarters by foreign companies. The United States took a particular interest in Bahrain because the Fifth Fleet is headquartered there. There were significant political reforms undertaken in 2002, but as the decade wore on Shia groups expressed increasing dissatisfaction with the pace of change. The system largely collapsed after the Arab Spring revolts in 2011, when after mass protests in February and March the government increasingly closed political space and began repressing Shia desires for a greater political role. In response to criticism, the Bahrain Independent Commission of Inquiry (BICI) was established in July 2011 and issued its final report in December of that year.[2]

BICI's final report tells the story. "The demands expressed during the earlier demonstrations related mainly to political and constitutional reform, which was to pave the way for greater popular participation in governance, equal access to socio-economic opportunities and development, action against corruption, and termination of the alleged practice of political naturalization." (The last phrase refers to government efforts to change the Sunni-Shia balance by granting citizenship to foreign-born Sunnis.) But as demonstrations began and were repressed, demands grew and the sectarian nature of the demonstrations grew more marked as well. "Popular discontent was further heightened by what many considered to be the lack of both adequate and timely government responses to the protestors' demands and measures to address grievances." The situation spiraled downward, and "gradually, the chant 'the people demand the removal of the regime,' which was borrowed from other Arab countries that had witnessed similar mass uprisings, became one of the protestors' slogans." This did not mean overthrowing the royal family, the BICI report explains, but removing the prime minister, who is the king's uncle and is understood to lead the hard-line faction in the royal family. One opposition demand, accordingly, was a constitutional reform that would provide for an elected prime minister.

In March 2011 the protests and the government reaction grew more violent, and talks between the opposition and the crown prince failed. "By 12–13 March, the general state of law and order in Bahrain had significantly deteriorated. This, coupled with the failure of political negotiations between HRH the Crown Prince and the opposition, led the GoB [Government of Bahrain] to take steps to restore order and maintain security." Troops from other Gulf Cooperation Council (GCC) countries, primarily Saudi Arabia and the UAE, arrived on March 14 to assist the government. In the years since 2011, the internal situation has deteriorated, culminating in the government's decision in 2016 to disband entirely Al-Wefaq, the primary Shia political organization; imprison its political leader, Sheik Ali Salman, and numerous human rights activists; and prosecute Al-Wefaq's religious leader, Sheik Isa Qasim, and strip him of his citizenship.

I believe the United States might have helped prevent this deterioration of Bahrain's internal situation, had our policies been different, had we intervened more, and if we had the trust of Bahraini officials and neighboring royal families. But by 2011 the Obama administration had lost the confidence of Saudi and Emirati as well as Bahraini leaders due to the American withdrawal from Iraq and to what they viewed as accommodationist policies toward Iran and the abandonment of President Mubarak in Egypt.

How might we have acted differently? It is worthwhile to pursue a thought experiment: had the Bush administration been in power in a mythical third term, what might have been possible? It seems to me from the events just described that there was a possibility of a compromise in Bahrain and that the negotiations led by the crown prince were not without promise. The internal situation deteriorated slowly in 2011 and the years after, and there were moments when that deterioration could have been slowed or halted. Even as late as 2014 there were serious negotiations between the crown prince and the Shia opposition, including the now-imprisoned Ali Salman. The key issues were on the table: Shia representation in parliament, parliamentary powers, the composition and powers of the appointed upper house, the independence of the judiciary, and the conduct of the security forces. The royal family was split, and a key part of the problem was that the most capable, efficient, and hard-working public official was the prime minister, who has held that post since 1970 and who was the most recalcitrant member of the royal family – and the most corrupt, by all accounts. The crown prince sought a negotiated agreement, but was powerless. The king vacillated.[3]

But the United States did too little and had too little influence. In my thought experiment, President Bush, who had a very good relationship with the king, might have pressed and persuaded him to act and to lean in the direction of the crown prince. He might have appointed a special envoy, perhaps a former secretary of state or defense or chairman of the Joint Chiefs of Staff or chief of naval operations, to try to salvage the negotiations, influence the parties, and produce a deal. He might have enlisted others with positive reputations in the region, like Tony Blair, by then out of power in the United Kingdom. He himself might have tried to reassure the Saudis and Emiratis that a negotiated deal, something the Saudis themselves appeared to be encouraging in 2013, was the best outcome for the royal family and for Saudi Arabia. This was not a "Mission Impossible."

His argument would have been clear: the Shia and the royal family have a common interest in stability and prosperity. Because its population is unique in the GCC – a Shia majority – some compromises are needed to stabilize the political situation. Granting additional power to parliament has not destabilized Kuwait (or Morocco, to give another royal example) and should not be seen as somehow unacceptable in the GCC. The alternative to compromise is perpetual conflict, opening the door to Iranian meddling and true disaster. We would have tried to persuade and enlist the Saudis and Emiratis in convincing the king that what Bahrain needs is internal stability, that its neighbors need a stable Bahrain, and that reaching some deal is the best outcome. As Fredric Wehrey notes in a discussion of Saudi policies,

> In an admission that surprised me in its frankness, a senior Saudi diplomat told me in 2006 that Saudi Arabia could live with Bahrain having a Shia premier. He went on to say that continued dependence on Saudi subsidies plus differences between Bahraini Shia and Iran's ruling clerics would keep the island out of Tehran's orbit. Hyperbole about the Iranian threat is useful, however, both as a distraction from the Khalifa family's governance failings and corruption, and as a way of maintaining the support of the United States, which bases its Fifth Fleet on the island.... Riyadh has counseled the Khalifa monarchy to adopt limited reforms as a pressure-release tactic.[4]

Of course all of Bush's efforts might have failed, especially if the Bahraini opposition took intransigent positions that made an agreement impossible. Perhaps the king would always have been cowed and outmaneuvered by the prime minister; perhaps the Saudis would have been unwilling to accept an agreement giving the Shia anything at all, fearing that it would lead to similar demands from Saudi Arabia's Shia population. But the repeated negotiating efforts, the fact that it took years for opposition demands and regime repression to harden, and that at one point the Saudis and Emiratis favored a negotiated agreement all suggest that there were opportunities for the United States to intervene. If this argument is correct, it is a partial answer to the question of how the United States should act when there are demands for greater democracy in an allied Arab state. Knowing that an absolute failure to bend means the system may break, and that slow and steady steps toward a more open political system will produce more stability than "mere" repression, we should use our influence to produce that outcome.

EGYPT

It is worth adding that such an approach might have produced a far better outcome in Egypt than the current repressive regime. The pressure on Mubarak in 2004–2006 did lead to a more open political system – for a while. There was hope back then that, slowly but steadily, the political reforms would continue and that forthcoming elections would be increasingly honest.

It was a great mistake for the United States to abandon that pressure in 2007–2008, and an even greater mistake as Egypt moved toward a planned presidential election in 2011. Mubarak would have been eighty-three at the time of the election, and apparently he sought to make his son Gamal his successor. Gamal had been appointed to a top position in the ruling National Democratic Party and was accompanying his father to summit meetings; it seemed he was being groomed for the presidency. Whether this would have been acceptable to the military and how Gamal could win if there was a multiparty election as there had been in 2005, and if it were at all fair, were hotly debated topics in Egypt and among Egypt watchers. Meanwhile, as time passed the Mubarak regime became more repressive rather than less, but the United States in the new Obama administration seemed determined to ignore what was happening.

The Obama administration in essence ignored the crisis that was developing – and developing even before the outbreak of the Arab Spring in Tunisia. How could anyone see in 2010 that trouble was ahead? Some analysts did. I was part of the "Working Group on Egypt," a small bipartisan group of academics, former officials, NGO experts, and human rights activists, and as early as 2010 we urged the administration to see what was developing in Egypt and act to avoid it. In April of that year we wrote to Secretary of State Clinton to say this:

> Egypt is at a critical turning point. It faces substantial leadership changes in the near future without a fair and transparent political process. With three sets of elections coming up over the next eighteen months, Egypt now has the opportunity to energize a process of political, economic, and social reform. If the government responds to demands for responsible political change, Egypt can face the future as a more democratic nation with greater

domestic and international support. If, on the other hand, the opportunity for reform is missed, prospects for stability and prosperity in Egypt will be in doubt.... The choice is not between a stable and predictable but undemocratic Egypt on the one hand, and dangerous instability and extremism on the other. There is now an opportunity to support gradual, responsible democratic reform.[5]

Yet there was no change in Obama administration policy. As late as January 2011, amid the protests that in February led to Mubarak's resignation, we thought the situation could still be salvaged. The Working Group's statement made some suggestions at that time:

> In his State of the Union address, President Obama said that the United States "stands with the people of Tunisia, and supports the democratic aspirations of all people." These words are welcome. But if the administration truly wants that message to be received by the Mubarak government, and the Egyptian people, it needs to speak with greater clarity and back its words with actions. Noticeably absent from its reactions to the demonstrations in Egypt were specific calls for changes to Egypt's constitution, an end to the state of emergency, or other measures that would enable upcoming presidential elections this year to be actually democratic....
>
> The administration should also press for constitutional and administrative changes necessary for a free and competitive presidential election open to candidates without restrictions, supervised by judges and monitored by domestic and international observers.[6]

This would have been the right approach for the United States to take in 2009–2011. It is obviously impossible to know now whether it would have worked or how late in the game regime change in Egypt could have been prevented. But what would have happened if in 2010 or even at the start of 2011 Mubarak had said that he was then eighty-two and would never run for president again; that Egypt was not Syria and had no fake royal family and so none of his sons was going to run for office; that his only goal in these last years was to assure that the presidential election of 2011 would be honest and that the transition from his rule would be calm? It is certainly possible that Egypt's years of violence, military rule, a coup, and now increasing repression could have been avoided. It is possible that the parliamentary election of 2010 and the presidential election of 2011 might have been fairer and been seen as steps forward – and actually been steps forward toward a more stable and more open political system.

As the Working Group put it, the choice was not between a stable and predictable but undemocratic Egypt on the one hand, and dangerous instability and extremism on the other. Today Egypt is not stable, repression is vast, and extremism is growing. This is the classic case: simply ignoring impractical and foolish arguments about political openings because we need stability produces instead the opposite. A slow and steady political opening was the path toward stability. Of course, Mubarak would have resisted it, but in 2004–2005 we had seen that he could be moved. Moreover, we had seen that his reaction to pressure was not to move away from the United States, but to accommodate it. How far? Sadly, we will never know, because in the Obama years we did not try. The policy toward Mubarak, and then the SCAF (the Supreme Council of the Armed Forces, which ruled for a year), President Morsi, and finally President Sisi was the same: whoever was in power was seen as critical for stability, and protests or pressure for a more open political system were weak and formulaic. Yet to have followed the policy of 2004–2005 and the advice of the Working Group was neither impossible nor unrealistic.

DOES DICTATORSHIP PREVENT ISLAMISM?

The Arab cases from this decade should also show persuasively that chaos results when a dictatorship falls and a void replaces it – consider Iraq or Libya, for example. Both were extreme forms of dictatorship, with no political institutions that could fill that void. The way to avoid such terrible situations is precisely to work at building political institutions. But what of the Islamist threat? It is real and extremely dangerous, but Islamist victories are not inevitable – especially when Islamists become part of a larger political system where the populace has a genuine opportunity to weigh and to reject their claims. In Muslim nations in Asia, the Islamist parties have not done well and have not won power. The Arab cases in which they have won power through legitimate elections are Tunisia and Egypt. The Tunisia story is a positive one, where a coalition government was formed and the Islamist party proved willing to live in a democratic system. Moreover, in follow-on elections the Islamist party, Ennahda, quickly lost much of the popularity it had won in the first post-dictatorship election. In fact, theory and history demonstrate that Islamists will always do best in the first election and then begin to lose the popularity they had won as victims of regime oppression untainted by power or corruption.

So the question becomes what alternatives exist in the political system at that point, after the old regime has fallen and the Islamists begin to lose their appeal to many citizens. In Tunisia, the void was filled by a large middle class, a group of moderate politicians, and not least a powerful trade union movement. In Egypt, the second case, the Islamists won power fairly and immediately squandered it by alienating millions of voters with their power grab. But the only alternative was the army, so as I write Egypt is back where it started under Hosni Mubarak. The country simply lacked the parties, groups, individuals, democratic political patterns, institutions, and experiences to build a powerful political center fast enough.

Egypt's story is again an argument for an American policy of promoting democracy, so that if and when regimes fall, the open space will not be filled by non- or anti-democratic movements that will then seize power. It is also a cautionary tale that reminds us of the cases of Iran in 1979, Cuba in 1959, and Russia in 1917 as well: even if the security forces were a bulwark of the old regime, it is critical that they remain intact to ensure order and to prevent the state from falling into the hands of extremist groups.

This is a version of the old Cold War security question:

In the context of the Cold War, the willingness of the United States to pressure its authoritarian allies was closely related to the risk that destabilizing the incumbent dictatorship would facilitate its replacement with a Marxist or pro-Soviet regime. Today, the willingness of the United States to exert pressure relates closely to the risk that destabilizing the incumbent dictatorship will facilitate its replacement with a hostile Islamic regime. The fundamental dilemma is the same. How can democratic governments promote democratic transitions abroad without compromising their own security?[7]

A powerful answer to the question is supplied by Fukuyama:

> [I]n making calculations of power, democracies have to remember that legitimacy is a form of power as well, and that strong states frequently hide grave internal weaknesses. This means that democracies that choose their friends and enemies by ideological considerations – that is, whether they are democratic – are likely to have stronger and more durable allies in the long run. And in dealing with enemies, they should not forget the abiding moral differences between their societies or sweep aside questions of human rights in pursuit of the powerful.[8]

ESCAPING THE "SECURITY DILEMMA"

The argument, then, is that the security dilemma is less awful than it may appear. "Incumbent dictatorships" will destabilize themselves as citizens become less and less willing to tolerate abuse and to accept the absolute closing off of the political system. *Realpolitik* will suggest that backing dictatorships is a losing game in the long run and even the medium run, as shown in Egypt and Tunisia. *Realpolitik* approaches turn out to be faulty because they are theories of international politics that ignore domestic politics and do not account for the increasing role in the twentieth and twenty-first centuries of the broad masses of citizens, as Tony Smith explains:

> They therefore could not appreciate the importance of the efforts to remake Japan and Germany domestically after the war, the practical seriousness of Kennedy's Alliance for Progress in the early 1960s, the political dynamic of European integration long sponsored by the United States, the depth of the appeal generated by Carter's human rights campaign in the late 1970s, or the political effectiveness of the enduring claims of Wilsonianism put forth by Reagan in the 1980s.[9]

In fact, repressive regimes may pave the way for Islamist victories, suggesting that the security dilemma points to the need for political openings, rather than support for decrepit dictatorships. Natan Sharansky put the point clearly: "If it were true that stability could be guaranteed by nondemocratic regimes, then the case for democracy across the world would be a dealt a fatal blow. For when given the choice between promoting morals and promoting interests, democratic nations will almost always choose the latter."

"If it were true . . . ." But it is not true. There would have been no huge expansion of the so-called Islamic State without the brutal repression of the Sunni majority by the Assad regime in Syria, nor a way for the Muslim Brotherhood to win power had the Mubarak regime not worked decade after decade to destroy the political center in Egypt. Such regimes are inept at fighting Islamism and terrorism and in fact often provide the platform from which those forces leap forward. This is true for several reasons. Such regimes sometimes deliberately provide these groups space to operate, using their existence as an argument for why regime repression is actually essential to preserve stability. The regimes themselves are illegitimate, lacking dynastic, democratic, or "performance" legitimacy, which allows alternative theories of legitimacy such as Islamism room to grow. As Jamie O'Connell concludes,

> When it comes to defusing the power of political Islam, democracy may be the worst form of government – except all the others. Arab autocrats' repression of opposition is widely considered to have been among the most important contributors to Islamists' popularity . . . . Supporting Arab autocrats is therefore likely to strengthen Islamists in the long run, unless they are repressed with a thoroughness that would require extreme brutality.[10]

And if that is the autocrats' game, as it may be in today's Egypt, Islamism may be repressed at the cost of growing terrorism when previously peaceful Islamists turn to violence – with predictable effects on economic progress, law and order, and regime stability.

The security dilemma is real, to be sure, but a slow, steady, careful expansion of political space is less likely to lead to extremist victories than pure repression and situations where Arab "countries continue to stagnate and fester politically."[11] This was the argument of the George W. Bush administration in the National Security Strategy of 2006:

> Transnational terrorists are recruited from people who have no voice in their own government and see no legitimate way to promote change in their own country. Without a stake in the existing order, they are

vulnerable to manipulation by those who advocate a perverse vision based on violence and destruction.[12]

O'Connell notes that this approach was the sole long-term component of the counterterror strategy promulgated in 2006, and explains it this way: "Democratization of Arab countries would reduce the number of their citizens who found foreign terrorism appealing for these reasons by giving them a peaceful, legal, and less dangerous means for shaping their governments' policies."[13]

So the expansion of democracy, the slow and steady approach that George W. Bush called "the work of generations" to increase political space and provide a stable path forward, does not require abandonment of security interests. It is not an approach whose moralistic claims are exceeded only by its blind optimism and disregard of the need to prevent extremist takeovers. Rather, it is an argument that repression will not work, that excluding the masses of citizens from any political role will produce a dangerous counterreaction likely to enable extremist gains.

A BETTER AMERICAN POLICY

We turn then to the question of how American foreign policy might sensibly try to promote democracy in the Arab world. Here are some guidelines for the coming years. The logic of these approaches should, I hope, emerge clearly from the preceding chapters.

PROMOTING DEMOCRACY, NOT ONLY DEFENDING HUMAN RIGHTS, SHOULD BE AT THE HEART OF U.S. POLICY Promoting democracy, not only defending human rights, should be at the heart of U.S. policy. This means challenging not only individual abuses and taking an interest in individual cases but also promoting systemic change.

As a veteran of the Reagan administration and its review of the Carter human rights policy, I was part of the move from human rights policy as a kind of foreign assistance we gave poor benighted nations to a policy of pressing for systemic change. I told this story in the introduction to this book. The goal was ultimately not to get one individual or another out of prison (although we certainly tried that), but the adoption of democratic systems where human rights were respected and peaceful pro-democracy activists were not jailed in the first place.[14] To paraphrase the *Arab Human Development Report* of 2002, political freedom is not only the goal but also the guarantor of human rights.[15] Fundamentally the American argument should be that governments must be legitimate and that those that do not respect the rights of the people, and which the people have not chosen and do not want, have compromised or nonexistent legitimacy. Such governments are unstable and should not have American support, for they will have to rule solely by force.

Accordingly, the United States should press for gradual but real political openings in Arab states. We should favor not only liberalization – small reforms that often have the purpose and effect of strengthening nondemocratic systems – but also a change in "core political structures" that bridges the gap (as Thomas Carothers puts it) between "liberalization" and "democratization" by addressing the issue of political contestation. What does this mean? The United States should "encourage and pressure Arab governments to strengthen and gradually broaden the processes of organized political contestation in their countries" by allowing elections for some posts and allowing the creation of political parties. The United States would then try to help such fledgling parties develop their skills to explain themselves to voters and to create political coalitions; would urge and assist in the development of election administration agencies; and would press for the ability of domestic and international election monitors to guarantee that elections are free and fair.[16]

This does not mean urging all monarchs to give up power tomorrow and live in golden exile someplace. It is instead an argument that, over time, regimes will be more stable if the monarchic principle – and good performance in power – are buttressed by increasing displays of public support for the system and by a sharing of power with the populace. The long-run goal would be constitutional monarchy, but that run can be very long indeed, and our goal is the same as that of monarchic regimes that are friends of the United States: stability and effective, legitimate government.

Promoting democracy in nondemocratic states can mean taking sides, abandoning a position of neutrality on what are the most sensitive matters of political power. In monarchies that are in fact legitimate today, the

American argument would be that legitimacy can increase or decrease and that they need to guard against its decline by developing a partnership with the populace and giving them some role in their own country's governance. This is happening in various ways and to various degrees in Jordan, Morocco, and Kuwait. The cases of Qatar and the UAE are unique because, quite simply, their populations are small and their wealth very great. In Saudi Arabia, Bahrain, and Oman after the passing of Sultan Qaboos, there will be a need to address these matters. In what I have called the "fake republics" whose governments lack democratic legitimacy, the need is more pressing.

But even here the United States would not be suggesting where and with whom power should lie; instead we would be suggesting that this issue should be resolved increasingly over time by the people. Of course, those who hold power will see this as a direct challenge, trying to get them to give up something they alone now hold. There is no way around this if we take not only democracy but even legitimacy seriously. The alternative is to back regimes that have no real legitimacy and so rule by force, and that is simply too dangerous. That policy is likely to alienate the United States from the people of the country and leave us extremely unpopular, it will not in the long run lead to stability, and by denying the possibility of creating strong democratic institutions it will leave a wide opening for extremists to take power when the regime eventually falls.

Nor can security forces provide a permanent victory over Islamist extremism. They cannot provide an alternative ideology nor explain why the Islamist version of life, history, and politics is wrong. Only an open debate in which opponents of the Islamists can join freely will be able to achieve that. The case of Turkey provides insight here: the military coups and outlawing of Islamist parties did keep the Islamists out of power for a long time, but outlawing the Islamists did little to persuade Turks that their ideas were dangerous. A coup can end a debate, but it cannot win one.

It should be obvious that the United States will benefit, and our goals are more likely to be achieved, when there is broad international support for them. This is not to say that we should refrain from acting out of fear that we will "taint" causes we support. There is some evidence that our support does not have that effect and that U.S. endorsements do not delegitimize the reforms we back.[17] In any event there is a clear fail-safe mechanism here: when groups in Arab lands have this fear, they will simply refuse American assistance and involvement with U.S. officials, and can counsel us about which causes to adopt and how to do so most effectively.

But it will always help when other governments, and their embassies on the ground, share the political burden and join in the practical work of democracy promotion. Internationalization of support for democratization is always welcome, though it is hardest to find in the Arab region. The role of the EU with respect to Eastern and Central Europe, demanding democratic reforms as the price of admission, and the efforts of the OAS under the Inter-American Democratic Charter of 2001 (for a while anyway, until those efforts were abandoned) were salutary, but the Arab League has never played such a role. Nor has the UN Human Rights Council been an effective influence. Instead democratic countries must work together informally, and U.S. efforts will be greatly reinforced when this happens. The visit of ambassadors to a foreign minister or prime minister or president, statements of protest or concern by ambassadors, visits to prisons, support for political groups – all are far more likely to have the desired impact when they are multilateral. Opposition political activities are always dangerous in nondemocratic settings, and the support of a wide range of foreign embassies and governments constitutes a form of protection. So long as the desire to expand such foreign support for democracy assistance activities does not become an excuse for U.S. inaction, it should always be an American objective. Achieving that objective will be more likely if the United States leads.

SUPPORT FOR DEMOCRACY MUST START AT THE TOP American diplomacy can be effective only when it is clear that the president and secretary of state are behind whatever diplomatic moves or statements an official in Washington or a U.S. ambassador is making. Assistance programs, press releases, and all other forms of American activity are undermined if they appear to be products of the bureaucratic machine, rather than expressions of the will and intentions of top officials.

That is why messages to Chun Doo Hwan and Ferdinand Marcos worked in the Reagan years and why Hosni Mubarak felt it necessary to allow some reforms in 2004–2005: the pressure came directly from the president. As several scholars conclude in a look at transatlantic cooperation regarding the Middle East, "What is needed is high-level political championing of the region's longer-term development within EU and US policy circles. This is not a region where technical fixes delivered by diligent public servants can get close to exerting the necessary leverage."[18]

We moved away from that over the Obama years, as Tom Carothers wrote in 2016: "Broadly speaking, U.S. engagement on democracy issues has shifted. There was a time when democracy promotion occupied policymakers at all levels – from the 'high policy' end of the spectrum (which involves top-level engagement that seeks transformative change in strategically important countries) to the 'low policy' realm of quiet, low-key methods that seek long-term, iterative change in countries of lesser policy relevance. Today, it's mostly the 'low policy' side that's left."[19] This is a mistake that deprives the United States of the pressure and leadership that are needed to make human rights policy work. Moreover, it is a mistake to believe that "low policy" tools can work effectively when it is obvious that there is no support at the highest levels.

Once the support at the very top is clear, many tools can be employed effectively. In South Korea, public and private messages from Washington and from the American ambassador, speeches and press conferences and secret letters, the ambassador's meeting and appearance schedule, and resolutions in Congress combined to send an effective message.[20] Moreover, such an American stance can often embolden the voices of other democratic nations, adding to the pressure.[21] As the Mubarak case in 2004–2006 makes clear, it was vocal public pressure that changed Egyptian behavior, not an increase in aid for democracy-promoting programming. Such programming can be blocked or slowed down and is, in any event, a very slow means of changing regime conduct.

In fact, democracy programming is not aimed at changing regime conduct, but at the slow accretion of knowledge and experience with democratic institutions and practices. It works best when the regime in power wants to open the political space – which is a rare occurrence. To open the space when the regime is reluctant, top-level pressure will always be necessary. The effectiveness of aid programs will in fact depend in part on whether they have "top cover" – protection from Washington that allows them to do what they are intended to do and opens a space in which they can operate. Carothers' critique of Obama policy was that "the 'low policy' of democracy support remains in place, but it often cannot count on the 'high-policy' side for backing when it matters."[22] That point is a guide for all administrations. U.S. support for democracy must start at the top or it will not be effective. Programming and enlarged budgets are no substitute for policy support from the White House.

STOP ASSISTING AUTOCRATS TO SLOW OR PREVENT POLITICAL OPENINGS Sometimes the most effective thing the United States can do is to stop reinforcing autocracy and strengthening illegitimate regimes. As Saad Eddin Ibrahim put it during the Mubarak years, "Democracy's advance in Egypt itself would be easier if the Mubarak regime did not get so much aid, trade, technology, and training from the West, especially the United States and France. This is not to say that democracy can be exported, but it can be supported. One way to support Arab democrats in the left-behind third of the Muslim world would be simply to stop sending so much help to autocrats."[23]

Even after the end of the Cold War competition with the Soviets, U.S. strategic interests were thought to require supporting any regime that had a pro-American foreign policy. This was true even when there were really no alternatives: what, after all, was Ben Ali going to do in Tunisia? Ally with Qadhafi and the terrorist groups he was hosting? The advent of the Morsi government in Egypt provided an interesting test case, for American support to Mubarak had long been defended as a means of maintaining his peace treaty with Israel. But even Morsi did not, at least in his brief year in power, challenge the treaty or diminish Egyptian-Israeli security cooperation. And today we see that Egyptian-Israeli security cooperation is stronger than ever and appears unrelated to the ups and downs of U.S. support for or criticism of the Sisi government. Egyptian policy does not reflect rising and falling American military aid, but instead the view in Cairo of where Egypt's real security interests lie in the face of jihadi activities in the region.

It is critical that we not revert to a Cold War pattern of backing almost any dictatorship that seeks our friendship or assistance, making them "our son of a bitch." In the aftermath of 9/11 and the rise of al-Qaeda and the so-called Islamic State that temptation has arisen again. But from the collapse of the shah's regime in Iran in 1979 to those of the Ben Ali and Mubarak dictatorships in 2011, we should learn the lesson that "our son of a bitch" may be illegitimate and unstable – and a weak bulwark against and even a contributor to extremism. And that the American role in sustaining such dictatorships can do lasting damage to American interests in the countries in question.

Jason Brownlee's point about the U.S. role is telling: in many cases, the United States is in essence a part of the ruling structure, and like the Ministry of the Interior or the police or intelligence service, with which American officials often work closely, Americans help in "shaping the calculations, priorities, and resources of the regime."[24] So it is fair to ask: Do American officials in that context express opposition to or dismay about repression? Do they argue for political openings? Are assistance programs, and especially those directed at security organs, conditioned on increasing respect for human rights, and do they try to modernize and professionalize the security forces so as to reduce the use of repressive tactics?

There are two easy cases in which the answer to such questions is often yes. When a government is not friendly to the United States or the country in question does not much matter to American security interests, promoting human rights and democracy is a much easier policy option. When I was assistant secretary of state for inter-American affairs in Reagan's second term, I found that the Department of Defense and CIA resisted pressure on the Panamanian dictator Manuel Noriega; however, no one in Washington strongly resisted pressure on and criticism of the Paraguayan dictator Alfredo Stroessner. That was because Paraguay was not an important country, had few linkages to the United States, hosted no U.S. military base, and, of course, had no canal.

The hard cases are those of countries aligned with the United States, but that, of course, is exactly where American pressure may be most effective. The principle "first, do no harm" that is ensconced in the Hippocratic Oath might be a good guide in such cases. Is the net effect of official relations with the United States – considering economic aid programs, democracy assistance programs, official visits at all levels, military-to-military and intelligence relationships, and statements by U.S. officials – to strengthen and deepen the dictatorship, to weaken human rights protections, to lengthen the path to democratic reforms, and accordingly to deepen public resentment of the United States for support of the regime? If the answer is yes, the gains the United States achieves from its official relations with such a regime should be very large indeed to justify maintaining the existing policy.

One can envision moments when the balance still favors silence or inaction on reform, as well as close cooperation with deeply repressive regimes; the classic case is our alliance with Stalin's Soviet Union from 1941 to 1945. But that was during a world war. The cases of cooperation with the "Stans" necessitated by the war in Afghanistan can also be defended. But the alliance with Stalin ended in 1945, and the alliances with the "Stans" should have ended when the U.S. role in the Afghan war became much smaller. Such extreme circumstances are not the norm and do not last for decades. When repressive Arab regimes are working, year after year and decade after decade, to destroy the political center, they are laying a foundation for resentment of the United States for our support and creating a situation where eventual regime collapse leaves no alternative political institutions. In those cases, even with governments viewed as friendly to the United States, our medium- and longer-term interests require that we stop helping the autocrats and start helping those trying to build democratic institutions.

TARGET BACKSLIDERS AND PROTECT MINORITIES Even a major expansion of U.S. democracy assistance programming would not obviate the need to prioritize and to target such aid. One key target, chosen because our chances of being effective are higher, should be those cases where there has been significant democratic reform but now there is backsliding. Turkey under Recep Tayyip Erdogan as prime minister and then president is a good non-Arab example, because Turkey achieved democracy but began to lose it. When democratic institutions exist but are being compromised, there will still exist a substantial reservoir of public support for democracy, opposition political parties will fight for themselves, newspapers will struggle to remain independent, and other democratic nations are more likely to join the United States in trying to prevent the loss of democracy and the compromise of human rights. The struggle will appear far from hopeless, and the achievement of stable democracy will appear possible in the near term. In the Arab world, this would suggest that we should be alert to regression in Tunisia or in countries such as Morocco, Kuwait, and Jordan, as shown by elections that are less free, greater restrictions on the press, and similar backsliding. It may seem somehow unfair that we would be more critical of such moves than of worse situations in, say, Saudi Arabia or Algeria, but it is essential to maintain the existing models of full or partial democratization in the Arab world. Moreover, urging friends in the Arab world against backsliding is not, and need not be done in a way that appears as, an attack that undermines stability.

These same principles should have been applied to the backsliding that took place under Mohammed Morsi in Egypt, who won a free election and proceeded to use state power to narrow the political opening. When journalists and other critics of the Muslim Brotherhood were arrested, the United States and other Western nations made only feeble protests. But Egypt had tasted open political debate, and Morsi's efforts to restrict it were widely unpopular – ultimately helping lead to his overthrow. American protests against backsliding might have slowed Morsi down and would have met with considerable popular support. More recently, as I write, President Sisi is engaging in the same practices, including the jailing of critics who are liberals, moderates, democrats, and in no sense Islamists, and once again American and Western protests are feeble. We appear to have learned nothing.

We should also target, in our own statements and activities, those situations where democracy is not itself a solution and may become part of the problem. Democracy, as we conceive it, is a system not only of popular sovereignty but also of constitutional limits on government and of constitutional protections of certain inalienable rights. The United States must be careful to assert that we do not see as truly democratic those majoritarian systems that simply allow election winners to rule without limits. Where this is a critical matter is in the protection of minorities – who will never win elections. For religious and ethnic minorities in the Arab world, such as Christians, Druze, Yazidis, and indeed Sunnis and Shia in various places, democracy is not a solution to the problem of minority rights. Until those systems are protected by established and agreed constitutional provisions and effective mechanisms, those in danger must look elsewhere for protection – especially to democratic nations abroad who in theory and in practice protect minority rights.

In the Arab Middle East, this means arguing strongly for religious freedom. I argued in Chapter 2 that religious freedom will not in any foreseeable future mean the absolute equality of religions at law and the absolute neutrality of the state. Those are unrealistic goals. But religious freedom is all the more important as an American objective in the context of the Arab Middle East, where religious minorities will be disadvantaged and increasingly democratic structures and practices may not protect them. Foreign pressure is a critical ingredient, and the United States – which does treat Islam neutrally and without discrimination – is in an especially good position to make the argument that Christians and others deserve the right to practice their religion. This means the right to build and repair places of worship, teach the religion to their children, and receive benefits from the state without discrimination. All these principles are violated on a wholesale basis in the region.

SEEK TO BUILD A CONSTITUENCY FOR DEMOCRACY, AND FOCUS ON THE PROTECTION OF LIBERAL/MODERATE VOICES

Democracy without democrats is impossible, or at best unsustainable, as is liberalism without liberals. But how does a foreign government (the United States) create liberals or democrats?

There are three answers to that question: first, by trying and working on spreading liberal (in the old-fashioned sense) ideas about human rights, politics, and democracy; second, by acknowledging that the effort will require decades and not a few years; and third, by building on whatever level of support and understanding actually exists.

There are very few Arab countries where there is no community of democracy and human rights supporters who believe in something very close to our own political principles. In many countries there are activists: men and women working in NGOs where political parties are banned, people struggling to build political parties where they are permitted, academics or journalists or lawyers seeking to teach certain principles and get them into the public square. The first thing the United States (and other democracies) can do is to strengthen and protect them, as noted earlier. But can we also help them in their work?

It is critical to use our influence to protect political voices that may be isolated, unpopular, and sometimes the special targets of nondemocratic regimes, and that are closest to representing our own views of politics: these are the voices of the liberal and moderate actors in Arab society. Regimes often see them as especially dangerous, as we saw in the Egyptian case. As Larry Diamond describes it,

> Authoritarian crackdowns have had another common feature: a fanatical crusade to sever ties between indigenous democratic actors and international sources of financial, technical, and moral support.... This "resistance to democracy programs" cuts off grants and aid to NGOs, think tanks, media, and political parties. Legal and regulatory obstacles impede work and shut down institutions. Representatives of international democracy assistance organizations have been expelled, while their civil society partners have been denounced, physically attacked, and imprisoned.[25]

There are many reasons why U.S. democracy assistance should try especially to assist such groups, beginning with philosophical affinity: they want the kind of political systems in which we believe. Moreover, due to their repression by the regimes in power these groups are badly in need of our help. The danger of Islamist victories is also greater when liberal or moderate parties are weak, which is sometimes the precise goal of regimes in power: to scare democracies into believing that the only choice is between the regime in place or ferocious Islamist alternatives. Helping create other options than rapacious dictatorships and Islamist extremes should obviously be a central U.S. objective. Tarek Masoud says it well: "Rather than wondering whether Islamists are not as bad as we think they are," we should "bend [our] efforts toward lifting the government yoke off parties whose democratic bona fides are not the objective of anguished speculation."[26]

Is this possible? Sometimes it is, as the Mubarak example shows. In the parliamentary elections of 2005 and 2010, the regime paid more attention to repressing centrist, liberal, moderate, and moderate Islamist groups than in keeping the Brotherhood out of parliament. There was no particular American reaction to this, although it would have been easy to construct an argument for treating these moderates (secular and Islamist, leftist and rightist) better. The regime would have been hard put to defend such tactics under resolute foreign pressure, but that pressure was absent.

Is this "picking winners" and interfering in foreign political systems? To some degree it is, but the alternative is indifference and a mindless form of neutrality. In any event, there is no way to calculate every statement of protest mathematically so that every repressed group gets equal treatment. And at least in the Egyptian case, we could have argued that we were merely seeking a level playing field, because the regime was unfairly tilting it toward its own party and the Brotherhood and against all other comers. Indeed the accusation of special U.S. concern for certain parties will be accurate only when the playing field is in fact tilted against them, and in those cases we have a very good explanation for why our own efforts are targeted at assisting them.

Stephen R. Grand argues powerfully that the old Middle East, dominated by secular tyrants like Saddam Hussein and Hosni Mubarak and Zine El Abidine Ben Ali, is gone; any replacements will necessarily be even less stable than their predecessors. So, he says,

the United States should throw its support firmly behind the forces of change in the region. It should align itself squarely with those Arab democrats seeking to build more just, participatory, and accountable political systems. In whatever ways possible, it should assist the citizens and countries of the region to make the difficult transition from an order based on coercion to one based on individual choice. That does not mean that the United States should abandon its long-standing allies tomorrow, but it should recognize that the future of the region will be determined by the region's citizens.[27]

The goal, he explains, is precisely to build a "political constituency for democracy."

There is a contradiction here: how do we know that (as he puts it) "there is no going back" to the old order and that democracy is possible if there is such a weak constituency for it? Grand argues that much of our work should be on the "supply side:" helping to craft effective constitutions, develop democratic political institutions, train government officials to staff those institutions, create vibrant political parties, convene free and fair elections, and ensure civilian oversight of the military." But he acknowledges this work will never be enough: such "institutional design is just one piece of a much larger puzzle. U.S. efforts to build effective political institutions will come to naught unless citizens demand that those institutions function as intended. If the United States wants democracy to succeed around the globe, it must help create public demand."[28] So he urges a "grand strategy designed specifically to cultivate effective political constituencies for democracy in the region."

But there is a constituency for democracy of varying power, size, cohesiveness, and effectiveness in each country in the Arab Middle East. It is obviously larger in Tunisia than in Saudi Arabia, but the Arab Barometer and other polls cited in previous chapters show widespread support for what those polled call "democracy." Enlarging that constituency and especially educating it are the tasks of Arab democrats, and they have many enemies. Some are Islamists who place the Koran over any man-made legal or constitutional limits; some are "fellouls" or relics of the old regime, seeking to hang on to shreds of power or return fully to the old system. At best it will take many years for the democrats to rise in strength and build an educated public that truly grasps and supports the liberal democratic principles the United States espouses. On some issues the Arab societies may never get there, for democracies vary as they approach questions like the role of religion in society. (France practices a form of secularism that would be widely unacceptable in the United States; several European democracies continue to have a state church.) This variation is not a roadblock to democratization, for after all democracies are more different in form and content than are dictatorships, which tend to use the same tools to stay in power.

Helping local democrats increase the "demand" for democracy will always be a very difficult task for outsiders, but we can be sure that providing them with some political protection will be appreciated, as will providing them with the resources their rivals have in greater measure.

One way for the United States to promote these goals is through wider education about democracy. The later section on economic development aid notes the downsides of economic assistance to dictatorships. Such aid might better be diverted in part to working to create a larger constituency for democracy by such steps as circulating liberal ideas about government through the publication of books, making more texts available in Arabic online, encouraging university courses on democratic politics, and helping and pressuring for revisions in school texts.

If we truly believe that expansion of democracy is the work of generations, we know that many battles will be lost and that there will be years when democracy appears to be losing out in some or all Arab lands. The democratic trend lines in Latin America were all positive in the 1980s, but later setbacks in Venezuela, Ecuador, Bolivia, and Nicaragua surely reduced the optimism that had earlier been widespread. The lesson was not to abandon struggling democrats in those countries, but to acknowledge that it would be a very long time before democracy was permanently sustainable. Arab democrats have not reacted to the failure of the Arab Spring to produce sustainable democracies by abandoning their principles or their struggle. Neither should we.

Of the various ways to assist Arab democrats facing the worst and most repressive situations, direct financial support can be one of the most important. As repression escalates, those struggling for human rights and democracy can lose their jobs, be imprisoned, or be exiled (or, in the most extreme cases, be killed). They and/or their families may need ways to support themselves. Dissidents often find that they are no longer employable as journalists or lawyers. If they need to be outside their own countries in a safer space at least for a time, they will need a way to earn their keep that does not require abandoning their political activities.

Financial support from foreign governments and NGOs may be the only possible sources of such funds. Obviously there can be many complications of such aid. Can money be safely transferred? Does accepting it constitute another offense under local laws? Who is truly deserving, and who will do the triage of what are likely to be inadequate funds? Nevertheless, making some money available to dissidents at home, and if need be outside their own countries, is an absolutely critical aspect of supporting democracy. Not only can it be essential to allowing activists to keep working but it can also be essential to keeping up both their and their families' morale, and that of others who fear that they are next and wonder how they will cope. More broadly, this kind of direct support can be a key to sustaining the morale of democratic activists around the world – who can see that in dire trouble they will not be abandoned and that help may be available.

SHIFT EMPHASIS IN FOREIGN AID PROGRAMS FROM CIVIL SOCIETY TO POLITICAL PARTIES, AND MOVE TOWARD THE PRIVATE FOUNDATION MODEL INSTEAD OF USAID PROGRAM-MING When countries are clearly on the path to democracy and government officials are guiding this move themselves, there is no need for the United States to be pressing them for democratization. In these cases, the society and its political elites have made the decision, and the turning point is now in the rear-view mirror. They may well need, and seek, foreign assistance and expertise in translating their decision into a workable and permanent shift to democracy, but they need U.S. help rather than U.S. pressure. But where that turning point has yet to be reached, the United States must do more in supporting people struggling to build democratic institutions and lead their country toward a real political opening.

Support for NGOs and civil society groups is important, but just as clearly inadequate if we truly seek democratization. In many cases, the political system will be closed and political activity illegal. There may be no alternative to working exclusively with civil society groups. But we should be aware that this approach avoids the central political issue of who rules. Regimes can absorb a lot of civil society activity without permitting any real contestation for power, which is the essence of democracy. What is more, we can never predict exactly how brittle a regime may be and when it may fall. The existence of civil society groups may in fact help bring about the collapse, but experience suggests that they will be unable to organize effective and broad political coalitions to take advantage of the political space that then opens. That is what politicians and political parties do, so we should, to the maximum extent possible, shift aid funds and attention to political activity. Where political activity is impossible, we should favor aid recipients whom we believe will be most likely to make the move into democratic politics and give them training not to be better NGOs but to understand and master politics. That is the lesson taught by Nelson Mandela, as Princeton Lyman explained it (see the discussion in Chapter 4).

Unlike NGOs and civil society groups, political parties can propose comprehensive policies, seek wide and inclusive national popular support, compete in elections, prepare to govern, and understand the necessity for public accountability. As Seymour Martin Lipset summarizes it, "Citizen groups must become the bases of – the sources of support for – the institutionalized political parties which are a necessary condition for – part of the very definition of – a modern democracy."[29] Only political party work teaches how to formulate and explain the entire policy agenda, do wide outreach, and organize nationally. Civil society groups do invaluable work, but they are no substitute for political parties. This means that the National Endowment for Democracy (NED) and the National Democratic Institute for International Affairs (NDI) and International Republican Institute (IRI), as well as the Agency for International Development, should adjust the portion of their budgets dedicated to civil society and political work in favor of the latter. It means that NDI and IRI political work should expand, and that more NED funds should be passed to the two party institutes, rather than being used by the NED itself for civil society work.

Whatever the success of USAID's work on issues like health or economic development, it is an unwieldy bureaucracy when it comes to promoting democracy. As Melinda Haring writes, "It's hardly news that the democracy bureaucracy is uncoordinated, redundant, and counterproductive."[30] More and more of the democracy-promotion activity should be shifted to the "private foundation" model and away from AID and the large, for-profit "beltway bandit" companies it hires to conduct programming. "The U.S. government should leave democracy assistance in countries that Freedom House ranks as 'not free' ... to the independent grant-making model exemplified by the National Endowment for Democracy (NED) – because in-country offices in authoritarian countries entail all sorts of compromises, dilute programs, and are far more expensive," Haring adds.

The decades of useful work by the German political party foundations, the "stiftungen," are more evidence that this model works better than direct programming by national government agencies. The first German party foundation opened in 1925, and in the post–World-War II period such foundations have made especially important contributions to democratization in Latin America in the 1960s and in Spain and Portugal in the 1970s. Today the six party foundations have 300 offices around the world (compared to the roughly 130 offices of the two American party-linked foundations). While they engage broadly with civil society organizations, such as trade unions, and work to train people in mass media in developing countries, their approach has wherever possible centered on aid to like-minded political parties, helping institutionalize them and "strengthen the internal party democracy of political parties as well as their capability to support the democratic consolidation of transformation states and young democracies."[31]

By contrast, USAID and those for-profit "consultants" are by nature and training (and economic interest) the least likely institutions to challenge autocracy and undertake the long and difficult task of helping support protection for human rights and the expansion of democracy. By definition USAID is a government agency relying on ties to other governments, which alone will make its programs too "tame," as Sarah Bush warns. As she argues, groups that are somewhat insulated from government agencies are likely to be nimbler and more effective.[32]

CONDITION ISLAMIST PARTY PARTICIPATION – BUT DO NOT EXCLUDE IT The absolute and unconditional exclusion of any Islamist party from political participation is unrealistic and unhealthy in most Arab cases. Islamist groups vary greatly in their beliefs, popular support, and attitudes toward democracy. Their strength can be a barrier to anything we would recognize as democracy, or they can become part of a democratic system. In Morocco, Jordan, and Kuwait, as we have seen, they have participated in politics and represented the views of many voters without subverting the political system. Nor are "secular" parties automatically repositories of democracy: in many cases they will be connected to the security institutions or the old repressive regimes, and will internally be undemocratic.

Some groups and parties should be barred from getting any American help. One critical test is their degree of internal democracy, a test that would, for example, have rightly kept any U.S. assistance from going to the Muslim Brotherhood in Egypt – and equally to Mubarak's National Democratic Party. The best test of whether a party would rule democratically when in power is whether it rules itself democratically when out of power. And the United States should not assist any party or group whose goals are antithetical to our own beliefs – groups whose goal, for example, is a theocracy or any other nondemocratic form of government or that espouse the discriminatory and unequal treatment of citizens. For example, the United States should not offer training to, and thereby presumably help succeed, a party that believes that only Muslims or only males can hold high office.

But there are two questions here: which groups does the United States help, and which groups does the United States argue should be included in or excluded from politics entirely? While we may not wish to use our own limited political clout and our programs to protect or assist a group that argues that only a Muslim can be president or prime minister, should such a group be barred from politics? What are realistic preconditions to impose on parties?

For the United States, it is perfectly fair to impose our own beliefs on aid recipients, to whatever degree we think possible. But to urge the exclusion from politics of groups that disagree with our current views on social issues – views that our own country arrived at only recently and after two hundred and fifty years of democracy – would be foolish. To suggest, for example, that any party that holds traditional Muslim views on women's rights or homosexual conduct, or believes that Islam should be the religion of the state, is an illegitimate participant in elections would hurt, not help, the development of democratic politics.

So what legal conditions should the United States support and indeed promote with respect to Islamist political participation? That parties must pledge to support the existing constitution and act within it to seek any changes they may desire; that they govern themselves democratically; and that they abjure the use of violence entirely. Any party that meets these standards should be permitted to present candidates and participate in elections, and the United States should oppose efforts to exclude Islamist parties that meet these standards – even if we believe their platforms to be offensive in a thousand ways.

This is principled and practical advice. Experience suggests that Islamist parties will lose support over time, especially when they win it in the first post-dictatorship elections where their advantages are greatest. The best way to defeat Islamism and maintain democracy is, of course, at the ballot box, by defeating Islamist ideas in open political debate rather than by preventing Islamists from speaking. Closing the political system to disfavored ideas will not build a sound basis for democracy.

Democratic principles and practices must be learned – through open debate, free elections, and the political education that comes from long experience.

CONDITION SECURITY ASSISTANCE ON SECURITY REFORM

The question of security reform in Arab states relates directly to issues such as police and military violations of human rights, but it goes as well to the heart of building democracies in the Middle East. As Robert Springborg puts it,

> Building competent, inclusive states requires subordination of coercive forces to civilian institutions . . . . Bolstering civilian organizations and institutions and facilitating political compromises need far more attention and resources, while militaries, militias, national guards, and other coercive forces need less. Western-inspired and supported counterinsurgency and counterterrorism strategies have been stripped of their humanitarian support and state building components, leaving only coercion as the means by which order is to be restored. The sad history of postcolonial Arab states should be sufficient demonstration that imbalance between coercive and non-coercive forces undermines states and the political order and development only they can deliver. Arab militaries have broken states, not successfully built them. Before they break any more it is time to seek other, or at least additional, means of building Arab states.[33]

With jihadi groups like al-Qaeda and the "Islamic State" at large in the Middle East, conditioning security assistance – aid to military, police, and intelligence institutions – on anything at all may seem dangerous. But there are practical and principled reasons to do so.

For one thing, as I have argued throughout this book, the best answer to Islamist extremism is not government-backed or government-imposed terrorism and vast repression. Military action against jihadis and terrorists is a necessary but not sufficient step, but if it is part of a broad campaign of suppressing all political activity and political protest it will eventually end up recruiting more cadres for those violent groups. Security forces that employ torture instead of intelligence, that cannot distinguish violent from nonviolent protesters and movements, and that violate legal, constitutional, and human rights with impunity are not going to add to the long-term or medium-term stability of the governments they serve. As I write, for example, the repressive activities of the Egyptian Army in the Sinai Peninsula have achieved little except perhaps to alienate its residents, mostly Bedouin, even further. That does not help defeat the jihadis who seek to use Sinai as a safe house and launching point. And jihadi activity in Sinai appears to be growing steadily.

Conditioning security assistance has three goals. The human rights goal is to disconnect the United States from acts of repression. We may not be able to cure the security institutions of bad practices, but we may be able to reduce the sense that the United States is complicit in them, approves of them, or at least accepts them without protest. Money talks, so occasional verbal protests against official abuses will carry no weight if those abuses do not affect the size and nature of security assistance. Back in the 1980s, the Reagan administration would sometimes say we would sell a regime the F-5 jet but not cattle prods, and the reasoning was obvious: F-5s were useful for protecting air space and national security, but not internal security; they were not instruments of repression. The United States has followed this path in many other cases. The sensible conditions to be imposed will be as varied as the cases: sometimes it may mean the denial of certain purchases, and other times it might be an insistence on human rights training for police and soldiers or on disciplining officers involved in abuses.

And that suggests the second goal of conditioning security assistance: making the security forces more effective in achieving their actual objective, which is combatting terrorism, criminality, and violence and maintaining law and order. In many Arab states, the police are undereducated and undertrained, resorting to violence themselves to seek confessions and punish citizens without any sort of trial. They are underresourced as well, lacking the sort of modern equipment needed to do their job well. They are part of a criminal justice system that works poorly at best, especially for the mass of citizens who are themselves poor. That contributes to the distance between the citizen and the state, the belief that law does not exist or cannot be enforced, and the sense of regime illegitimacy.

Third, democracy is itself illusory when there is no civilian control of the military. Robert Springborg writes of the Arab world that "[c]ontrol based on law and exercised by civilian institutions of the state and civil society is nowhere to be found. A, if not the, challenge facing the movements that brought about the Arab spring is to establish such control."[34] In many Arab states the security forces, military and police, have been laws unto themselves. Neither the military nor the *mukhabarat* are actually under any kind of civilian control except in monarchies – and sometimes not even then. They exist as separate internal empires. When Arab states move toward democracy, whether as republics or constitutional monarchies in form, this situation presents a huge challenge. New parliamentarians or ministers have no information about these key state institutions.

Yet this is not a new challenge, and any country moving from military dictatorship to civilian government faces it. We saw this in the 1980s and 1990s in Latin America, for example, as newly elected presidents appointed new ministers of defense who confronted the closed ranks of the military. There are no quick solutions, but there are ways to help. The United States probably has far more information about each Arab military than the citizens of Arab countries (including the new ministers) and could offer to inform new officials about budgets, strengths and weaknesses, organizational structures, personal links, and other critical information – at least as we understand them. We can put them in contact with officials who have faced this challenge in other countries that democratized in recent decades – from Brazil or Chile or Argentina in Latin America, to the Czech Republic and Poland, to South Africa – and provide for a forum for these exchanges. We should speak out publicly in defense of civilian control of the military as a principle of democratic government. We can insist that our military education and training programs include serious discussions of civilian control, and pointedly include civilians from the relevant ministries in Arab countries.

We can ensure that American military officers make these points publicly and privately – including the explanation that civilian control means civilian responsibility – thereby lifting a burden from military officers for actions that prove unpopular. Moreover, we can try to explain to soldiers that their own institution is ultimately at risk when its purpose is vastly enlarged to include not only protecting the state from armed enemies but also replacing the state.

The problems we should be trying to address are well summarized in an article called "Getting to Democracy" in *Foreign Affairs*:

> Senior civilian officials charged with overseeing security forces should be knowledgeable about security matters and respectful of their peers in the military, the police, and the intelligence services. This can be difficult where democratic movements have clashed violently with the security services, where mutual distrust persists, and where there is little respect for civilian expertise in military affairs.[35]

In most Arab countries the affairs of the military and police have long been regarded as unfit for public discussion and so have been subject to censorship. The time to begin preparing for civilian control of the military is as soon as possible. Perhaps courses on the subject can be introduced at universities like American University Cairo and in the branches of American colleges that are now spreading in the region. Journalists can be offered special training in covering the subject, as can parliamentarians. Part of the goal is to make the entire subject a safe one for discussion and to enhance that discussion; the other part is to convey actual skills and information.

The response to these suggestions from many U.S. government officials may be that we already condition security assistance and support civilian control of the military. But a cursory glance at the region will suggest that far more can be done. As Springborg concludes, "Although the Arab world received a disproportionate amount of U.S. funding to promote democracy, it received virtually no support to enhance civilian control of the militaries."[36]

**REEVALUATE THE ACHIEVEMENTS OF ECONOMIC DEVELOP-
MENT AID TO DICTATORSHIPS** Providing economic assistance to dictatorships can help them remain in power. When the purpose of the
aid is purely humanitarian – disaster assistance, prevention of famine,
prevention of the spread of epidemics like AIDS or Ebola – it can easily
be defended. But what of longer-term development assistance?

Typically the goals of such programs are purely economic, without
sufficient thought being given to their political impact in strengthening autocratic regimes. And similarly, insufficient thought is given to
whether different programming might actually help advance political
development. The critical insight here is that economic development
is not an independent variable unrelated to a nation's political structures. Economic policies are chosen by rulers, and in undemocratic
regimes the rulers will likely choose policies that benefit themselves –
not national development or the alleviation of poverty. Policies will benefit those within the charmed circle rather than expanding that circle.
There are exceptions, such as Lee Kuan Yew's Singapore, but they are
rare.

What is the goal of American economic assistance? There are strong
arguments that economic crisis can create sharp pressure for political
reform, so should American foreign aid be trying to help avoid crises
absent political reform? Isobel Coleman and Terra Lawson-Remer argue
in *Pathways to Freedom*, "What does not seem to promote democracy . . . is
economic development in authoritarian states. Economic crises, not
growth, spur democratization."[37] As they note, in the cases of Indonesia,
Brazil, and Mexico "deteriorating economic conditions were an unmis-
takable trigger of change. This continues to be the case around the world,
as is clear from the Arab uprisings of recent years, which were sparked in
part by rising food prices and frustrated economic ambitions."[38] There
is a familiar argument that economic development must come first, laying a foundation for political change, but that argument assumes that
economic reform is possible without political change. As Carothers puts
it, "Although the idea that economic change should precede political
change is very appealing the sticky fact remains that the lack of political
reform and political accountability is precisely what undermines efforts
to motivate Arab governments to undertake far-reaching economic

structural reform."[39] Egypt is a prime example: its army's economic role is vast, and open competition against "private" companies owned by the military is never permitted. There have been several exceptions to this rule in Asia, and Chile's Augusto Pinochet brought about an extraordinary economic change – but that was possible in part because the Chilean military had never had any economic role.[40]

A rich discussion of this issue is found in *Why Nations Fail*, where Daren Acemoglu and James A. Robinson argue that the roots of poverty lie in the economic and political institutions that govern a country and make choices about economic policy. There can, of course, be substantial "authoritarian growth," and China may be the best example. But they warn, "[C]ontrary to the claims of modernization theory, we should not count on authoritarian growth leading to democracy or inclusive political institutions."[41] Nor is conditionality, they suggest, the best approach: it merely seeks to get those in power to make a few concessions on economic policy. It has long been understood that famines are the product of policy choices rather than of natural disasters. Acemoglu and Robinson take that understanding further: "poor countries are poor because those who have power make choices that create poverty. They get it wrong not by mistake or ignorance but on purpose. To understand this, you have to go beyond economics and expert advice on the best thing to do and, instead, study how decisions actually get made, who gets to make them, and why those people decide to do what they do. This is the study of politics and political processes."[42]

Economic and political progress are linked, but they are not sequential. Sometimes an economic breakthrough has come under a dictatorship, especially in Asia, but there are no Arab cases. In the Arab world, those in power have skewed economic policy to keep themselves in power and enrich themselves further. Corruption is vast and systemic, and political as well as economic structures protect the system. The lack of freedom of the press means that corruption cannot be exposed, and the lack of free elections means that corrupt officials cannot be thrown out of office peacefully. Foreign assistance programs that secure a few concessions in economic policy but help sustain dictatorships in power should be reconsidered, and more emphasis placed on a push toward more open political systems where economic policy can be debated.

**KEEP FREE ELECTIONS AT THE CENTER OF DEMOCRACY PRO-
MOTION, AND DO NOT ASSUME THE UNITED STATES CAN
INSIST ON "GRADUAL" CHANGE** In theory, gradual change toward
democracy would work best, but is often unlikely. Gradual change
assumes perfect conditions, such as enlightened rulers whose goal is precisely a steady move toward democratic government. It may be that in certain monarchies, such as Morocco or Jordan, gradual change is possible
and will come about. But in other monarchic and "republican" (such as
Bahrain, and Algeria and Egypt, respectively) cases, ruling elites appear
to see gradual change as a danger – and to see its advocates as especially dangerous actors who must be harshly repressed. Top-down political change toward real democracy has been extremely rare; it is far more
common, as Carothers describes it, that "the accumulated failures of an
authoritarian or semi-authoritarian regime may provoke a loss of political
legitimacy, which leads to the regime being driven out of power (by spontaneous public demonstrations, an organized opposition movement, or
disenchanted political elites) and to an attempt to create a democratic
system to take the place of the discredited, ousted regime."[43]

The pace of change will reflect local conditions, and so our overall
preference for gradual change must give way to reality. When the mass
of citizens wants change *now*, it would be folly for the United States
to adopt a policy of opposition where we urge delay in moving to free
speech, free press, independent courts, and above all free elections. This
is why the many criticisms of the Obama administration for "throwing
Mubarak under the bus" are foolish. Once Egyptians had gone to the
streets by the millions and the regime's legitimacy had been destroyed,
an argument for "gradualism" was impossible and the United States had
to accept that. The time to have argued for gradual reform was in the
previous decade, when this was done by the Bush administration in
2004–2006, but then was largely forgotten in the last Bush years and
entirely abandoned in the Obama years. The last decade of Mubarak's
rule might have been a time for gradual reform, and Mubarak could have
promised and slowly introduced freer and freer elections – but instead
he chose to position his son Gamal as his successor, a move that the
vast majority of Egyptians saw as illegitimate, and to return to stealing
elections.

What the United States can more effectively do under both autocratic regimes and at moments of political opening is to argue strongly about the *nature* of free elections: the conditions that permit elections to be free. Here we may have an audience and a role to play. A level playing field, equal access for all democratic parties to the populace through media and party organizational work, civil liberties such as freedom of speech and press that allow criticism of incumbent parties and leaders and the free expression of reform proposals, a better organized and independent electoral commission, the presence of an adequate number of foreign and domestic observers – these are what turn a phony or flawed election into a reliable expression of voters' desires. American explanations of these preconditions and assistance in achieving them will be far better received than any arguments that the country is not "ready for elections."

The United States and other democracies are engaged in such activities in dozens of countries around the globe, especially when it comes to election observation. And in recent years, observation missions have begun to visit countries holding elections far in advance of the election date, and to comment on the playing field and whether elections are really fair *even if* the votes are being counted fairly on Election Day itself. What we have done less effectively and less often is to offer the political training and assistance that are required in the years before political openings occur, concentrating too much on civil society instead. To take two examples, in the 2006 Palestinian elections the Fatah Party made an error that Hamas did not commit. In some electoral districts Fatah presented more than one candidate, who then split the non-Hamas vote and allowed Hamas to win the seat. This kind of simple error turned Hamas's 44–41 percent victory over Fatah in the popular vote into a 45–17 rout when it came to winning constituency seats. In the 2012 Egyptian parliamentary elections, the Muslim Brotherhood was better at selecting attractive individual candidates early, telling voters about them, learning about voter preferences, describing its own beliefs, and getting voters to the polls than non-Islamist parties and coalitions.[44] The Brotherhood's long experience with political organization made it unlikely that the small and diverse parties opposing it could fully match its performance, but they might have done better – especially with more advice and training.

The solution was surely not to say, in Egypt and Palestine, that elections should simply not be held – and had they been postponed for perhaps a year little would likely have changed. (In fact, the Palestinian parliamentary elections had actually been postponed from 2005 to 2006.) Outside political advice can urge one form of sequencing over another: for example, writing a new constitution before holding parliamentary elections, a sequence that helped stabilize post-Ben Ali Tunisia. But any population emerging from a dictatorship will seek elections, and arguments for some sort of lengthy transition without the introduction of new democratic institutions will always lose. This should lead us to the conclusion that the gradual change must start earlier and that a key American role should be to push for small and partial political openings – as much as the traffic will bear – even when democracy itself seems far off.

RECOGNIZE THAT THE FATE OF ARAB DEMOCRACY IS LINKED TO THE FUTURE OF AMERICAN LEADERSHIP The National Security Strategy of 2002, issued by George W. Bush, stated, "We seek instead to create a balance of power that favors human freedom."[45] It is not coincidental that the period when democracy expanded most broadly in the world was also a period of maximum American influence and power.

Scholars have repeatedly noted the impact of outside influences on domestic political developments, and not only when there is direct intervention. In "Diffusion and the International Context of Democratization," for example, Professors Kristian Skrede Gleditsch and Michael D. Ward argue that "international factors influence the prospects for democracy, and that transitions are not simply random but are more likely in the wake of changes in the external environment," and note that events in neighboring countries and regions are critical.[46] But how can whole regions move toward democracy, as Latin America and East Asia did in certain decades?

Robert Kagan sums up a key explanation in discussing the "third wave" of democratization (occurring from roughly 1974 to 2000):

> What explained the prolonged success of democratization over the last quarter of the twentieth century? Nations moved into a democratic phase and stayed there. But why? The answer is related to the configuration of

power and ideas in the world. The international climate from the mid-1970s onward was simply more hospitable to democracies.

Kagan next quotes the late Samuel Huntington: "the pervasiveness of democratic norms rested in large part on the commitment to those norms of the most powerful country in the world." Kagan then adds, "The United States, in fact, played a critical role in making the explosion of democracy possible." He continues,

> In the 1980s as in the 1840s, liberal movements arose for their own reasons in different countries, but their success or failure was influenced by the balance of power at the international level. In the era of U.S. predominance, the balance was generally favorable to democracy, which helps to explain why the liberal revolutions of that later era succeeded. Had the United States not been so powerful, there would have been fewer transitions to democracy, and those that occurred might have been short-lived. It might have meant a shallower and more easily reversed third wave.[47]

Arab democracy may fail while democracy advances in other parts of the world, a phenomenon we saw in the "third wave" decades. But it is extremely unlikely that democracy will flourish in Arab lands when it is collapsing elsewhere and when the cause of democracy is itself under assault. That the fate of democracy internationally is inevitably tied to U.S. influence in the world is a descriptive rather than normative statement. In a world where the power and influence of countries such as China and Russia are growing, we can at best expect a slower and narrower expansion of democracy and of liberal government more generally. The very association of democracy with progress and success and prosperity, which was so important during the "third wave," is absent when the United States appears to be diminishing as a power and as a model.

This is not an argument for seeking forms of international leadership that may contradict U.S. economic or security interests, but rather a caution. In periods of perceived American decline, the struggle for democracy will be significantly harder. That might, tactically, suggest that American efforts to promote democracy in periods of declining U.S. power and influence should concentrate on preventing backsliding in countries where there has been some progress. In periods of American leadership, our tactics might change and we might decide to press harder for more advances. The point is that linkage exists. It is not determinative of the outcome in any single country, because variables such as national leadership, economic developments, and the regional security picture will be more significant. But as we consider ways to advance the cause of freedom, it is folly to blind ourselves to the fact that the cause and perceptions of American power and success have been linked for two centuries and remain connected.

ARAB DEMOCRACY AND ARAB LEGITIMACY The collapse of the Arab Spring and, with it, widespread hopes for democracy in the Arab world has been depressing to watch. Certainly a massive dose of realism has been added to counteract optimism about the pace and direction of political change. There will be no wave of democratization such as the "third wave" of 1974–2000 in Latin America, parts of East Asia, and Europe. Professors Brownlee, Masoud, and Reynolds close their book *The Arab Spring* with a grim prognosis, describing its "modest harvest" as "a bitter litany of failed uprisings, brutal crackdowns, flawed elections, and endemic violence" that emphasizes not change in the region but the power of "inherited . . . social and economic structures impeding democratic development." They conclude that the Arab Spring will come to be understood as "a momentary break in a longer, more dismal story."[48]

But my subject in this book has been the American role in that story, even if one shares their pessimism about the years to come. When does a policy that is believed to be a form of *realpolitik* become self-defeating and unrealistic, setting back the long-term prospects for democracy and abandoning both Arab democrats and our own principles?

The failure of the Arab Spring has led many to question whether Arab democracy is even possible and, if possible, whether it is desirable. The argument here has been that both questions should elicit positive answers. Legitimate regimes in the Arab world can in theory derive that legitimacy from monarchy, democracy, or effective performance. But where in the Arab world has there ever been a republican dictatorship whose political and economic performance was inspiring? With no feedback loops, whether from free elections or a free press, such regimes become calcified and corrupt and often increasingly repressive. Entrenched economic interests, whether of the ruling family, the army, or economic elites, move to protect and enhance their own wealth, not toward a more productive free market economy with wider social and economic mobility. If there have on occasion been something like philosopher-kings, monarchic rulers who had the people's interests at heart and did in fact advance them, there have in the Arab world been no philosopher-dictators. There is no Arab version of Singapore's Lee Kuan Yew.

So it is folly to expect that there will be slow and gradual, but real and measurable, progress toward democracy in such dictatorships. There may be in the monarchies, and there are indeed several cases of steady if slow liberalization. The United States should support such progress in the monarchies, and call for democracy in the republics – because it is realistically the only form whereby legitimate government can take root in those countries. The argument against such an American position is the "security dilemma," the view that more open political systems are simply too dangerous because Islamist extremists will use any political opening to seize and retain power. That argument, I have shown, overstates the problem and the danger. In the struggle against violent and nonviolent forms of Islamist extremism, repression is sometimes a useful and indeed a necessary tool. But Islamists have no magic to sell, and their fellow citizens soon judge them by their fruits when they have a share of power. To build democratic institutions, enhance the rule of law, protect an independent judiciary, establish a free press, and hold free elections is the best basis for limiting Islamist excesses and holding them to constitutional limits. Forceful suppression may be needed when violent extremists seek to seize or retain power unlawfully, but Islamist ideas will not be defeated by policemen and soldiers. Only better ideas can achieve that goal, and the dictatorships have usually worked hardest to suppress the ideas and the people who might most effectively defeat Islamism because the same ideas and people might also undermine the dictatorship itself.

Despite all the recent setbacks to political liberalization in the Arab world and the dangers of jihadism and Islamist extremism that abound, is Arab democracy possible and desirable? It is – and our own interests are best served by Arab governments that are legitimate, decent, and stable and are able to combat extremism effectively. Whether those are republics or monarchies that bring the citizenry into a partnership for the governance of the country through representative institutions, they cannot in the long run be autocracies that prevent all political debate and exclude the people from any role in governing themselves. Not only will such regimes prove unstable but they will also create conditions where moderate and liberal voices are crushed while extremists and extremism thrive. Tyranny in the Arab world is dangerous and should itself be viewed as a form of political extremism that is likely to feed other forms. It is up to Arabs to determine their political fate, but outside influences matter – including the attitude we in the United States take and the support we give or withhold. Our principles and our security interests both suggest that we should be giving repression and tyranny far more effective opposition, and freedom and democracy far more effective support.

Notes

PREFACE

1. Fareed Zakaria, "A New Middle East," *Time*, May 1, 2011, http://content.time.com/time/magazine/article/0,9171,2069033,00.html.
2. Paul Cruickshank, "Why Arab Spring Could Be al Qaeda's Fall," *CNN*, February 21, 2011, www.cnn.com/2011/WORLD/meast/02/21/arab.unrest.alqaeda.analysis/.
3. Olivier Roy, "End of the old Arab Strongman," *New Statesman*, March 3, 2011, www.newstatesman.com/middle-east/2011/02/israel-iran-movement-arab.
4. Jean-Marie Guéhenno, "The Arab Spring Is 2011, Not 1989," *New York Times*, April 21, 2011, www.nytimes.com/2011/04/22/opinion/22iht-edguehenno22.html?_r=0.
5. Daniel Byman, "After the Hope of the Arab Spring, the Chill of an Arab Winter," *Washington Post*, December 1, 2011, www.washingtonpost.com/opinions/after-the-hope-of-the-arab-spring-the-chill-of-an-arab-winter/2011/11/28/gIQABGqHIO_story.html.
6. Tarek Masoud, "Has the Door Closed on Arab Democracy?" *Journal of Democracy* 26, no. 1 (2015): 74, http://muse.jhu.edu/article/565640/pdf.

INTRODUCTION: FORTY YEARS OF HUMAN RIGHTS POLICY

1. Woodrow Wilson, "Address to a Joint Session of Congress on the Conditions of Peace," January 8, 1918, transcript, American Presidency Project, University of California-Santa Barbara, www.presidency.ucsb.edu/ws/?pid=65405.
2. John F. Kennedy, "Address at a White House Reception for Members of Congress and for the Diplomatic Corps of the Latin American Republics," March 13, 1961, transcript, John F. Kennedy Presidential Library and Museum, www.jfklibrary.org/Research/Research-Aids/JFK-Speeches/Latin-American-Diplomats-Washington-DC_19610313.aspx.
3. John F. Kennedy, "Address on the First Anniversary of the Alliance for Progress," March 13, 1962, transcript, American Presidency Project, University of California-Santa Barbara, www.presidency.ucsb.edu/ws/?pid=9100.
4. Matthew Berke, "The Disputed Legacy of Reinhold Niebuhr," *First Things*, November 1992, www.firstthings.com/article/1992/11/004-the-disputed-legacy-of-reinhold-niebuhr.

5. Daniel P. Moynihan, "The United States in Opposition," *Commentary*, March 1975, www.commentarymagazine.com/articles/the-united-states-in-opposition/.

6. George McGovern, "Address Accepting the Presidential Nomination of the Democratic National Convention," July 14, 1972, transcript, American Presidency Project, University of California-Santa Barbara, www.presidency.ucsb.edu/ws/?pid=25967.

7. Henry M. Jackson, "Speech on Behalf of Norwegian Independence Day," May 10, 1948, cited in Robert G. Kaufman, *Henry M. Jackson: A Life in Politics* (Seattle: University of Washington Press, 2000), 49.

8. David Samuels, "A Fourth of July Story, *Tablet*, June 30, 2016, www.tabletmag.com/jewish-news-and-politics/191785/a-fourth-of-july-story.

9. Adam Nagourney, "In Tapes, Nixon Rails about Jews and Blacks," *New York Times*, December 10, 2010, www.nytimes.com/2010/12/11/us/politics/11nixon.html?_r=0.

10. William Korey, "The Struggle over Jackson-Mills-Vanik," *American Jewish Yearbook* 75 (1974–1975), www.bjpa.org/Publications/downloadFile.cfm?FileID=20308.

11. *The Jackson Amendment on East-West Trade & Freedom of Emigration*, Amendment No. 79, Inside the Cold War, http://insidethecoldwar.org/sites/default/files/documents/Jackson-Vanik%20Amendment%20to%20the%20trade%20reform%20act%20of%201972,%20january%204,%201975.pdf.

12. George Perkovich, "Soviet Jewry and American Foreign Policy,"*World Policy Journal* 5, no. 3 (Summer 1988): 458, www.jstor.org/stable/40209090.

13. Memorandum of Conversation, "Cabinet Meeting," February 21, 1974, National Security Adviser's Memoranda of Conversations, 1973–1977, Box 3, Gerald R. Ford Library, http://fordlibrarymuseum.gov/library/document/memcons/1552663.pdf.

14. Memorandum of Conversation, "Cabinet Meeting: Briefing on Middle East," March 8, 1974, National Security Adviser's Memoranda of Conversations, 1973–1977, Box 3, Gerald R. Ford Library, http://fordlibrarymuseum.gov/library/document/0314/1552668.pdf.

15. Elliott Abrams, *Security and Sacrifice: Isolation, Intervention, and American Foreign Policy* (Indianapolis: Hudson Institute, 1995), 84.

16. David Samuels, "A Fourth of July Story."

17. Kaufman, *Henry M. Jackson*, 294.

18. Frederic C. Hof, "A Bad Defense for a Mistaken Policy," *Syria Source*, Atlantic Council, August 29, 2016, www.atlanticcouncil.org/blogs/syriasource/a-bad-defense-for-a-mistaken-policy.

19. "Clinton: Chinese Human Rights Can't Interfere with Other Crises," CNN, February 21, 2009, www.cnn.com/2009/POLITICS/02/21/clinton.china.asia/?iref=nextin.

20. Hillary Rodham Clinton, "Remarks on Development in the 21st Century," January 6, 2010, transcript, U.S. Department of State, www.state.gov/secretary/20092013clinton/rm/2010/01/134838.htm.

21. Natan Sharansky with Ron Dermer, *The Case for Democracy* (New York: Public Affairs Books, 2006), 95.

22. Natan Sharansky, "Peace Will Only Come after Freedom and Democracy," *Middle East Quarterly* 12, no. 1 (Winter 2005), www.meforum.org/666/natan-sharansky-peace-will-only-come-after.

23. Sandra Vogelgesang, "What Price Principle? U.S. Policy on Human Rights," *Foreign Affairs* 56, no. 4 (January 1978): 820, www.foreignaffairs.com/articles/1978–07–01/what-price-principle-us-policy-human-rights.

24. Ibid., 825.

25. Quoted in Jeane J. Kirkpatrick, "Human Rights and Foreign Policy," in *Human Rights and American Foreign Policy*, Fred E. Baumann, ed. (Gambier, Kenyon College, 1982), 1.

26. William F. Buckley Jr., "Human Rights and Foreign Policy: A Proposal," *Foreign Affairs* 58, no. 4 (Spring 1980): 780, www.foreignaffairs.com/articles/1980–03–01/human-rights-and-foreign-policy-proposal.

27. Ibid., 783.

28. Jimmy Carter, "Inaugural Address," January 20, 1977, transcript, American Presidency Project, University of California-Santa Barbara, www.presidency.ucsb.edu/ws/?pid=6575.

29. Jimmy Carter, "Address at Commencement Exercises at University of Notre Dame," May 22, 1977, transcript, American Presidency Project, University of California-Santa-Barbara, www.presidency.ucsb.edu/ws/?pid=7552.

30. Presidential Directive NSC-30, February 17, 1978, Jimmy Carter Presidential Library, http://www.jimmycarterlibrary.gov/documents/pddirectives/pd30.pdf.

31. Lincoln Bloomfield, "From Ideology to Program to Policy: Tracking the Carter Human Rights Policy," *Journal of Policy Analysis and Management* 2, no. 1 (Autumn 1982): 8, www.jstor.org/stable/3323646?seq=1#page_scan_tab_contents.

32. Jimmy Carter and Reza Pahlavi, "Tehran, Iran, Toasts of the President and the Shah at a State Dinner," December 31, 1977, transcript, American Presidency Project, University of California-Santa Barbara, www.presidency.ucsb.edu/ws/?pid=7080

33. Bloomfield, "From Ideology to Program to Policy," 9.

34. Karen de Young, "Newly Declassified Papers Reveal U.S. tensions regarding Argentina's 'Dirty War,'" *Washington Post*, August 8, 2016, www.washingtonpost.com/world/national-security/newly-declassified-papers-reveal-us-tensions-regarding-argentinas-dirty-war/2016/08/08/4227fbee-5db1–11e6-af8e-54aa2e849447_story.html.

35. Cyrus Vance, "Human Rights and Foreign Policy," April 30, 1977, transcript, U.S. Department of State, https://history.state.gov/historicaldocuments/frus1977–80v01/d37.

36. Jimmy Carter, "Address at Commencement Exercises at University of Notre Dame."

37. Kirkpatrick, "Human Rights and Foreign Policy," 4–5.

38. Jimmy Carter, "The President's News Conference," March 24, 1977, transcript, American Presidency Project, University of California-Santa Barbara, www.presidency.ucsb.edu/ws/index.php?pid=7229.

39. Jimmy Carter, "The President's News Conference," June 13, 1977, transcript, American Presidency Project, University of California-Santa Barbara, www.presidency.ucsb.edu/ws/index.php?pid=7670.

40. "Carter in Warsaw, Starting 9-Day Tour," *New York Times*, December 30, 1977, www.nytimes.com/1977/12/30/archives/new-jersey-pages-carter-in-warsaw-starting-9day-tour-says-old.html.

41. Paul C. Warnke, "Apes on a Treadmill," *Foreign Policy* no. 18 (Spring 1975): 12–29, www.jstor.org/stable/1147960.

42. Edward C. Burks, "Moynihan: How He Won His Senate Spurs," *New York Times*, April 5, 1977, www.nytimes.com/1977/04/05/archives/moynihan-how-he-won-his-senate-spurs-initiation-of-senator-moynihan.html.

43. Jimmy Carter, "Visit of President Josip Broz Tito of Yugoslavia, Remarks at the Welcoming Ceremony," March 7, 1978, transcript, American Presidency Project, the University of California-Santa Barbara, www.presidency.ucsb.edu/ws/?pid=30462.

44. Jimmy Carter, "Visit of President Nicolae Ceausescu of Romania, Remarks at the Welcoming Ceremony," April 12, 1978, transcript, American Presidency Project, the University of California-Santa Barbara, www.presidency.ucsb.edu/ws/?pid=30655.

45. Henry M. Jackson, "The Balance of Power and the Future of Freedom," April 24, 1978, quoted in Kaufman, *Henry M. Jackson*, 371.

46. Kaufman, *Henry M. Jackson*, 370–371.

47. "Dr. Condoleezza Rice Discusses President's National Security Strategy," October 1, 2002, transcript, George W. Bush Presidential Library, National Archives, https://georgewbush-whitehouse.archives.gov/news/releases/2002/10/20021001-6.html.

48. Robert Kagan and William Kristol, "National Interest and Global Responsibility," in *Present Dangers: Crisis and Opportunity in American Foreign and Defense Policy*, eds. Robert Kagan and William Kristol (San Francisco: Encounter Books, 2000), 24.

49. Quoted in Shirley Christian, *Nicaragua: Revolution in the Family* (New York: Random House, 1985), 69, 76.

50. Patricia Derian, *Secret Memorandum from Assistant Secretary of State Patricia Derian to Acting Secretary Warren Christopher*, June 18, 1979, cited in Robert Kagan, *A Twilight Struggle: American Power and Nicaragua, 1977–1990* (New York: Free Press, 1996), 746.

51. Jeane Kirkpatrick, "Dictatorships and Double Standards, *Commentary*, November 1, 1979, www.commentarymagazine.com/articles/dictatorships-double-standards.

52. Irving Kristol, "'Moral Dilemmas' in Foreign Policy," *Wall Street Journal*, February 28, 1980, http://search.proquest.com/hnpwallstreetjournal/docview/134428824/B92EDC12A92841CFPQ/1?accountid=10986.

53. Irving Kristol, "Toward a Moral Foreign Policy," *Wall Street Journal*, November 15, 1983, http://search.proquest.com/hnpwallstreetjournal/docview/134793803/5D26C45BA614B39PQ/1?accountid=10986.

54. Irving Kristol, "In Search of Our National Interest," *Wall Street Journal*, June 7, 1990, http://search.proquest.com/hnpwallstreetjournal/docview/135463649/FDBAB5EC80204B8EPQ/1?accountid=10986.

55. Justin Vaïsse, *Neoconservatism: The Biography of a Movement* (Cambridge, MA: Harvard University Press, 2011), 223.

56. "October 28, 1980 Debate Transcript," Commission on Presidential Debates, www .debates.org/index.php?page=october-28–1980-debate-transcript.

57. "Excerpts from Secretary of State Alexander M. Haig's News Conference," *New York Times*, January 28, 1981, www.nytimes.com/1981/01/29/world/excerpts-from-haig-s-remarks-at-first-news-conference-as-secretary-of.html?pagewanted=all.

58. *Testimony before House Foreign Affairs Committee, Subcommittee on International, Economic Policy and Trade*, July 12, 1979, quoted in Iain Guest, *Behind the Disappearances: Argentina's Dirty War against Human Rights and the United Nations* (Philadelphia: University of Pennsylvania Press, 1990), 280.

59. U.S. Department of State, *Action Memorandum from the Director of Policy Planning to the Secretary of State*, "The Human Rights Policy: An Interim Assessment," January 20, 1978, https://history.state.gov/historicaldocuments/frus1977–80v02/d105.

60. Hal Brands, *Making the Unipolar Moment* (Ithaca: Cornell University Press, 2016), 38.

61. Ibid., 79.

62. Multilateral development banks such as the World Bank or Inter-American Development Bank.

63. Kaufman, *Henry M. Jackson*, 408.

64. U.S. Department of State, *Country Reports on Human Rights Practices, 1981*, https://babel .hathitrust.org/cgi/pt?id=ien.35556011424686;view=1up;seq=22.

65. Ronald Reagan, "Address to Members of the British Parliament," June 8, 1982, transcript, Ronald Reagan Presidential Library, National Archives, https://reaganlibrary .archives.gov/archives/speeches/1982/60882a.htm.

66. Hauke Hartmann, "US Human Rights Policy under Carter and Reagan, 1977–1981," *Human Rights Quarterly* 23, no. 2, (May 2001): 403, http://muse.jhu.edu/article/ 13768.

67. Tamar Jacoby, "The Reagan Turnaround on Human Rights," *Foreign Affairs* 64, no. 5 (Summer 1986): 1076, www.foreignaffairs.com/articles/1986–06–01/reagan-turnaround-human-rights.

68. U.S. Department of State, *Country Reports on Human Rights Practices for 1982*, February 1983, https://babel.hathitrust.org/cgi/pt?id=mdp.39015014164753;view=1up;seq=1.

69. Guest, *Behind the Disappearances*, 295.

70. George P. Shultz, "Remarks to Conference on Democratization of Communist Countries," October 18, 1982, quoted in Kaufman, *Henry M. Jackson*, 125.

71. Ronald Reagan, "Remarks on Central America and El Salvador at the Annual Meeting of the National Association of Manufacturers," March 10, 1983, transcript, Ronald Reagan Presidential Library, National Archives, https://reaganlibrary.archives.gov/archives/ speeches/1983/31083a.htm.

72. George P. Shultz, *Turmoil and Triumph: My Years as Secretary of State* (New York: Charles Scribner's Sons, 1993), 404.

73. Brands, *Making the Unipolar Moment*, 138.

74. I have told that story in full in "The Gringos Are with Us," *Commentary Magazine*, April 2013.

75. Ibid., 147.

76. John M. Poindexter, *Memorandum for John M. Poindexter from Jacqueline Tillman, NSC Meeting on Chile, November 18, 1986*, cited in Morris Morley and Chris McGillion, *Reagan and Pinochet: The Struggle over US Policy toward Chile* (New York: Cambridge University Press, 2015), 194.

77. Peter Kornbluh and Marian Schlotterbeck, "How U.S. President Reagan Broke with Chile's Pinochet," *Santiago Times* (Santiago), November 30, 2010, www.santiagotimes .cl/2010/11/30/how-us-president-reagan-broke-with-chiles-pinochet/.

78. Quoted in Jacoby, "The Reagan Turnaround on Human Rights," 107–108.

79. Ibid.

80. "October 21, 1984 Debate Transcript," transcript, Commission on Presidential Debates, www.debates.org/index.php?page=october-21-1984-debate-transcript.

81. Brands, *Making the Unipolar Moment*, 159.

82. Editorial, "Mr. Reagan's Human Rights Conversion," *New York Times*, December 10, 1988, www.nytimes.com/1988/12/10/opinion/mr-reagan-s-human-rights-conversion .html.

83. Nestor Ratesh, "The American Connection," in *Romania, 40 Years (1944–1984)*, ed. Vlad Georgescu (New York: Praeger, 1985), 68; John Newhouse, *War and Peace in the Nuclear Age* (New York: Alfred A. Knopf, 1989), 339.

84. Shultz, *Turmoil and Triumph*, 1094.

85. Ibid., 586–587.

86. Ibid., 887.

87. Ronald Reagan, "Remarks at the Annual Convention of the National Association of Evangelicals," March 8, 1983, Ronald Reagan Presidential Library, National Archives, https://reaganlibrary.archives.gov/archives/speeches/1983/30883b.htm.

88. Ronald Reagan, "Remarks on East-West Relations at the Brandenburg Gate," June 12, 1987, transcript, Ronald Reagan Presidential Library, National Archives, https:// reaganlibrary.archives.gov/archives/speeches/1987/061287d.htm.

89. Quoted in Tom Wicker, *George Herbert Walker Bush* (New York: Penguin, 2004), 128–129.

90. Quoted in James Traub, *The Freedom Agenda: Why America Must Spread Democracy* (New York: Farrar, Straus and Giroux, 2009), 65.

91. U.S. Department of State, "Themes," June 29, 1989, Document 33 in "Tiananmen Square, 1989: The Declassified History," National Security Archive Electronic Briefing Book No. 16, National Security Archive, George Washington University, http:// nsarchive.gwu.edu/NSAEBB/NSAEBB16/docs/doc34.pdf.

92. "George H. W. Bush: Foreign Affairs."

93. Quoted in Tony Smith, *America's Mission: The United States and the Worldwide Struggle for Democracy* (Princeton: Princeton University Press, 1994), 320.

94. "The 1992 Campaign; Excerpts From Speech by Clinton on U.S. Role," *New York Times*, October 2, 1992, www.nytimes.com/1992/10/02/us/the-1992-campaign-excerpts-from-speech-by-clinton-on-us-role.html.

95. Susan L. Woodward, "Upside-Down Policy: The U.S. Debate on the Use of Force and the Case of Bosnia," in *The Use of Force after the Cold War*, ed. H. W. Brands (College Station: Texas A&M University Press, 2000), 115.

96. United Nations General Assembly (GA), Sixtieth Session, 2005 World Summit Outcome, ¶138–139, September 15, 2005, www.globalr2p.org/media/files/wsod_2005 .pdf.

97. Scott Neuman, "Clinton Aides Weighed Fallout of Calling Rwanda Killing 'Genocide,'" National Public Radio, August 31, 2016, www.npr.org/sections/thetwo-way/2014/06/ 06/319563918/clinton-aides-mulled-fallout-of-calling-rwanda-killing-genocide.

98. David Remnick, "The Wandered," *New Yorker*, September 18, 2006, www.newyorker .com/magazine/2006/09/18/the-wanderer-3.

99. Alan D. Hertzke, *Freeing God's Children: The Unlikely Alliance for Global Human Rights* (New York: Rowman & Littlefield, 2004), 239–240.

100. Ivo Daalder, "Decision to Intervene: How the War in Bosnia Ended," Brookings Institution, December 1, 1998, www.brookings.edu/articles/decision-to-intervene-how-the-war-in-bosnia-ended.

101. William Kristol and Robert Kagan, "Toward a Neo-Reaganite Foreign Policy," *Foreign Affairs* 75, no. 4 (July/August 1996), www.foreignaffairs.com/articles/1996–07–01/ toward-neo-reaganite-foreign-policy.

102. Kagan and Kristol, eds., *Present Dangers*, 17–20.

103. "October 11, 2000 Presidential Debate," October 11, 2000, transcript, Commission on Presidential Debates, www.debates.org/index.php?page=october-11–2000-debate-transcript.

104. Condoleezza Rice, "Campaign 2000: Promoting the National Interest," *Foreign Affairs* (January/February 2000), www.foreignaffairs.com/articles/2000–01–01/campaign-2000-promoting-national-interest.

105. "Condi Rice Talks Freedom, War, Working for Bush," Author Interviews, NPR, November 2, 2011, www.npr.org/2011/11/02/141931702/condi-rice-talks-freedom-war-working-for-bush.

106. Rice, *No Higher Honor: A Memoir of My Years in* Washington (New York: Crown Publishers, 2001), 307.

107. Ibid., 93–94.

108. George W. Bush (43rd President of the United States), in discussion with the author, November 2016.

109. George W. Bush, "Address Before a Joint Session of the Congress on the United States Response to the Terrorist Attacks of September 11," September 20, 2001, transcript, American Presidency Project, University of California-Santa Barbara, www.presidency .ucsb.edu/ws/index.php?pid=64731&st=&st1=.

110. George W. Bush, "State of the Union Address," January 29, 2002, transcript, George W. Bush Presidential Library, National Archives, https://georgewbush-whitehouse .archives.gov/news/releases/2002/01/20020129–11.html.

111. "U.S. President Bush's Speech to United Nations," CNN, November 10, 2001, http:// edition.cnn.com/2001/US/11/10/ret.bush.un.transcript/index.html.

112. The story of the *Karine A* and its influence on U.S. policy is told in my book *Tested by Zion: The Bush Administration and the Israeli-Palestinian Conflict* (New York: Cambridge University Press, 2013), 25–27.

113. "George W. Bush's Statement on the Middle East," *New York Times*, April 2, 2002, www.nytimes.com/2002/04/04/international/bushs-statement-on-the-middle-east .html.

114. George W. Bush, "President Bush Calls for New Palestinian Leadership," June 24, 2002, transcript, George W. Bush Presidential Library, National Archives, https:// georgewbush-whitehouse.archives.gov/news/releases/2002/06/20020624-3.html.

115. George W. Bush, "President George W. Bush Speaks at AEI's Annual Dinner," February 28, 2003, transcript, American Enterprise Institute, www.aei.org/publication/ president-george-w-bush-speaks-at-aeis-annual-dinner/.

116. George W. Bush, "Remarks by President George W. Bush at the Twentieth Anniversary of the National Endowment for Democracy," November 6, 2003, transcript, National Endowment for Democracy, www.ned.org/remarks-by-president- george-w-bush-at-the-20th-anniversary/.

117. Douglas Feith, quoted in Traub, *The Freedom Agenda*, 104.

118. Ibid., 125.

119. Ibid., 5.

120. Rice, *No Higher Honor*, 328.

121. Anne Marie Slaughter, "How to Succeed in a Networked World," *Foreign Affairs* 95 no. 6 (November/December, 2016): 89, www.foreignaffairs.com/articles/world/ 2016–10–04/how-succeed-networked-world.

122. "President Bush Delivers Remarks in Prague," *Washington Post*, June 5, 2007, www .washingtonpost.com/wp-dyn/content/article/2007/06/05/AR2007060500647 .html.

123. Ty McCormick, "Unmade in the USA," *Foreign Policy*, February 25, 2015, http:// foreignpolicy.com/2015/02/25/unmade-in-the-usa-south-sudan-bush-obama/.

124. Michael Abramowitz, "Olympics Notwithstanding, Trip Won't Be All Fun and Games," *Washington Post*, August 8, 2008, www.washingtonpost.com/wp-dyn/content/article/ 2008/08/03/AR2008080301785.html.

125. George W. Bush, "State of the Union Address," January 23, 2007, transcript, George W. Bush Presidential Library, National Archives, https://georgewbush-whitehouse .archives.gov/news/releases/2007/01/20070123-2.html.

126. George W. Bush, "State of the Union Address," January 28, 2008, transcript, George W. Bush Presidential Library, National Archives, https://georgewbush-whitehouse .archives.gov/news/releases/2008/01/20080128-13.html.

127. The story is told in more detail in my book, Tested by Zion: The Bush Administration and the Israeli-Palestinian Conflict, chapter 7.

128. Christine Spolar, "Egypt Reformer Feels Iron Hand of the Law," *Chicago Tribune*, March 6, 2006, http://articles.chicagotribune.com/2006–03–06/news/0603060129_ 1_ayman-nour-president-hosni-mubarak-egypt.

129. "President Bush Meets with President Hosni Mubarak of Egypt," January 16, 2008, transcript, George W. Bush Presidential Library, National Archives, https://georgewbush-whitehouse.archives.gov/news/releases/2008/01/20080116–2.html.

130. Matt Latimer, "When Bush Caved to Egypt," *Daily Beast*, January 30, 2011, www.thedailybeast.com/articles/2011/01/30/president-bush-pulled-his-punches-on-egypts-mubarak-too.html.

131. "President Bush Attends World Economic Forum," May 18, 2008, transcript, George W. Bush Presidential Library, National Archives, https://georgewbush-whitehouse.archives.gov/news/releases/2008/05/20080518–6.html.

132. Sheryl Gay Stolberg, "Bush's Speech Prods Middle Eastern Leaders," *New York Times*, May 19, 2008, www.nytimes.com/2008/05/19/world/middleeast/19prexy.html.

133. Latimer, "When Bush Caved to Egypt."

134. "President Bush Visits Prague, Czech Republic, Discusses Freedom," June 5, 2007, transcript, George W. Bush Presidential Library, National Archives, https://georgewbush-whitehouse.archives.gov/news/releases/2007/06/20070605–8.html.

135. George W. Bush (43rd President of the United States), in discussion with the author, November 2016.

136. Rice, *No Higher Honor*, 328.

137. See the discussion in Abrams, *Security and Sacrifice*, 95–143.

138. Rice, *No Higher Honor*, 325–326.

139. This is the argument Stephen Sestanovich makes in *Maximalist: America in the World from Truman to Obama* (New York: Knopf, 2014).

CHAPTER 1: THE ARAB SPRING

1. Marc Lynch, "Introduction," in *The Arab Uprisings Explained*, ed. Marc Lynch (New York: Columbia University Press, 2014), 4.

2. George W. Bush, "President Bush Discusses Freedom in Iraq and Middle East," White House, Office of the Press Secretary, November 6, 2003, http://georgewbush-whitehouse.archives.gov/news/releases/2003/11/20031106–2.html.

3. United Nations Development, *Arab Human Development Report 2002: Creating Opportunities for Future Generations* (New York: United Nations Publications, 2002), 2, 18. www.arab-hdr.org/publications/other/ahdr/ahdr2002e.pdf.

4. Seymour Martin Lipset, "Some Social Requisites of Democracy: Economic Development and Political Legitimacy," *American Political Science Review* 53 (1959): 86, www.jstor.org/stable/1951731.

5. Bernard Lewis, "Free at Last: The Arab World in the Twenty-First Century," *Foreign Affairs* 88, no. 2 (2009): 86–87, www.foreignaffairs.com/articles/middle-east/2009–03–01/free-last.

6. "2015 Edelman Trust Barometer," 2016. www.edelman.com/insights/intellectual-property/2016-edelman-trust-barometer/executive-summary. 2016.

7. "Towards the End of Poverty," *The Economist*, June 1, 2013, www.economist. com/news/leaders/21578665-nearly-1-billion-people-have-been-taken-out-extreme-poverty-20-years-world-should-aim.

8. Shantayanan Devarajan et al., "Inequality, Uprisings, and Conflict in the Arab World," *Middle East and North Africa Economic Monitor* (Washington, DC: World Bank Group, 2015): 25, 27, http://documents.worldbank.org/curated/en/303441467992017147/Inequality-uprisings-and-conflict-in-the-Arab-World.

9. Andrew Nathan, "China since Tiananmen: Authoritarian Impermanence," *Journal of Democracy* 20 (2009): 37–40, www.journalofdemocracy.org/sites/default/files/Nathan-20-3.pdf.

10. Ellen Lust, "Missing the Third Wave: Islam, Institutions, and Democracy in the Middle East," *Studies in Comparative International Development* 46 (2011): 165, http://link.springer.com/article/10.1007/s12116–011–9086-z

11. Khairi Abaza, "Political Islam and Regime Survival in Egypt," *Policy Focus no. 51* (Washington, DC: Washington Institute for Near East Policy, 2006), 15, www.washingtoninstitute.org/html/pdf/PolicyFocus51.pdf.

12. Saad Eddin Ibrahim, "Toward Muslim Democracies," *Journal of Democracy* 18, no. 2 (2007): 9–10, www.journalofdemocracy.org/article/toward-muslim-democracies.

13. Stephen R. Grand, *Understanding Tahrir Square: What Transitions Elsewhere Can Teach Us about the Prospects for Arab Democracy* (Washington, DC: Brookings Institution Press, 2014), 22.

14. Lucan Way, "The Lessons of 1989," in *Democratization and Authoritarianism in the Arab World*, eds. Larry Diamond and Marc Plattner (Baltimore: Johns Hopkins University Press, 2014), 157.

15. Jason Brownlee, Tarek Masoud, and Andrew Reynolds, "Why the Modest Harvest?" *Journal of Democracy* 24, no. 4 (2013): 30, www.journalofdemocracy.org/article/tracking-arab-spring-why-modest-harvest.

16. Bahgat Korany, Rex Brynen, and Paul Noble, "Conclusion: Liberalization, Democratization, and Arab Experiences," in *Political Liberalization and Democratization in the Arab World* vol. II, eds. Bahgat Korany, Rex Brynen, and Paul Noble (Boulder: Lynne Rienner Publishers, 1998), 276.

17. Shadi Hamid, *Temptations of Power: Islamists and Illiberal Democracy in a New Middle East* (New York: Oxford University Press, 2014), 4.

18. CNN Wire Staff, "Muslim Brotherhood: 'We Are Not Seeking Power,'" *CNN*, February 10, 2011, www.cnn.com/2011/WORLD/africa/02/09/egypt.muslim.brotherhood/.

19. Jocelyne Cesari, *The Awakening of Muslim Democracy: Religion, Modernity, and the State* (New York: Cambridge University Press, 2014), 167.

20. Hamid, *Islamic Exceptionalism*, 49.

21. Amichai Magen, "On Political Order and the 'Arab Spring,'" *Israel Journal of Foreign Affairs* 6, no. 1 (2012): 4, http://portal.idc.ac.il/FacultyPublication.Publication?PublicationID=1986&FacultyUserName=YW1pY2hhaW0=.

22. Ibid., 5.

23. Ibid., 9–10.
24. Anne Cary Morris, ed., *The Diary and Letters of Gouverneur Morris: Minister of the United States to France; Member of the Constitutional Convention, etc.*, Vol. I (New York: Charles Scribner's Sons, 1888), 114.
25. Magen, "On Political Order and the 'Arab Spring,'" 5–6.
26. Samuel Tadros, *Reflections on the Revolution in Egypt* (Stanford, CA: Hoover Institution Press, 2014), 68–69.
27. Grand, *Understanding Tahrir Square*, 79.
28. Natan Sharansky and Ron Dermer, *The Case for Democracy* (New York: Public Affairs Books, 2006), 38.
29. Michael Robbins and Mark Tessler, "Arab Views on Governance after the Uprisings," *Washington Post*, October 29, 2014, www.washingtonpost.com/blogs/monkey-cage/wp/2014/10/29/arab-views-on-governance-after-the-uprisings/.
30. Zogby Research Services, *Middle East 2016: Current Conditions and the Road Ahead*, prepared for the Sir Bani Yas Forum, November 2016, 10–11.
31. Robin Yassin-Kassab, "Burning Country: Syrians in Revolution and War," *The National*, July 25, 2016, www.thenational.ae/opinion/comment/against-all-odds-village-republics-take-hold-in-syria.
32. Michael Robbins, "After the Arab Spring: People Still Want Democracy," *Journal of Democracy* 26, no. 4 (2015), 80–83, www.journalofdemocracy.org/article/after-arab-spring-people-still-want-democracy.
33. Mark Tessler, Amaney Jamal, and Michael Robbins, "New Findings on Arabs and Democracy," in *Democracy and Authoritarianism in the Arab World*, eds. Larry Diamond and Marc Plattner (Baltimore: Johns Hopkins University Press, 2014), 55.
34. Amaney Jamal and Mark Tessler, "Measuring Support for Democracy in the Arab World and across the Globe," *Arab Barometer*, arabbarometer.org/sites/default/files/files/measuringsupport.pdf.
35. Grand, *Understanding Tahrir Square*, 176–177.
36. Ibid., 180.

CHAPTER 2: ARAB AND MUSLIM DEMOCRACY

1. Francis Fukuyama, *The End of History and the Last Man* (New York: Free Press, 1992), 42–48.
2. Ibid., 45–46.
3. Alfred Stepan and Graeme Robertson, "An 'Arab' More than 'Muslim' Electoral Gap," *Journal of Democracy* 14, no. 3 (2003): 33, https://muse.jhu.edu/article/44541.
4. Alfred Stepan and Graeme B. Robertson, "Arab, Not Muslim, Exceptionalism," *Journal of Democracy* 15, no. 4 (2004): 146, https://muse.jhu.edu/article/174006.
5. Sanford Lakoff, "The Reality of Muslim Exceptionalism," *Journal of Democracy* 15, no. 4 (2004): 138, www.journalofdemocracy.org/article/reality-muslim-exceptionalism.

6. Stepan and Robertson, "An 'Arab' More than 'Muslim' Electoral Gap," 41.

7. Etel Solingen, "Transcending Disciplinary Divides: A Comparative Framework on the International Relations of the Middle East," *Project on Middle East Political Science*, August 31, 2015, http://pomeps.org/2015/08/31/transcending-disciplinary-divides-a-comparative-framework-on-the-international-relations-of-the-middle-east.

8. Robert Springborg, "Arab Militaries," in *The Arab Uprisings Explained*, ed. Marc Lynch (New York: Columbia University Press, 2014), 143.

9. Robert Springborg, "Arab Armed Forces; State Makers or State Breakers," www.mei.edu/content/at/arab-armed-forces-state-makers-or-state-breakers.

10. Tadros, *Reflections on the Revolution in Egypt*, 68–69.

11. Courtney Freer, *The Rise of Pragmatic Islamism in Kuwait's Post-Arab Spring Opposition Movement* (Washington, DC: Brookings Institution, August 2015), www.brookings.edu/wp-content/uploads/2016/07/Kuwait_Freer-FINALE.pdf, 14.

12. Hamid, *Temptations of Power*, 30.

13. Cesari, *The Awakening of Muslim Democracy*, xiv.

14. Ibid., 3.

15. Freer, "The Rise of Pragmatic Islamism," 5.

16. Ibid., 11.

17. Olivier Roy, "The Transformation of the Arab World," in *Democracy and Authoritarianism in the Arab World*, eds. Larry Diamond and Marc Plattner (Baltimore: Johns Hopkins University Press, 2014), 16–17.

18. Fareed Zakaria, "The Rise of Illiberal Democracy," *Foreign Affairs* 76, no. 6 (1997): 22–43, www.foreignaffairs.com/articles/1997-11-01/rise-illiberal-democracy.

19. Roy, "The Transformation of the Arab World," 16–17.

20. Hamid, *Temptations of Power*, 26, 205.

CHAPTER 3: WILL THE ISLAMISTS ALWAYS WIN?

1. Hamid, *Temptations of Power*, 16.

2. Scott Shane, "Cables from American Diplomats Portray U.S. Ambivalence on Tunisia," *New York Times*, January 15, 2011, www.nytimes.com/2011/01/16/world/africa/16cables.html?_r=0.

3. Shadi Hamid, *Islamic Exceptionalism: How the Struggle over Islam Is Reshaping the World* (New York: Macmillan, 2016), 196–197.

4. Marwan Muasher, *The Second Arab Awakening and the Battle for Pluralism* (New Haven: Yale University Press, 2014), 34–35.

5. Steven Brooke, *The Muslim Brotherhood's Social Outreach after the Egyptian Coup* (Washington, DC: Brookings Institution, August 2015), www.brookings.edu/wp-content/uploads/2016/07/Egypt_Brooke-FINALE-2.pdf, 3.

6. Melanie Cammett and Pauline Jones Luong, "Is There an Islamist Political Advantage," *Annual Review of Political Science* 17 (2014): 8, www.annualreviews.org/doi/pdf/10.1146/annurev-polisci-071112-221207.

7. Ibid., 2.

8. Ibid.

9. Tarek Masoud, "Why Do Islamists Provide Services, and What Do Those Services Do?" *Project on Middle East Political Science* 9 (2014), 27. http://pomeps.org/wp-content/uploads/2014/10/POMEPS_Studies_9_SocialServices_web.pdf.

10. Cesari, *The Awakening of Muslim Democracy*, 211.

11. Cammett and Luong, "Is There an Islamist Political Advantage," 4, 15.

12. The exceptions, to which I will return, are labor unions and parties that are based on or include support from unions. They may well have broad outreach, and their role in Tunisia was critical in winning and maintaining a transition to democracy.

13. Catriona Croft-Cusworth, "Indonesia's Election: Surprise Success for Islamic Parties," *The Interpreter*, April 18, 2014, www.lowyinterpreter.org/post/2014/04/18/Indonesias-election-Surprise-success-for-Islamic-parties.aspx?COLLCC=3609281719&.

14. Eric Trager, *Arab Fall: How the Muslim Brotherhood Won and Lost Egypt in 891 Days* (Washington, DC: Georgetown University Press, 2016), 4.

15. Samuel Tadros, "Egypt's Elections: Why the Islamists Won," *World Affairs Journal* (2012), www.worldaffairsjournal.org/article/egypt%E2%80%99s-elections-why-islamists-won.

16. Elliott Abrams, "Is 'Insulting the President' or Converting to Christianity a Crime?" *Pressure Points* (blog), *Council on Foreign Relations*, January 23, 2013, http://blogs.cfr.org/abrams/2013/01/23/is-insulting-the-president-or-converting-to-christianity-a-crime/; Arabic Network for Human Rights Information, "The Crime of Insulting the President: A Crime of an Authoritarian Regime," January 20, 2013, http://anhri.net/?lang=en.

17. "Democrat or Sultan?" *The Economist*, June 8, 2013, www.economist.com/news/leaders/21579004-recep-tayyip-erdogan-should-heed-turkeys-street-protesters-not-dismiss-them-democrat-or-sultan.

18. Robbins and Tessler, "Arab Views on Governance after the Uprisings."

19. Muasher, *The Second Arab Awakening and the Battle for Pluralism*, 185.

20. Trager, *Arab Fall*, 155.

21. Hamid, *Temptations of Power*, 6.

22. Quinn Mecham, "Islamist Movements," in *The Arab Uprisings Explained*, ed. Marc Lynch (New York: Columbia University Press, 2014), 213–215.

23. Cesari, *The Awakening of Muslim Democracy*, 219–220.

24. Rachid Ghannouchi, *Tunisia's New Political Order* (Washington, DC: Woodrow Wilson Center, February 24, 2014), www.wilsoncenter.org/article/ghannouchi-tunisias-new-political-order.

25. Monica Marks, *Tunisia's Ennahda: Rethinking Islamism in the Context of ISIS and the Egyptian Coup* (Washington, DC: Brookings Institution, August, 2015), www.brookings.edu/wp-content/uploads/2016/07/Tunisia_Marks-FINALE-5.pdf, 12.

26. Monica Marks, "How Big Were the Changes Tunisia's Ennahda Party Just Made at Its National Congress?" *Washington Post*, May 25, 2016, www.washingtonpost.com/news/monkey-cage/wp/2016/05/25/how-big-were-the-changes-made-at-tunisias-ennahda-just-made-at-its-national-congress/

27. Monica Marks, "A Response to Sayida Ounissi's 'Ennahda from Within: Islamists or Muslim Democrats?'" in *Rethinking Political Islam* (Washington, DC: Brookings Institution, June 1, 2016), www.brookings.edu/~/media/research/files/reports/2015/07/rethinking-political-islam/reaction-essays/monicamarks_re2sayidaounissi3.pdf.
28. Ibid.
29. Sarah Souli, "Why Tunisia's Top Islamist Party Rebranded Itself," *Al-Monitor*, May 23, 2016, www.al-monitor.com/pulse/originals/2016/05/tunisia-ennahda-islamist-party-rebranding-congress.html.
30. Sayida Ounissi, "Ennahda from Within: Islamists or 'Muslim Democrats?'" in *Rethinking Political Islam* (Washington, DC: Brookings Institution, February 2016), www.brookings.edu/research/papers/2016/03/ennahda-islamists-muslim-democrats-ounissi.
31. David Siddartha Patel, *The More Things Change, the More They Stay the Same: Jordanian Islamist Responses to the Arab Spring* (Washington, DC: Brookings Institution, August 2015), 1–6, www.brookings.edu/wp-content/uploads/2016/07/Jordan_Patel-FINALE.pdf.
32. Freer, "The rise of Pragmatic Islamism," 2–12.
33. Avi Spiegel, *Succeeding by Surviving: Examining the Durability of Political Islam in Morocco* (Washington, DC: Brookings Institution August 2015), www.brookings.edu/wp-content/uploads/2016/07/Morocco_Spiegel-FINALE.pdf, 3–12.
34. Jamie O'Connell, "Common Interests, Closer Allies: How Democracy in Arab States Can Benefit the West," *Stanford Journal of International Law* 48, no. 2 (2012): 377, 387.
35. O'Connell, "Common Interests, Closer Allies," 395–396.
36. Hamid, *Temptations of Power*, 177.
37. Ibid., 188.
38. Ibid., 36.
39. Ibid., 117.
40. Steven Brooke, "The Muslim Brotherhood's Social Outreach after the Egyptian Coup," 1–4. But see Ammar Fayed, *Is the Crackdown on the Muslim Brotherhood Pushing the Group toward Violence?* (Washington, DC: Brookings Institution, March 2016), www.brookings.edu/research/papers/2016/03/muslim-brotherhood-crackdown-violence-fayed, arguing that violence is still not the Brotherhood's likely path.
41. "Foreign Travel Advice: Egypt," Government of the United Kingdom, www.gov.uk/foreign-travel-advice/egypt/terrorism.
42. "Egypt," Government of Canada, https://travel.gc.ca/destinations/egypt.
43. "Egypt Travel Warning, U.S. Department of State, https://travel.state.gov/content/passports/en/alertswarnings/egypt-travel-warning.html.
44. "Egypt," U.S. Department of State, Bureau of Consular Affairs, https://travel.state.gov/content/passports/en/country/egypt.html.
45. Samuel Tadros, "The Brotherhood Divided," Hudson Institute, August 20, 2015, www.hudson.org/research/11530-the-brotherhood-divided.
46. Roy, "The Transformation of the Arab World," 16–17.
47. Fayed, "Is the Crackdown on the Muslim Brotherhood Pushing The Group toward Violence?"

48. Eric Trager et al., "Islamists in Government: Do They Moderate once in Power?" Washington Institute for Near East Policy, May 1, 2014, www.washingtoninstitute.org/policy-analysis/view/islamists-in-government-do-they-moderate-once-in-power

49. Daniel Pipes, "Distinguishing between Islam and Islamism," June 30, 1998, www.danielpipes.org/954/distinguishing-between-islam-and-islamism.

50. Elie Kedourie, *Democracy and Arab Political Culture* (Portland: Frank Cass, 1994), 95.

51. Larry Diamond, *The Spirit of Democracy* (New York: Holt, 2008), 285.

52. Grand, *Understanding Tahrir Square*, 196.

53. Abrams, *Tested by Zion*, 143, 145.

54. Robbins and Tessler, "Arab Views on Governance after the Uprisings."

CHAPTER 4: THE TROUBLE WITH U.S. POLICY

1. Sarah Bush, "Forms of International Pressure and the Middle East," Project on Middle East Political Science, August 21, 2015, http://pomeps.org/2015/08/21/forms-of-international-pressure-and-the-middle-east/.

2. Alan B. Krueger and Jitka Maleckova, "Seeking the Roots of Terrorism," *Chronicle of Higher Education: The Chronicle Review* (2003).

3. See Michael McFaul and Francis Fukuyama, "Should Democracy Be Promoted or Demoted?," *Washington Quarterly* 31, no. 1 (2008), 23–45.

4. Shadi Hamid and Steven Brooke, "Promoting Democracy to Stop Terror, Revisited," *Policy Review*, Hoover Institution, February and March 2010, www.hoover.org/research/promoting-democracy-stop-terror-revisited. See also Alberto Abadie, "Poverty, Political Freedom, and the Roots of Terrorism," National Bureau of Economic Research, Working Paper 10859, May 2006, www.nber.org/papers/w10859.pdf, which found that "[o]ver most of the range of the political rights index, lower levels of political rights are associated with higher levels of terrorism."

5. George W. Bush, "Remarks By President Bush on the 20th Anniversary of the National Endowment for Democracy."

6. George W. Bush, Second Inaugural Address, January 20, 2005.

7. Thomas F. Farr, *World of Faith and Freedom* (New York: Oxford University Press, 2008), 205–207.

8. Michele Dunne, "Evaluating Egyptian Reform," Carnegie Endowment for International Peace, *Carnegie Papers* 66 (2006): 3, http://carnegieendowment.org/files/CP66.Dunne.FINAL.pdf.

9. Khairi Abaza, "Political Islam and Regime Survival in Egypt," Washington Institute for Near East Policy, *Policy Focus* 51 (2006): iv–vi, http://www.washingtoninstitute.org/html/pdf/PolicyFocus51.pdf.

10. George W. Bush, "Statement on President Congratulating Egyptian President Mubarak on Election," (Washington, DC: White House, Office of the Press Secretary, September 10, 2005), http://georgewbush-whitehouse.archives.gov/news/releases/2005/09/text/20050910–11.html.

11. Traub, *The Freedom Agenda*, 164.

12. Ibid., 164, 235.

13. Ibid., 131.

14. Ibid., 129–130.

15. Condoleezza Rice, "Remarks at the American University in Cairo," United States Department of State, June 20, 2005, http://2001–2009.state.gov/secretary/rm/2005/48328.htm.

16. "Bush Speaks with Libya's Gaddafi in Historic Phone Call," *Washington Post*, www.washingtonpost.com/wp-dyn/content/article/2008/11/17/AR2008111702975.html.

17. Helene Cooper, "Isolation over, Libyan Leader Meets with Rice," *New York Times*, September 5, 2008, www.nytimes.com/2008/09/06/world/africa/06diplo.html?_r=0.

18. Elise Labott, "Rice, Gadhafi's Son to Meet, Officials Say," *CNN*, November 17, 2008, www.cnn.com/2008/WORLD/africa/11/17/libya.rice.gadhafi.

19. Sudarsan Raghavan, "Saif al-Islam al-Gaddafi, a Proponent of Change, May One Day Lead Libya," *Washington Post*, May 26, 2010, www.washingtonpost.com/wp-dyn/content/article/2010/05/25/AR2010052505143.html.

20. Becky Anderson, *CNN*, May 26, 2010, http://transcripts.cnn.com/TRANSCRIPTS/1005/26/ctw.01.html.

21. In the Oval Office before the press, Bush called for freedom of the press and an "open political process," and the video was posted on YouTube as "humiliation of Ben Ali by Bush," www.youtube.com/watch?v=qlJ0Ic9nyFI?

22. *Country Reports on Human Rights Practices, 2004, Tunisia*, U.S. Department of State, www.state.gov/j/drl/rls/hrrpt/2004/41733.htm?

23. Abdul Karim Bangura, *Stakes in Africa-United States Cooperation: Proposals for Equitable Partnership* (New York: The African Institution, 2007), 77.

24. Jeremy M. Sharp, "Yemen: Background and U.S. Relations," Congressional Research Service, February 11, 2015, www.fas.org/sgp/crs/mideast/RL34170.pdf.

25. Simon Henderson, "Fighting al-Qaeda: The Role of Yemen's President Saleh," Washington Institute for Near East Policy, January 7, 2010, www.washingtoninstitute.org/policy-analysis/view/fighting-al-qaeda-the-role-of-yemens-president-saleh.

26. "Yemen President Leads Vote Count," *BBC*, September 20, 2006, http://news.bbc.co.uk/2/hi/middle_east/5362592.stm.

27. EU Election Observation Mission, Yemen 2006, "Final Report on the Presidential and Local Council Elections," www.eods.eu/library/FR%20YEMEN%202006_en.pdf?.

28. Gregory Johnsen, "The Election Yemen Was Supposed to Have," Middle East Research and Information Project, October 3, 2006, www.merip.org/mero/mero100306.

29. "President Bush Visits Prague, Czech Republic, Discusses Freedom," https://georgewbush-whitehouse.archives.gov/news/releases/2007/06/20070605–8.html.

30. Traub, *The Freedom Agenda*, 171.

31. Michele Dunne, Amr Hamzawy, and Nathan Brown, *Egypt – Don't Give up on Democracy Promotion*, Policy Brief no. 52 (Washington, DC: Carnegie Endowment for International Peace, 2007), 1, 4, http://carnegieendowment.org/files/pb_52_egypt_final.pdf.

32. The evolution of Egypt policy is discussed in the introduction.

33. Joel Brinkley, "How 'Democracy' Got to Be a Dirty Word," *SFGate*, April 5, 2009, www .sfgate.com/opinion/article/How-democracy-got-to-be-a-dirty-word-3165842.php.

34. Traub, *The Freedom Agenda*, 247.

35. "Clinton: Chinese Human Rights Can't Interfere with Other Crises," CNN, February 21, 2009, www.cnn.com/2009/POLITICS/02/21/clinton.china.asia/#cnnSTCText.

36. Fawaz A. Gerges, *Obama and the Middle East: The End of America's Moment?* (New York: Palgrave Macmillan, 2012), 9, 103–104, 158.

37. Jason Brownlee, *Democracy Prevention: The Politics of the U.S.-Egyptian Alliance* (New York: Cambridge University Press, 2012), 170.

38. Katie Sanders, "Chris Wallace: Hillary Clinton Defended Syria's Assad as a 'Possible Reformer,'" *Politifact*, June 1, 2014, www.politifact.com/punditfact/statements/2014/ jun/01/chris-wallace/chris-wallace-hillary-clinton-defended-syrias-assa/.

39. Trager, *The Freedom Agenda*, 88, 170, 185.

40. Thomas Carothers, "Why Is the United States Shortchanging Its Commitment to Democracy?" *Washington Post*, December 22, 2014, www.washingtonpost.com/ opinions/falling-usaid-spending-shows-a-lack-of-commitment-to-fostering-democracy/ 2014/12/22/86b72d58–89f4–11e4-a085–34e9b9f09a58_story.html?wpisrc=nl_opin& wpmm=1.

41. Thomas Carothers, "Democracy Aid at 25: A Time to Choose," *Journal of Democracy* 26, no. 1 (2015): 71, http://muse.jhu.edu/article/565639/pdf.

42. Peter Baker and Jacey Fortin, "Obama, in Ethiopia, Calls Its Government 'Democrat- ically Elected,'" *New York Times*, July 27, 2015, www.nytimes.com/2015/07/28/world/ africa/obama-calls-ethiopian-government-democratically-elected.html?_r=0.

43. Frances Burwell, Danya Greenfield, and Amy Hawthorne, *A Transatlantic Approach to the Arab World, Issue in Focus* (Washington, DC: Atlantic Council, 2015), 1, www .atlanticcouncil.org/images/files/Transatlantic_Approach_to_the_Arab_World_ 1–14–15_web.pdf.

44. McCormick, "Unmade in the USA."

45. Thomas Carothers, *Democratization Policy under Obama: Revitalization or Retreat?* (Wash- ington, DC: Carnegie Endowment for International Peace, 2012), 37, http:// carnegieendowment.org/files/democracy_under_obama.pdf.

46. Burwell, Greenfield, and Hawthorne, *A Transatlantic Approach to the Arab World*, 2.

47. Grand, *Understanding Tahrir Square*, 199.

48. Ibid., 180, 184.

49. Thomas Carothers and Saskia Brechenmacher, *Closing Space: Democracy and Human Rights Support under Fire* (Washington, DC: Carnegie Endowment for International Peace, 2014), 27–28.

50. See Michele Dunne, "Caught in History's Crossroads," *Journal of Democracy* 26, no. 4, (2015): 75–79; and Mieczyslaw P. Boduszyński, Kristin Fabbe, and Christopher Lam- ont, "After the Arab Spring: Are Secular Parties the Answer?" *Journal of Democracy* 26, no. 4 (2015): 125–139, www.journalofdemocracy.org/article/after-arab-spring-are- secular-parties-answer.

51. Princeton N. Lyman, "Mandela's Legacy at Home and Abroad," *Journal of Democracy* 25, no. 2 (2014): 22–31, www.journalofdemocracy.org/article/mandela%E2%80%99s-legacy-home-and-abroad.

52. Marina Ottaway, *Democracy and Constituencies in the Arab World*, Carnegie Papers, Middle East Series, No. 48, July 2004, 4.

53. Thomas Carothers, *Aiding Democracy Abroad: The Learning Curve* (Washington, DC: Carnegie Endowment for International Peace, 1999), 248, http://carnegieendowment.org/1999/12/31/aiding-democracy-abroad-learning-curve-pub-99.

54. Thomas Carothers, *Critical Mission: Essays on Democracy Promotion Curve* (Washington, DC: Carnegie Endowment for International Peace, 2004), 100–101.

55. Carothers, *Aiding Democracy Abroad*, 247–248.

56. Quinn Mecham, "Islamist Movements," 190. See also Vickie Langhor, "Labor Movements or Organizations," in Marc Lynch, *The Arab Uprisings Explained*, 180–181.

57. See, for example, Sarah Chayes, *How a Leftist Labor Union Helped Force Tunisia's Political Settlement* (Washington, DC: Carnegie Endowment for International Peace, March 27, 2014), http://carnegieendowment.org/2014/03/27/how-leftist-labor-union-helped-force-tunisia-s-political-settlement; and Hala al-Youssoufi, "Tunisia Labor Union Serves as Political mediator," *al-Monitor*, March 14, 2014, www.al-monitor.com/pulse/politics/2014/03/tunisia-labor-union-political-balance.html.

58. Marc Lynch, "Media, Old and New," in *The Arab Uprisings Explained*, ed. Marc Lynch (New York: Columbia University Press, 2014), 93–109.

59. Bayard Rustin, "From Protest to Politics: The Future of the Civil Rights Movement," *Commentary Magazine*, February 1965, www.commentarymagazine.com/articles/from-protest-to-politics-the-future-of-the-civil-rights-movement/.

60. Larry Diamond, "From Activism to Democracy," in *Taking to the Streets: The Transformation of Arab Activism*, eds. Lina Khatib and Ellen Lust (Baltimore: Johns Hopkins University Press, 2014), 324.

61. Jason Brownlee, Tarek Masoud, and Andrew Reynolds, *The Arab Spring* (New York: Oxford University Press, 2015), 186.

62. Dankwart Rustow, "Transitions to Democracy: Towards a Dynamic Model," *Comparative Politics* 2 (1970): 337, www.jstor.org/stable/421307.

63. Brownlee, Masoud, and Reynolds, *The Arab Spring*, 204.

64. Steven Levitsky and Lucan A. Way, *Competitive Authoritarianism: Hybrid Regimes after the Cold War* (New York: Cambridge University Press, 2010), 42.

65. United Nations Development Program, *Arab Human Development Report 2004*.

66. Larbi Sadiki, *Rethinking Arab Democratization: Elections without Democracy* (New York: Oxford University Press, 2011), 81, 277, 156.

67. Grand, *Understanding Tahrir Square*, 169.

68. Isobel Coleman and Terra Lawson-Remer, *Pathways to Freedom: Political and Economic Lessons from Democratic Transitions* (New York: Council on Foreign Relations Press, 2013), 5–6, 22.

69. Levitsky and Way, *Competitive Authoritarianism*, 358.

70. Carothers, *Critical Mission*, 222.

71. Kenneth Wollack, "Retaining the Human Dimension," in *Critical Mission: Essays on Democracy Promotion Curve*, ed. Thomas Carothers (Washington, DC: Carnegie Endowment for International Peace, 2004), 201–202.

72. Samuel Tadros, *Reflections on the Revolution in Egypt*, 25, 64, 62–63.

73. Quintan Wiktorowicz, "Civil Society as Social Control: State Power in Jordan," *Comparative Politics* 33:1 (2000): 43–45, 57–58, www.jstor.org/stable/422423.

74. Carothers, *Closing Space*, 28.

75. Sarah Sunn Bush, *The Taming of Democracy Assistance: Why Democracy Promotion Does Not Confront Dictators* (New York: Cambridge University Press, 2015).

76. Office of Inspector General, "Audit of USAID/Egypt's Democracy and Governance Activities," Audit Report No. 6–263–10–001-P, October 27, 2009, 7, 11.

77. Sarah Bush, "Confront or Conform? Rethinking U.S. Democracy Assistance," Policy Brief, Project on Middle Eastern Democracy (2013), http://pomed.org/pomed/new-pomed-policy-brief-confront-or-conform-rethinking-u-s-democracy-assistance/.

78. Bush, *The Taming of Democracy Assistance*, 232.

79. Thomas Carothers, *The Closing Space Challenge: How Are Funders Responding* (Washington, DC: Carnegie Endowment for International Peace, 2015), 15, http://carnegieendowment.org/2015/11/02/closing-space-challenge-how-are-funders-responding-pub-61808.

80. "Congressional Budget Justification Fiscal Year 2016," Department of State, www.usaid.gov/sites/default/files/documents/9276/FY16CBJStateFORP.pdf.

81. "Political Parties," National Democratic Institute, www.ndi.org/political-parties?quicktabs_functional_area_tabs=0#quicktabs-functional_area_tabs.

82. Project on Middle East Democracy, "The Federal Budget and Appropriations for Fiscal Year 2017," April 2016, http://pomed.org/pomed-publications/fy17-budget-report/.

83. Congressional Research Service, "Millenium Challenge Corporation," April 5, 2016, www.fas.org/sgp/crs/row/RL32427.pdf.

84. A. David Adesnik and Sunhyuk Kim, "South Korea: *The Puzzle of Two Transitions*," in *Transitions to Democracy: A Comparative Perspective*, eds. Kathryn Stoner and Michael McFaul (Baltimore: Johns Hopkins University Press, 2013), 267–268.

CHAPTER 5: WHAT IS TO BE DONE?

1. Efraim Inbar, "The European Peace Offensive," *Israel Hayom*, June 1, 2015, www.israelhayom.com/site/newsletter_opinion.php?id=12739.

2. *Report of the Bahrain Independent Commission of Inquiry*, Bahrain Independent Commission of Inquiry, December 10, 2011, www.bici.org.bh/BICIreportEN.pdf.

3. Simon Henderson, "Royal Rivalry: Bahrain's Ruling Family and the Island's Political Crisis," *Policywatch 2198*, Washington Institute for Near East Policy, January 24, 2014, www.washingtoninstitute.org/policy-analysis/view/royal-rivalry-bahrains-ruling-family-and-the-islands-political-crisis. See also the discussion of the Bahraini crisis in Robert Gates's memoir, *Duty: Memoirs of a Secretary at War* (New York: Vintage, 2014).

4. Fredric Wehrey, "Saudi Arabia's Anxious Autocrats," in Larry Diamond, Marc F. Plattner, and Christopher Walker, eds. *Authoritarianism Goes Global* (Baltimore: Johns Hopkins University Press, 2016), 105.

5. Working Group on Egypt, "A Letter to Secretary Clinton from the Working Group on Egypt," April 7, 2010, http://carnegie-mec.org/2010/04/06/letter-to-secretary-clinton-from-working-group-on-egypt-pub-40535

6. Working Group on Egypt, "Protests in Egypt," Carnegie Endowment for International Peace, January 27, 2011, http://carnegieendowment.org/publications/index.cfm?fa=view&id=42387.

7. Adesnik and Kim, "South Korea: The Puzzle of Two Transitions," 286.

8. Fukuyama, *The End of History and the Last Man*, 280.

9. Smith, *America's Mission*, 355.

10. O'Connell, "Common Interests, Closer Allies," 395–396.

11. Thomas Carothers, "Is Gradualism Possible: Choosing a Strategy for Promoting Democracy in the Middle East," Carnegie Endowment for International Peace Democracy and Rule of Law Project 39, 2003, 13, http://carnegieendowment.org/files/wp39.pdf.

12. White House, "Strengthen Alliances to Defeat Global Terrorism and Work to Prevent Attacks against Us and Our Friends," http://georgewbush-whitehouse.archives.gov/nsc/nss/2006/sectionIII.html.

13. O'Connell, "Common Interests, Closer Allies," 377.

14. This distinction is explained very clearly in Adesnik and Kim, "South Korea: The Puzzle of Two Transitions," 266–289.

15. United Nations, *Arab Human Development Report 2002*, 18.

16. The quotation and the suggestion of possible demands are from Carothers, *Critical Mission*, 246.

17. Sarah Bush and Amaney Jamal, "Anti-Americanism, Authoritarianism, and Attitudes about Women in Politics: Evidence from a Survey Experiment in Jordan," paper presented at the 2011 Annual Meeting of the Middle East Studies Association, Washington, DC, December 2011.

18. Burwell, Greenfield, and Hawthorne, *A Transatlantic Approach to the Arab World*, 3–4.

19. Thomas A. Carothers, "Is the United States Giving up on Supporting Democracy Abroad?" *Foreign Policy*, September 8, 2016, http://foreignpolicy.com/2016/09/08/is-the-united-states-giving-up-on-supporting-democracy-abroad.

20. Adesnik and Kim, "South Korea: The Puzzle of Two Transitions," 274.

21. See, for example, Joel D. Barkan, "U.S. Human Rights Policy and Democratization in Kenya," in *Implementing U.S. Human Rights Policy: Agendas, Policies, and Practices*, ed. Debra Liang-Fenton (Washington, DC: USIP Press, 2004). He describes how the German and Scandinavian envoys followed the lead of the U.S. ambassador in making public demands for respect for democratic norms.

22. Carothers, "Democracy Aid at 25: A Time to Choose," 9.

23. Ibrahim, "Toward Muslim Democracies," 5–13.

24. Quoted in Shadi Hamid, *Temptations of Power*, 22–23; Jason Brownlee, *Democracy Prevention*, 10.

25. Diamond, *The Spirit of Democracy*, 85.
26. Tarek Masoud, "Islamist Parties and Democracy: Are They Democrats? Does It Matter?" *Journal of Democracy* 19, no. 3 (2008): 23, http://muse.jhu.edu/article/241790/pdf.
27. Grand, *Understanding Tahrir Square*, 203.
28. Ibid., 208.
29. Lipset, "The Social Requisites of Democracy Revisited," 12.
30. Melinda Haring, "Can Washington Stop Doing Dumb Democracy Promotion, Please?" *Foreign Policy*, December 15, 2015, http://foreignpolicy.com/2015/12/15/can-washington-stop-doing-dumb-democracy-promotion-please-usaid/.
31. Kristina Weissenbach, "Promoting Internal Party Democracy: Party Assistance of the German Political Foundations in Sub-Saharan Africa," NRW School of Governance, Universitat Duisburg Essen, https://ecpr.eu/Filestore/PaperProposal/0f72a5c2-8fc4-43b3-92ad-cff5fcf8226f.pdf. See also Michael Pinto-Duschinsky, "Foreign Political Aid: The German Political Foundations and Their US Counterparts," *International Affairs* 67, no. 1 (January 1991): 33–63.
32. Bush, "Confront or Conform? Rethinking U.S. Democracy Assistance."
33. Springborg, "Arab Armed Forces: State Makers or State Breakers."
34. Springborg, "Arab Militaries," 152.
35. Abraham F. Lowenthal and Sergio Bitar, "Getting to Democracy," *Foreign Affairs* 95, no. 1 (2016): 140, www.foreignaffairs.com/articles/2015-12-14/getting-democracy.
36. Ibid., 143.
37. Coleman and Lawson-Remer, *Pathways to Freedom*, 30.
38. Ibid., 4.
39. Carothers, *Critical Mission*, 100–101.
40. Elliott Abrams, "Sissi Is No Pinochet," *Washington Post*, April 24, 2015, www.washingtonpost.com/opinions/hes-no-pinochet/2015/04/24/8c8d642e-e212-11e4-905f-cc896d379a32_story.html.
41. Daren Acemoglu and James A. Robinson, *Why Nations Fail* (New York: Random House, 2012), 445.
42. Ibid., 68.
43. Carothers, *Critical Mission*, 240.
44. See the comments of Samuel Tadros in Chapter 3, fn. 13.
45. "The National Security Strategy of the United States of America," U.S. Department of State, September 2002, www.state.gov/documents/organization/63562.pdf.
46. Kristian Skrede Gleditsch and Michael D. Ward, "Diffusion and the International Context of Democratization," *International Organization* 60, no. 4 (2006): 912, www.jstor.org/stable/3877851.
47. Robert Kagan, "The Weight of Geopolitics," *Journal of Democracy* 26, no. 1 (2015): 24–29, www.journalofdemocracy.org/article/weight-geopolitics.
48. Brownlee, Masoud, and Reynolds, *The Arab Spring*, 228.

Bibliography

"The 1992 Campaign; Excerpts from Speech by Clinton on U.S. Role." *New York Times*, October 2, 1992. www.nytimes.com/1992/10/02/us/the-1992-campaign-excerpts-from-speech-by-clinton-on-us-role.html.

"2015 Edelman Trust Barometer." Edelman, January 15, 2016. www.slideshare.net/EdelmanInsights/2015-edelman-trust-barometer-global-results.

Abadie, Alberto. "Poverty, Political Freedom, and the Roots of Terrorism." National Bureau of Economic Research, Working Paper 10859, May 2006, http://www.nber.org/papers/w10859.pdf.

Abaza, Khairi. *Political Islam and Regime Survival in Egypt.* Washington, DC: Washington Institute for Near East Policy, 2006. www.washingtoninstitute.org/html/pdf/PolicyFocus51.pdf.

Abramowitz, Michael. "Olympics Notwithstanding, Trip Won't Be All Fun and Games." *Washington Post*, August 8, 2008. www.washingtonpost.com/wp-dyn/content/article/2008/08/03/AR2008080301785.html.

Abrams, Elliott. "Is 'Insulting the President' or Converting to Christianity a Crime?" *Pressure Points*, January 23, 2013. http://blogs.cfr.org/abrams/2013/01/23/is-insulting-the-president-or-converting-to-christianity-a-crime/.

"The Gringos Are with Us." *Commentary Magazine*, April 2013.

Security and Sacrifice: Isolation, Intervention, and American Foreign Policy. Indianapolis: Hudson Institute, 1995.

"Sissi Is No Pinochet." *Washington Post*, April 24, 2015, www.washingtonpost.com/opinions/hes-no-pinochet/2015/04/24/8c8d642e-e212–11e4–905f-cc896d379a32_story.html.

Tested by Zion: The Bush Administration and the Israeli-Palestinian Conflict. New York: Cambridge University Press, 2013.

Acemoglu, Daron, and James A. Robinson. *Why Nations Fail: The Origins of Power, Prosperity, and Poverty.* New York: Crown Publishing, 2012.

Adesnik, A. David, and Sunhyuk Kim. "South Korea: The Puzzle of Two Transitions." In *Transitions to Democracy: A Comparative Perspective*, edited by Kathryn Stoner and Michael McFaul, 266–289. Baltimore: Johns Hopkins University Press, 2013.

Arab Center for Research and Policy Studies. "The ACRPS Announces the Results of the 2012/2013 Arab Opinion Index." June 13, 2013. Doha, Qatar.

Arabic Network for Human Rights Information. "The Crime of Insulting the President: A Crime of an Authoritarian Regime." January 20, 2013. http://bit.ly/1NlEZrz.

Arango, Tim. "Prospect of Instability Looms as Turkish Voters Deny Erdogan a Majority." *New York Times*, June 8, 2015. www.nytimes.com/2015/06/09/world/europe/in-turkish-election-a-foe-recep-erdogan-could-not-beat-voter-fatigue.html?_r=0.

Bangura, Abdul Karim. *Stakes in Africa-United States Cooperation: Proposals for Equitable Partnership.* New York: African Institution, 2007.

Barkan, Joel D. "U.S. Human Rights Policy and Democratization in Kenya." In *Implementing U.S. Human Rights Policy: Agendas, Policies, and Practices*, edited by Debra Liang-Fenton, 51–84. Washington, DC: United States Institute of Peace Press, 2004.

Ben-Dor, Gabriel. "Prospects of Democratization in the Arab World: Global Diffusion, Regional Demonstration, and Domestic Imperatives." In *Democratization in the Arab World: Vol. 1, Theoretical Perspectives*, edited by Rex Brynen, Bahgat Korany, and Paul Noble, 307–332. Boulder: Lynne Rienner, 1995.

Berke, Matthew. "The Disputed Legacy of Reinhold Niebuhr." *First Things*, November 1992. www.firstthings.com/article/1992/11/004-the-disputed-legacy-of-reinhold-niebuhr.

Bloomfield, Lincoln. "From Ideology to Program to Policy: Tracking the Carter Human Rights Policy." *Journal of Policy Analysis and Management* 2, (Autumn 1982): 1–12. www.jstor.org/stable/3323646?seq=1#page_scan_tab_contents.

Boduszyński, Mieczyslaw P., Kristin Fabbe, and Christopher Lamont. "After the Arab Spring: Are Secular Parties the Answer?" *Journal of Democracy* 26, no. 4 (2015): 125–139. www.journalofdemocracy.org/article/after-arab-spring-are-secular-parties-answer.

Brands, Hal. *Making the Unipolar Moment.* Ithaca: Cornell University Press, 2016.

Brooke, Steven. *The Muslim Brotherhood's Social Outreach after the Egyptian Coup.* Washington, DC: Brookings Institution, 2015. www.brookings.edu/wp-content/uploads/2016/07/Egypt_Brooke-FINALE-2.pdf.

Brownlee, Jason. *Democracy Prevention: The Politics of the U.S.–Egyptian Alliance.* New York: Cambridge University Press, 2012.

Brownlee, Jason, Tarek Masoud, and Andrew Reynolds. *The Arab Spring.* New York: Oxford University Press, 2015.

———. "Tracking the 'Arab Spring:' Why the Modest Harvest?" *Journal of Democracy* 24, no. 4 (2013): 29–44. www.journalofdemocracy.org/article/tracking-arab-spring-why-modest-harvest.

Buckley, William F., Jr. "Human Rights and Foreign Policy: A Proposal." *Foreign Affairs* 58 (Spring 1980). www.foreignaffairs.com/articles/1980–03–01/human-rights-and-foreign-policy-proposal.

Burks, Edward C. "Moynihan: How He Won His Senate Spurs." *New York Times*, April 5, 1977. www.nytimes.com/1977/04/05/archives/moynihan-how-he-won-his-senate-spurs-initiation-of-senator-moynihan.html.4

Burwell, Frances, Danya Greenfield, and Amy Hawthorne. *A Transatlantic Approach to the Arab World*. Washington, DC: Atlantic Council, 2015.

Bush, George W. In discussion with the author, November 7, 2016. Transcript. Offices of President George W. Bush. Dallas.

"Address before a Joint Session of the Congress on the United States Response to the Terrorist Attacks of September 11." September 20, 2001. Transcript. American Presidency Project, University of California-Santa Barbara. www .presidency.ucsb.edu/ws/index.php?pid=64731&st=&st1=.

"President Bush Calls for New Palestinian Leadership." June 24, 2002. Transcript. George W. Bush Presidential Library, National Archives. https://georgewbush-whitehouse.archives.gov/news/releases/2002/06/ 20020624–3.html.

"President George W. Bush Speaks at AEI's Annual Dinner." February 28, 2003. Transcript. American Enterprise Institute. www.aei.org/publication/ president-george-w-bush-speaks-at-aeis-annual-dinner/.

"Remarks by President George W. Bush at the Twentieth Anniversary of the National Endowment for Democracy." November 6, 2003. Transcript. National Endowment for Democracy. www.ned.org/ remarks-by-president-george-w-bush-at-the-20th-anniversary/.

"State of the Union Address." January 29, 2002. Transcript. George W. Bush Presidential Library, National Archives. https://georgewbush-whitehouse .archives.gov/news/releases/2002/01/20020129–11.html.

"State of the Union Address." January 23, 2007. Transcript. George W. Bush Presidential Library, National Archives. https://georgewbush-whitehouse .archives.gov/news/releases/2007/01/20070123–2.html.

"State of the Union Address." January 28, 2008. Transcript. George W. Bush Presidential Library, National Archives. https://georgewbush-whitehouse .archives.gov/news/releases/2008/01/20080128–13.html.

Bush, Sarah. "Confront or Conform? Rethinking U.S. Democracy Assistance." *POMED Policy Brief* (2013). http://pomed.org/pomed/new-pomed- policy-brief-confront-or-conform-rethinking-u-s-democracy-assistance/.

"Forms of International Pressure and the Middle East." *Project on Middle East Political Science*, August 21, 2015. http://pomeps.org/2015/08/21/ forms-of-international-pressure-and-the-middle-east/.

The Taming of Democracy Assistance: Why Democracy Promotion Does Not Confront Dictators. New York: Cambridge University Press, 2015.

Bush, Sarah, and Amaney Jamal. "Anti-Americanism, Authoritarianism, and Attitudes about Women in Politics: Evidence from a Survey Experiment in Jordan." Paper presented at the 2011 Annual Meeting of the Middle East Studies Association, Washington, DC, December 2011.

Byman, Daniel. "After the Hope of the Arab Spring, the Chill of an Arab Winter." *Washington Post*, December 1, 2011. www.washingtonpost.com/opinions/ after-the-hope-of-the-arab-spring-the-chill-of-an-arab-winter/2011/11/28/ gIQABGqHIO_story.html.

Cammett, Melani. "Development and Underdevelopment in the Middle East and North Africa." In *Oxford Handbook of Development*, edited by Carol Lancaster and Nicholas van de Walle. New York: Oxford University Press, 2013.

Cammett, Melani, and Pauline Jones Luong. "Is There an 'Islamist Political Advantage'?" *Annual Review of Political Science* 17 (2014): 187–206. www .annualreviews.org/doi/pdf/10.1146/annurev-polisci-071112-221207.

Carothers, Thomas. *Aiding Democracy Abroad: The Learning Curve.* Washington, DC: Carnegie Endowment for International Peace, 1999.

The Closing Space Challenge: How Are Funders Responding? Washington, DC: Carnegie Endowment for International Peace, 2015. http:// carnegieendowment.org/files/CP_258_Carothers_Closing_Space_Final .pdf.

Critical Mission: Essays on Democracy Promotion. Washington, DC: Carnegie Endowment for International Peace, 2004.

"Democracy Aid at 25: A Time to Choose," *Journal of Democracy* 26, no. 1 (2015): 59–73. http://muse.jhu.edu/article/565639/pdf.

Democracy Policy under Obama: Revitalization or Retreat? Washington, DC: Carnegie Endowment for International Peace, 2012. http:// carnegieendowment.org/files/democracy_under_obama.pdf.

"Is Gradualism Possible? Choosing a Strategy for Promoting Democracy in the Middle East." *Carnegie Endowment for International Peace Democracy and Rule of Law Project* 39 (2003). http://carnegieendowment.org/files/wp39.pdf.

"Why Is the United States Shortchanging Its Commitment to Democracy?" *Washington Post,* December 22, 2014. www.washingtonpost.com/opinions/ falling-usaid-spending-shows-a-lack-of-commitment-to-fostering-democracy/ 2014/12/22/86b72d58–89f4–11e4-a085–34e9b9f09a58_story.html? wpisrc=nl_opin&wpmm=1.

Carothers, Thomas, and Saskia Brechenmacher. *Closing Space: Democracy and Human Rights Support under Fire.* Washington, DC: Carnegie Endowment for International Peace, 2014. http://carnegieendowment.org/files/closing_ space.pdf.

"Carter in Warsaw, Starting 9-Day Tour." *New York Times,* December 30, 1977. www.nytimes.com/1977/12/30/archives/new-jersey-pages-carter-in-warsaw- starting-9day-tour-says-old.html.

Carter, Jimmy. "Address at Commencement Exercises at University of Notre Dame." May 22, 1977. Transcript. American Presidency Project, University of California-Santa-Barbara. www.presidency.ucsb.edu/ws/?pid= 7552.

"Inaugural Address." January 20, 1977. Transcript. American Presidency Project, University of California-Santa Barbara. www.presidency.ucsb.edu/ ws/?pid=6575.

"The President's News Conference." June 13, 1977. Transcript. American Presidency Project, University of California-Santa Barbara. www.presidency.ucsb .edu/ws/index.php?pid=7670.

"The President's News Conference." March 24, 1977. Transcript. American Presidency Project, University of California-Santa Barbara. www.presidency .ucsb.edu/ws/index.php?pid=7229.

"Visit of President Josip Broz Tito of Yugoslavia, Remarks at the Welcoming Ceremony." March 7, 1978. Transcript. American Presidency Project, University of California-Santa Barbara. www.presidency.ucsb.edu/ws/?pid=30462.

"Visit of President Nicolae Ceausescu of Romania, Remarks at the Welcoming Ceremony." April 12, 1978. Transcript. American Presidency Project, University of California-Santa Barbara. www.presidency.ucsb.edu/ws/?pid=30655.

Carter, Jimmy, and Reza Pahlavi. "Tehran, Iran, Toasts of the President and the Shah at a State Dinner." December 31, 1977. Transcript. American Presidency Project, University of California-Santa Barbara. www.presidency.ucsb .edu/ws/?pid=7080.

Cesari, Jocelyne. *The Awakening of Muslim Democracy: Religion, Modernity, and the State.* New York: Cambridge University Press, 2014.

Chayes, Sarah. *How a Leftist Labor Union Helped Force Tunisia's Political Settlement.* Washington, DC: Carnegie Endowment for International Peace, 2014. http://carnegieendowment.org/2014/03/27/how-leftist-labor-union-helped-force-tunisia-s-political-settlement.

Christian, Shirley. *Nicaragua: Revolution in the Family.* New York: Random House, 1985.

"Clinton: Chinese Human Rights Can't Interfere with Other Crises." *CNN*, February 21, 2009. www.cnn.com/2009/POLITICS/02/21/clinton.china.asia/? iref=nextin.

Clinton, Hillary Rodham. "Remarks on Development in the 21st Century." January 6, 2010. Transcript. U.S. Department of State. www.state.gov/secretary/ 20092013clinton/rm/2010/01/134838.htm.

CNN Wire Staff. "Muslim Brotherhood: 'We Are Not Seeking Power.'" *CNN*, February 10, 2011. www.cnn.com/2011/WORLD/africa/02/09/egypt .muslim.brotherhood/.

Coleman, Isobel, and Terra Lawson-Remer, eds. *Pathways to Freedom: Political and Economic Lessons from Democratic Transitions.* New York: Council on Foreign Relations Press, 2013.

"Condi Rice Talks Freedom, War, Working for Bush." Author Interviews. *NPR*, November 2, 2011. www.npr.org/2011/11/02/141931702/condi-rice-talks-freedom-war-working-for-bush.

Croft-Cusworth, Catriona. "Indonesia's Election: Surprise Success for Islamic Parties." *The Interpreter*, April 18, 2014. www.lowyinterpreter.org/post/ 2014/04/18/Indonesias-election-Surprise-success-for-Islamic-parties.aspx? COLLCC=3609281719&.

Cruickshank, Paul. "Why Arab Spring Could Be al Qaeda's Fall." CNN.com, February 21, 2011. www.cnn.com/2011/WORLD/meast/02/21/arab .unrest.alqaeda.analysis/

Daalder, Ivo. "Decision to Intervene: How the War in Bosnia Ended." *Brookings Institution*, December 1, 1998. www.brookings.edu/articles/ decision-to-intervene-how-the-war-in-bosnia-ended/.

"Democrat or Sultan?" *The Economist*, June 8, 2013. www.economist.com/news/ leaders/21579004-recep-tayyip-erdogan-should-heed-turkeys-street-protesters-not-dismiss-them-democrat-or-sultan.

Derian, Patricia. "Secret Memorandum from Assistant Secretary of State Patricia Derian to Acting Secretary Warren Christopher." June 18, 1979. In *A Twilight Struggle: American Power and Nicaragua, 1977–1990* by Robert Kagan, 746. New York: Free Press, 1996.

Devarajan, Shantayanan, et al. "Inequality, Uprisings, and Conflict in the Arab World." *Middle East and North Africa Economic Monitor.* Washington, DC: World Bank Group, October 2015. http://documents.worldbank.org/curated/en/303441467992017147/pdf/99989-REVISED-Box_393220B-OUO-9-MEM-Fall-2015-FINAL-Oct-13–2015.pdf.

deYoung, Karen. "Newly Declassified Papers Reveal U.S. Tensions regarding Argentina's 'Dirty War.'" *Washington Post,* August 8, 2016. www.washingtonpost.com/world/national-security/newly-declassified-papers-reveal-us-tensions-regarding-argentinas-dirty-war/2016/08/08/4227fbee-5db1–11e6-af8e-54aa2e849447_story.html.

Diamond, Larry. "From Activism to Democracy." In *Taking to the Streets: The Transformation of Arab Activism,* edited by Lina Khatib and Ellen Lust, 322–334. Baltimore: Johns Hopkins University Press, 2014.

  The Spirit of Democracy: The Struggle to Build Free Societies throughout the World. New York: Holt Paperbacks, 2008.

Diamond, Larry and Marc F. Plattner (eds.). *Democratization and Authoritarianism in the Arab World.* Baltimore: Johns Hopkins University Press, 2014.

Dobson, William J. *The Dictator's Learning Curve: Inside the Global Battle for Democracy.* New York: Doubleday, 2012.

Dunne, Michele. "Caught in History's Crossroads." *Journal of Democracy* 26, no. 4 (2015): 75–79.

  "Evaluating Egyptian Reform." *Carnegie Papers* 66 (2006). http://carnegieendowment.org/files/CP66.Dunne.FINAL.pdf.

Dunne, Michele, Amr Hamzawy, and Nathan Brown, "Egypt – Don't Give up on Democracy Promotion." *Carnegie Endowment for International Peace Policy Brief* 52 (2007).

Dunne, Michele and Robert Kagan. "Obama Needs to Support Egyptians as Well as Mubarak." *Washington Post,* June 4, 2010. www.washingtonpost.com/wp-dyn/content/article/2010/06/03/AR2010060303935.html

Editorial. "Mr. Reagan's Human Rights Conversion." *New York Times,* December 10, 1988. www.nytimes.com/1988/12/10/opinion/mr-reagan-s-human-rights-conversion.html.

"Excerpts from Secretary of State Alexander M. Haig's News Conference." *New York Times,* January 28, 1981. www.nytimes.com/1981/01/29/world/excerpts-from-haig-s-remarks-at-first-news-conference-as-secretary-of.html?pagewanted=all.

Farr, Thomas F. *World of Faith and Freedom.* New York: Oxford University Press, 2008.

Fayed, Ammar. "Is the Crackdown on the Muslim Brotherhood Pushing the Group toward Violence?" *Brookings Institution,* March 2016, www.brookings.edu/research/papers/2016/03/muslim-brotherhood-crackdown-violence-fayed.

Filali-Ansary, Abdou. "The Languages of the Arab Revolutions." *Journal of Democracy* 23, no. 2 (2012): 5–18. www.journalofdemocracy.org/sites/default/files/Filali-23–2.pdf.

Freedom House. "Freedom in the World 2015." https://freedomhouse.org/report/freedom-world/freedom-world-2015#.VWc1Yuu4mX1.

Freer, Courtney. *The Rise of Pragmatic Islamism in Kuwait's Post-Arab Spring Opposition Movement.* Washington, DC: Brookings Institution, August 2015. www .brookings.edu/wp-content/uploads/2016/07/Kuwait_Freer-FINALE.pdf.

Fukuyama, Francis. *The End of History and the Last Man.* New York: Free Press, 1992.

Garfinkle, Aram. "How to Think about the Middle East before the 'Arab Spring' – and After." *FootNotes* (2013). www.fpri.org/articles/2013/11/ how-think-about-middle-east-arab-spring-and-after

"George H. W. Bush: Foreign Affairs." Miller Center, University of Virginia. http://millercenter.org/president/biography/bush-foreign-affairs.

"George W. Bush's Statement on the Middle East." *New York Times,* April 2, 2002. www.nytimes.com/2002/04/04/international/bushs-statement-on-the-middle-east.html.

Gerges, Fawaz A. *The End of America's Moment? Obama and the Middle East.* New York: Palgrave Macmillan, 2012.

Ghalioun, Burhan and Philip J. Costopoulos. "The Persistence of Arab Authoritarianism." *Journal of Democracy* 15, no. 4 (2004): 126–132. http://muse.jhu .edu/article/174001/pdf.

Ghannouchi, Rachid. "Tunisia's New Political Order." Woodrow Wilson Center, Washington, DC, February 24, 2014. www.wilsoncenter.org/article/ ghannouchi-tunisias-new-political-order.

Gleditsch, Kristian Skrede and Michael D. Ward. "Diffusion and the International Context of Democratization." *International Organization* 60.4 (2006): 911–933.

Gouverneur Morris. *The Diary and Letters of Gouverneur Morris: Vol. 1.* New York: Charles Scribner's Sons, 1888.

Grand, Stephen R. *Understanding Tahrir Square: What Transitions Elsewhere Can Teach Us about the Prospects for Arab Democracy.* Washington, DC: Brookings Institution Press, 2014.

Guéhenno, Jean-Marie. "The Arab Spring Is 2011, Not 1989." *New York Times,* April 21, 2011. www.nytimes.com/2011/04/22/opinion/22iht-edguehenno22.html?_r=0.

Guest, Iain. *Behind the Disappearances: Argentina's Dirty War against Human Rights and the United Nations.* Philadelphia: University of Pennsylvania Press, 1990.

Hamid, Shadi. *Islamic Exceptionalism: How the Struggle Over Islam Is Reshaping the World.* New York: Macmillan, 2016.

"Political Party Development before and after the Arab Spring," in *Beyond the Arab Spring: The Evolving Ruling Bargain in the Middle East,* edited by Mehran Kamrava, 131–150. New York: Oxford University Press, 2014.

"The Rise of the Islamists." *Foreign Affairs* 90, no. 3 (2011): 40–47.

Temptations of Power: Islamists and Illiberal Democracy in a New Middle East. New York: Oxford University Press, 2014.

Hamid, Shadi and Steven Brooke, "Promoting Democracy to Stop Terror, Revisited," *Policy Review,* Hoover Institution, February and March 2010, www .hoover.org/research/promoting-democracy-stop-terror-revisited

Haring, Melinda. "Can Washington Stop Doing Dumb Democracy Promotion, Please?" *Foreign Policy,* December 15, 2015.

http://foreignpolicy.com/2015/12/15/can-washington-stop-doing-dumb-democracy-promotion-please-usaid/.

Hartmann, Hauke. "US Human Rights Policy under Carter and Reagan, 1977–1981." *Human Rights Quarterly* 23.2 (May 2001): 402–430. http://muse.jhu.edu/article/13768.

Henderson, Simon. "Fighting al-Qaeda: The Role of Yemen's President Saleh," Washington Institute for Near East Policy, January 7, 2010, www.washingtoninstitute.org/policy-analysis/view/fighting-al-qaeda-the-role-of-yemens-president-saleh.

"Royal Rivalry: Bahrain's Ruling Family and the Island's Political Crisis." *Policywatch 2198*. Washington Institute for Near East Policy, January 24, 2014.

Hertzke, Alan D. *Freeing God's Children: The Unlikely Alliance for Global Human Rights*. New York: Rowman & Littlefield, 2004.

Hof, Frederic C. "A Bad Defense for a Mistaken Policy." *Syria Source*. Atlantic Council, August 29, 2016. www.atlanticcouncil.org/blogs/syriasource/a-bad-defense-for-a-mistaken-policy.

Huntington, Samuel P. *The Clash of Civilizations and the Remaking of World Order*. New York: Simon and Schuster, 2007.

Ibrahim, Saad Eddin. "Toward Muslim Democracies." *Journal of Democracy* 18 (2007): 5–13.

Inbar, Efraim. "The European Peace Offensive." *Israel Hayom*, June 1, 2015, www.israelhayom.com/site/newsletter_opinion.php?id=12739.

Inglehart, Ronald and Christian Welzel. "Changing Mass Priorities: The Link between Modernization and Democracy." *Perspectives on Politics* 8, no. 2 (2010): 551–567. www.jstor.org/stable/25698618.

"Islam in a Changing Middle East: Islamist Social Services." *Project on Middle East Political Science* 9 (2014). http://pomeps.org/wp-content/uploads/2014/10/POMEPS_Studies_9_SocialServices_web.pdf.

Jackson Amendment on East-West Trade & Freedom of Emigration, Amendment No. 79. Inside the Cold War. http://insidethecoldwar.org/sites/default/files/documents/Jackson-Vanik%20Amendment%20to%20the%20trade%20reform%20act%20of%201972,%20january%204,%201975.pdf.

Jacoby, Tamar. "The Reagan Turnaround on Human Rights." *Foreign Affairs* 64 (Summer 1986): 1065–1086. www.foreignaffairs.com/articles/1986-06-01/reagan-turnaround-human-rights.

Jamal, Amaney and Mark Tessler. "Measuring Support for Democracy in the Arab World and across the Globe," *Arab Barometer*, arabbarometer.org/sites/default/files/files/measuringsupport.pdf.

Johnsen, Gregory. "The Election Yemen Was Supposed to Have." *Middle East Research and Information Project*, October 3, 2006, www.merip.org/mero/mero100306.

Kagan, Robert. "The Weight of Geopolitics," *Journal of Democracy* 26, no. 1 (2015): 21–31. www.journalofdemocracy.org/article/weight-geopolitics.

Kagan, Robert and Michele Dunne. "U.S. Needs to Show Egypt Some Tough Love." *Washington Post*, February 20, 2013. www.washingtonpost.com/opinions/time-to-get-tough-with-egypt-and-morsi/2013/02/20/7e1343c6-7aba-11e2-82e8-61a46c2cde3d_print.html.

"Why Egypt has to be the U.S. Priority in the Middle East." *Washington Post*, March 7, 2011. www.brookings.edu/opinions/why-egypt-has-to-be-the-u-s-priority-in-the-middle-east/.

Kagan, Robert and William Kristol, eds. *Present Dangers: Crisis and Opportunity in American Foreign and Defense Policy*. San Francisco: Encounter Books, 2000.

Kaufman, Robert G. *Henry M. Jackson: A Life in Politics*. Seattle: University of Washington Press, 2000.

Kedourie, Elie. *Democracy and Arab Political Culture*. Portland, OR: Frank Cass, 1994.

Kennedy, John F. "Address at a White House Reception for Members of Congress and for the Diplomatic Corps of the Latin American Republics." March 13, 1961. Transcript. John F. Kennedy Presidential Library and Museum. www.jfklibrary.org/Research/Research-Aids/JFK-Speeches/Latin-American-Diplomats-Washington-DC_19610313.aspx.

"Address on the first Anniversary of the Alliance for Progress." March 13, 1962. Transcript. American Presidency Project, University of California-Santa Barbara. www.presidency.ucsb.edu/ws/?pid=9100.

Khatib, Lina and Ellen Lust, eds. *Taking to the Streets: The Transformation of Arab Activism*. Baltimore: Johns Hopkins University Press, 2014.

Kirkpatrick, Jeane J. "Dictatorships and Double Standards, *Commentary*, November 1, 1979. www.commentarymagazine.com/articles/dictatorships-double-standards

"Human Rights and Foreign Policy." In *Human Rights and American Foreign Policy*, edited by Fred E. Baumann, 1–5. Gambier: Kenyon College, 1982.

Korany, Bahgat, Rex Brynen, and Paul Noble, eds. *Political Liberalization and Democratization in the Arab World: Vol. 2, Comparative Experiences*. Boulder, CO: Lynne Rienner, 1998.

Korey, William. "The Struggle over Jackson-Mills-Vanik." *American Jewish Yearbook* 75 (1974–19755): 82. www.bjpa.org/Publications/downloadFile.cfm?FileID=20308.

Kornbluh, Peter and Marian Schlotterbeck. "How U.S. President Reagan Broke with Chile's Pinochet." *Santiago Times*, November 30, 2010. www.santiagotimes.cl/2010/11/30/how-us-president-reagan-broke-with-chiles-pinochet/.

Kristol, Irving. "In Search of Our National Interest." *Wall Street Journal*, June 7, 1990. http://search.proquest.com/hnpwallstreetjournal/docview/135463649/FDBAB5EC80204B8EPQ/1?accountid=10986.

Kristol, Irving. "Moral Dilemmas' in Foreign Policy." *Wall Street Journal*, February 28, 1980. http://search.proquest.com/hnpwallstreetjournal/docview/134428824/B92EDC12A92841CFPQ/1?accountid=10986.

"Toward a Moral Foreign Policy." *Wall Street Journal*, November 15, 1983. http://search.proquest.com/hnpwallstreetjournal/docview/134793803/5D26C45BA614B39PQ/1?accountid=10986.

Kristol, William and Robert Kagan. "Toward a Neo-Reaganite Foreign Policy." *Foreign Affairs* 75, (July/August 1996): 18–32. www.foreignaffairs.com/articles/1996–07–01/toward-neo-reaganite-foreign-policy.

Krueger, Alan B. and Jitka Maleckova. "Seeking the Roots of Terrorism." *Chronicle of Higher Education* (2003).

Kubba, Laith. "Institutions Make the Difference." *Journal of Democracy* 19, no. 3 (2008): 37–42. https://muse.jhu.edu/article/241796.

Lakoff, Sanford A. "The Reality of Muslim Exceptionalism." *Journal of Democracy* 15, no. 4 (2004): 133–139. http://muse.jhu.edu/article/174004/pdf.

Langhor, Vickie. "Labor Movements or Organizations," in *The Arab Uprisings Explained: New Contentious Politics in the Middle East,* edited by Marc Lynch, 180–181. New York: Columbia University Press, 2014.

Latimer, Matt. "When Bush Caved to Egypt." *Daily Beast,* January 30, 2011. www.thedailybeast.com/articles/2011/01/30/president-bush-pulled-his-punches-on-egypts-mubarak-too.html.

Levitsky, Steven and Lucan Way. *Competitive Authoritarianism: Hybrid Regimes After the Cold War.* New York: Cambridge University Press, 2010.

"International Linkage and Democratization." *Journal of Democracy* 16, no. 3 (2005): 20–34. https://muse.jhu.edu/article/185273.

Lewis, Bernard. "Democracy and the Enemies of Freedom." *Wall Street Journal,* December 22, 2003. www.wsj.com/articles/SB107205654377356100.

"Free at Last: The Arab World in the Twenty-First Century." *Foreign Affairs* 88, no. 2 (2009): 86–87. www.foreignaffairs.com/articles/middle-east/2009-03-01/free-last.

Liang-Fenton, Debra, ed. *Implementing U.S. Human Rights Policy: Agendas, Policies, and Practices.* Washington, DC: United States Institute of Peace Press, 2004.

Lipset, Seymour Martin. "The Social Requisites of Democracy Revisited." *American Sociological Review* 59 (1994): 1–22. www.jstor.org/stable/2096130.

"Some Social Requisites of Democracy: Economic Development and Political Legitimacy." *American Political Science Review* 53, no. 1 (1959): 69–105. www.jstor.org/stable/1951731.

Lowenthal, Abraham F. and Bitar, Sergio. "Getting to Democracy." *Foreign Affairs* 95, no. 1 (2016): 134–144. www.foreignaffairs.com/articles/2015-12-14/getting-democracy.

Lust, Ellen. "Missing the Third Wave: Islam, Institutions, and Democracy in the Middle East." *Studies in Comparative International Development* 46, no. 2 (2011): 163–190. http://link.springer.com/article/10.1007/s12116-011-9086-z.

Lyman, Princeton N. "Mandela's Legacy at Home and Abroad." *Journal of Democracy* 25, no. 2 (2014): 21–34. https://muse.jhu.edu/article/542443.

Lynch, Marc, ed. *The Arab Uprisings Explained: New Contentious Politics in the Middle East.* New York: Columbia University Press, 2014.

"Media, Old and New." In *The Arab Uprisings Explained: New Contentious Politics in the Middle East,* edited by Marc Lynch, 93. New York: Columbia University Press, 2014.

Magen, Amichai. "On Political Order and the 'Arab Spring.'" *Israel Journal of Foreign Affairs* 6, no. 1 (2012): 9–21. www.ict.org.il/UserFiles/ICTWPS%20-%20Amichai%20Magen%20-%201.pdf.

Marks, Monica. "A Response to Sayida Ounissi's 'Ennahda from Within: Islamists or Muslim Democrats.'" In *Rethinking Political Islam.*

Washington, DC: Brookings Institution, June 1, 2016. www.brookings.edu/
~/media/research/files/reports/2015/07/rethinking-political-islam/
reaction-essays/monicamarks_re2sayidaounissi3.pdf

"Tunisia's Ennahda: Rethinking Islamism in the Context of ISIS and the
Egyptian Coup." *Brookings Institution*, August 2015. www.brookings.edu/
wp-content/uploads/2016/07/Tunisia_Marks-FINALE-5.pdf.

Masoud, Tarek. "Has the Door Closed on Arab Democracy?" *Journal of Democracy*
26, no. 1 (2015): 74–87. http://muse.jhu.edu/article/565640/pdf.

"Islamist Parties and Democracy: Are they Democrats? Does it Matter?" *Journal
of Democracy* 19, no. 3 (2008): 19–24. http://muse.jhu.edu/article/241790/
pdf.

"Why Do Islamists Provide Services, and What Do Those Services Do?" *Project
on Middle East Political Science* 9. http://pomeps.org/wp-content/uploads/
2014/10/POMEPS_Studies_9_SocialServices_web.pdf.

McCormick, Ty. "Unmade in the USA." *Foreign Policy*, February 25, 2015.
http://foreignpolicy.com/2015/02/25/unmade-in-the-usa-south-sudan-
bush-obama/.

McFaul, Michael and Francis Fukuyama, "Should Democracy Be Promoted or
Demoted?" *Washington Quarterly* 31, no. 1 (2008), 23–45.

McGovern, George. "Address Accepting the Presidential Nomination of the
Democratic National Convention." July 14, 1972. Transcript. American
Presidency Project, University of California-Santa Barbara. www.presidency
.ucsb.edu/ws/?pid=25967.

Mecham, Quinn. "Islamist Movements." In *The Arab Uprisings Explained*,
edited by Marc Lynch, 201–217. New York: Columbia University Press,
2014.

Memorandum of Conversation. "Cabinet Meeting." February 21, 1974. National
Security Adviser's Memoranda of Conversations, 1973–1977. Box 3. Gerald R. Ford Library. http://fordlibrarymuseum.gov/library/document/
memcons/1552663.pdf.

Memorandum of Conversation. "Cabinet Meeting: Briefing on Middle East."
March 8, 1974. National Security Adviser's Memoranda of Conversations,
1973–1977. Box 3. Gerald R. Ford Library. http://fordlibrarymuseum.gov/
library/document/0314/1552668.pdf.

Morley, Morris and Chris McGillion. *Reagan and Pinochet: The Struggle over US Policy
toward Chile.* New York: Cambridge University Press, 2015.

Morris, Anne Cary, ed. *The Diary and Letters of Gouverneur Morris: Minister of the
United States to France; Member of the Constitutional Convention, etc.* vol. I. New
York: Charles Scribner's Sons, 1888.

Moynihan, Daniel P. "The United States in Opposition." *Commentary*, March 1975.
www.commentarymagazine.com/articles/the-united-states-in-opposition/.

Muasher, Marwan. *The Second Arab Awakening and the Battle for Pluralism.* New
Haven, CT: Yale University Press, 2014.

Nagourney, Adam. "In Tapes, Nixon Rails against Jews and Blacks." *New
York Times*, December 10, 2010. www.nytimes.com/2010/12/11/us/politics/
11nixon.html?_r=0.

Nathan, Andrew. "China since Tiananmen: Authoritarian Impermanence." *Journal of Democracy* 20, no. 3 (2009): 37–40. www.journalofdemocracy.org/sites/default/files/Nathan-20–3.pdf.

National Democratic Institute. "Political Parties." www.ndi.org/political-parties?quicktabs_functional_area_tabs=0#quicktabs-functional_area_tabs.

Neuman, Scott. "Clinton Aides Weighed Fallout of Calling Rwanda Killing 'Genocide.'" *National Public Radio*, August 31, 2016. www.npr.org/sections/thetwo-way/2014/06/06/319563918/clinton-aides-mulled-fallout-of-calling-rwanda-killing-genocide.

Newhouse, John. *War and Peace in the Nuclear Age*. New York: Alfred A. Knopf, 1989.

O'Connell, Jamie. "Common Interests, Closer Allies: How Democracy in Arab States Can Benefit the West." *Stanford Journal of International Law* 48, no. 2 (2012): 341–404. www.law.berkeley.edu/php-programs/faculty/facultyPubsPDF.php?facID=5697&pubID=6.

"October 28, 1980 Debate Transcript." October 28, 1980. Transcript. Commission on Presidential Debates. www.debates.org/index.php?page=october-28–1980-debate-transcript.

"October 21, 1984 Debate Transcript." October 21, 1984. Transcript. Commission on Presidential Debates. www.debates.org/index.php?page=october-21–1984-debate-transcript.

"October 11, 2000 Presidential Debate." October 11, 2000. Transcript. Commission on Presidential Debates. www.debates.org/index.php?page=october-11–2000-debate-transcript.

Office of the Inspector General. *Audit of USAID/Egypt's Democracy and Governance Activities*. Audit Report No. 6–263–10–001-P, October 27, 2009. Washington, DC: OIG.

Ounissi, Sayida. "Ennahda from Within: Islamists or 'Muslim Democrats?'" In *Rethinking Political Islam*. Washington, DC: Brookings Institution, February 2016. www.brookings.edu/research/papers/2016/03/ennahda-islamists-muslim-democrats-ounissi.

Patel, David Siddartha. "The More Things Change, the More They Stay the Same: Jordanian Islamist Responses to the Arab Spring." *Brookings Institution*, August 2015. www.brookings.edu/wp-content/uploads/2016/07/Jordan_Patel-FINALE.pdf.

Ottaway, Marina. "Democracy and Constituencies in the Arab World." *Carnegie Papers, Middle East Series*, no. 48 (July 2004).

Perkovich, George. "Soviet Jewry and American Foreign Policy." *World Policy Journal* 5 (Summer 1988): 458. www.jstor.org/stable/40209090.

Pevehouse, Jon C. "Democracy from the Outside-In? International Organizations and Democratization." *International Organization* 56, no. 3 (2002): 515–549. https://muse.jhu.edu/article/14326.

Pinto-Duschinsky, Michael. "Foreign Political Aid: The German Political Foundations and their US Counterparts." *International Affairs* 67, no. 1 (January 1991): 33–63.

Pipes, Daniel. "Distinguishing between Islam and Islamism." June 30, 1998. www.danielpipes.org/954/distinguishing-between-islam-and-islamism.

Poindexter, John M. "Memorandum for John M. Poindexter from Jacqueline Tillman, NSC Meeting on Chile." November 18, 1986. Cited in *Reagan and Pinochet: The Struggle over US Policy toward Chile* by Morris Morley and Chris McGillion, 194. New York: Cambridge University Press, 2015.

"President Bush Attends World Economic Forum." May 18, 2008. Transcript. George W. Bush Presidential Library, National Archives. https://georgewbush-whitehouse.archives.gov/news/releases/2008/05/20080518–6.html.

"President Bush Delivers Remarks in Prague." *Washington Post*, June 5, 2007. www.washingtonpost.com/wp-dyn/content/article/2007/06/05/AR2007060500647.html.

"President Bush Discusses Freedom in Iraq and Middle East." Office of the Press Secretary. http://georgewbush-whitehouse.archives.gov/news/releases/2003/11/20031106–2.html.

"President Bush Meets with President Hosni Mubarak of Egypt." January 16, 2008. Transcript. George W. Bush Presidential Library, National Archives. https://georgewbush-whitehouse.archives.gov/news/releases/2008/01/20080116–2.html.

"President Bush Visits Prague, Czech Republic, Discusses Freedom." June 5, 2007. Transcript. George W. Bush Presidential Library, National Archives. https://georgewbush-whitehouse.archives.gov/news/releases/2007/06/20070605–8.html.

Presidential Directive NSC-30. February 17, 1978. Jimmy Carter Presidential Library. www.jimmycarterlibrary.gov/documents/pddirectives/pd30.pdf.

Ratesh, Nestor. "The American Connection." In *Romania, 40 Years (1944–1984)*, edited by Vlad Georgescu. New York: Praeger, 1985.

Reagan, Ronald. "Address to Members of the British Parliament." June 8, 1982. Transcript. Ronald Reagan Presidential Library, National Archives. https://reaganlibrary.archives.gov/archives/speeches/1982/60882a.htm.

"Remarks at the Annual Convention of the National Association of Evangelicals." March 8, 1983. Ronald Reagan Presidential Library, National Archives. https://reaganlibrary.archives.gov/archives/speeches/1983/30883b.htm.

"Remarks on Central America and El Salvador at the Annual Meeting of the National Association of Manufacturers." March 10, 1983. Transcript. Ronald Reagan Presidential Library, National Archives. https://reaganlibrary.archives.gov/archives/speeches/1983/31083a.htm.

"Remarks on East-West Relations at the Brandenburg Gate." June 12, 1987. Transcript. Ronald Reagan Presidential Library, National Archives. https://reaganlibrary.archives.gov/archives/speeches/1987/061287d.htm.

Remnick, David. "The Wandered." *New Yorker*, September 18, 2006. www.newyorker.com/magazine/2006/09/18/the-wanderer-3.

Rice, Condoleezza. "Campaign 2000: Promoting the National Interest." *Foreign Affairs* (January/February 2000). www.foreignaffairs.com/articles/2000–01–01/campaign-2000-promoting-national-interest.

"Dr. Condoleezza Rice Discusses President's National Security Strategy." October 1, 2002. Transcript. National Archives. https://georgewbush-whitehouse.archives.gov/news/releases/2002/10/20021001–6.html.

No Higher Honor: A Memoir of My Years in Washington. New York: Crown Publishers, 2001.

"Remarks at the American University in Cairo." United States Department of State, June 20, 2005. http://2001–2009.state.gov/secretary/rm/2005/48328.htm.

Robbins, Michael. "People Still Want Democracy." *Journal of Democracy,* 26, no. 4 (2015): 80–89. http://muse.jhu.edu/article/595925/pdf.

Robbins, Michael and Mark Tessler. "Arab Views on Governance after the Uprisings." *Washington Post,* October 29, 2014. www.washingtonpost.com/blogs/monkey-cage/wp/2014/10/29/arab-views-on-governance-after-the-uprisings/.

Roy, Olivier. "End of the Old Arab Strongman." *New Statesman,* March 3, 2011. www.newstatesman.com/middle-east/2011/02/israel-iran-movement-arab.

"The Transformation of the Arab World." In *Democratization and Authoritarianism in the Arab World,* edited by Larry Diamond and Marc Plattner, 15–28. Baltimore: Johns Hopkins University Press, 2014.

Rustin, Bayard. "From Protest to Politics: The Future of the Civil Rights Movement." *Commentary Magazine* 39, no. 2 (1965). www.commentarymagazine.com/articles/from-protest-to-politics-the-future-of-the-civil-rights-movement.

Rustow, Dankwart. "Transitions to Democracy: Towards a Dynamic Model." *Comparative Politics* 2, no. 3 (1970): 337–363. www.jstor.org/stable/421307.

Sadiki, Larbi. *Rethinking Arab Democratization: Elections without Democracy.* New York: Oxford University Press, 2009.

Salzman, Philip Carl. "Why the Middle East Is the Way It Is." *Hedgehog Review: Critical Reflections on Contemporary Culture* 13, no. 3 (2011): 23–36. www.iasc-culture.org/THR/archives/Fall2011/Salzman_lo.pdf.

Sanders, Katie. "Chris Wallace: Hillary Clinton Defended Syria's Assad as a 'Possible Reformer.'" *Politifact,* June 1, 2014. www.politifact.com/punditfact/statements/2014/jun/01/chris-wallace/chris-wallace-hillary-clinton-defended-syrias-assa/.

Samuels, David. "A Fourth of July Story." *Tablet,* June 30, 2016. www.tabletmag.com/jewish-news-and-politics/191785/a-fourth-of-july-story.

Sestanovich, Stephen. *Maximalist: America in the World from Truman to Obama.* New York: Knopf, 2014.

Shane, Scott. "Cables from American Diplomats Portray U.S. Ambivalence on Tunisia." *New York Times,* January 15, 2011. www.nytimes.com/2011/01/16/world/africa/16cables.html?_r=0.

Sharansky, Natan. "Peace Will Only Come after Freedom and Democracy." *Middle East Quarterly* 12 (Winter 2005). www.meforum.org/666/natan-sharansky-peace-will-only-come-after.

Sharansky, Natan and Ron Dermer. *The Case for Democracy.* New York: Public Affairs Books, 2006.

Shultz, George P. *Turmoil and Triumph: My Years as Secretary of State.* New York: Charles Scribners' Sons, 1993.

Slaughter, Anne Marie. "How to Succeed in a Networked World." *Foreign Affairs* 95 (November/December 2016): 76–89. www.foreignaffairs.com/articles/ world/2016–10–04/how-succeed-networked-world.

Smith, Tony. *America's Mission: The United States and the Worldwide Struggle for Democracy in the Twentieth Century.* Princeton, NJ: Princeton University Press, 1995.

Solingen, Etel. "Transcending Disciplinary Divide/S: A Comparative Framework on the International Relations of the Middle East." *Project on Middle East Political Science.* http://pomeps.org/2015/08/31/transcending-disciplinary-divides-a-comparative-framework-on-the-international-relations-of-the-middle-east/.

Spolar, Christine. "Egypt Reformer Feels Iron Hand of the Law." *Chicago Tribune,* March 6, 2006. http://articles.chicagotribune.com/2006–03–06/ news/0603060129_1_ayman-nour-president-hosni-mubarak-egypt.

Spiegel, Avi. "Succeeding by Surviving: Examining the Durability of Political Islam in Morocco." *Brookings Institution,* August 2015. www.brookings.edu/ wp-content/uploads/2016/07/Morocco_Spiegel-FINALE.pdf.

Springborg, Robert. "Arab Armed Forces; State Makers or State Breakers." *Middle East Institute,* July 14, 2015. www.mei.edu/content/at/arab-armed-forces-state-makers-or-state-breakers.

"Arab Militaries." In *The Arab Uprisings Explained,* edited by Marc Lynch, 142–159. New York: Columbia University Press, 2014.

Stepan, Alfred and Juan J. Linz. "Democratization Theory and the 'Arab Spring.'" *Journal of Democracy* 24, no. 2 (2013): 15–30. www.journalofdemocracy.org/ sites/default/files/Stepan-24–2.pdf.

Stepan, Alfred and Graeme B. Robertson. "An 'Arab' More Than 'Muslim' Electoral Gap." *Journal of Democracy* 14, no. 3 (2003): 30–44.

"Arab, Not Muslim, Exceptionalism." *Journal of Democracy* 15, no. 4 (2004): 140–146. https://muse.jhu.edu/article/44541.

Stolberg, Sheryl Gay. "Bush's Speech Prods Middle Eastern Leaders." *New York Times,* May 19, 2008. www.nytimes.com/2008/05/19/world/middleeast/ 19prexy.html.

Stoner, Kathryn and Michael McFaul, eds. *Transitions to Democracy: A Comparative Perspective.* Baltimore: Johns Hopkins University Press, 2013.

Tadros, Samuel. "The Brotherhood Divided." *Hudson Institute,* August 20, 2015. www.hudson.org/research/11530-the-brotherhood-divided.

"Egypt's Elections: Why the Islamists Won." *World Affairs Journal* (2012), www.worldaffairsjournal.org/article/egypt%E2%80%99s-elections-why-islamists-won.

Reflections on the Revolution in Egypt. Stanford, CA: Hoover Institution Press, 2014.

Tessler, Mark, Amaney Jamal, and Michael Robbins. "New Findings on Arabs and Democracy." In *Democracy and Authoritarianism in the Arab World,* edited by Larry Diamond and Marc Plattner, 54–68. Baltimore: Johns Hopkins University Press, 2014.

"Testimony before House Foreign Affairs Committee, Subcommittee on International, Economic Policy and Trade." July 12, 1979. Quoted in *Behind the*

Disappearances: Argentina's Dirty War against Human Rights and the United Nations by Iain Guest, 280. Philadelphia: University of Pennsylvania Press, 1990.

White House. "Statement on President Congratulating Egyptian President Mubarak on Election." George W. Bush White House Archives, September 10, 2005. http://georgewbush-whitehouse.archives.gov/news/releases/2005/09/text/20050910-11.html.

"Strengthen Alliances to Defeat Global Terrorism and Work to Prevent Attacks against Us and Our Friends." http://georgewbush-whitehouse.archives.gov/nsc/nss/2006/sectionIII.html.

Working Group on Egypt. "A Letter to Secretary Clinton From the Working Group on Egypt." Letter to Hillary Clinton. April 7, 2010. MS. Washington, DC. http://carnegie-mec.org/2010/04/07/letter-to-secretary-clinton-from-working-group-on-egypt-pub-40535

"A Need for Free and Fair Elections in Egypt: A Statement by the Working Group on Egypt." *Foreign Policy Initiative*, January 29, 2011. www.foreignpolicyi.org/content/statement-working-group-egypt-saturday-january-29-2011.

"Protests in Egypt: A Statement by the Working Group on Egypt." *Carnegie Endowment for International Peace*, January 27, 2011. www.foreignpolicyi.org/content/protests-egypt-statement-working-group-egypt.

"A Second Letter to Clinton from the Working Group on Egypt." Letter to Hillary Clinton. May 11, 2010. MS. Washington, DC. www.brookings.edu/wp-content/uploads/2016/06/20100511_clinton_letter.pdf.

"Statement by the Egypt Working Group." *Freedom House*, July 8, 2013.

"Violence in Egypt: A Statement by the Working Group on Egypt." *Carnegie Endowment for International Peace*, February 3, 2011. www.foreignpolicyi.org/content/violence-egypt-statement-working-group-egypt.

"Working Group on Egypt Writes to President Obama and Secretary Clinton." *Foreign Policy Initiative*, February 7, 2011. www.foreignpolicyi.org/content/working-group-egypt-writes-president-obama-and-secretary-clinton.

"Working Group on Egypt Letter to Secretary Clinton." Letter to Hillary Clinton. April 17, 2012. MS. Washington, DC.

"Working Group on Egypt Letter to the President." Letter to Barack Obama. January 29, 2014. MS. Washington, DC. www.humanrightsfirst.org/wp-content/uploads/Working-Group-on-Egypt-1-28-2014.pdf.

"Working Group on Egypt Writes to President Obama on the NGO Trial." Letter to Barack Obama. June 11, 2013. MS. Washington, DC. www.atlanticcouncil.org/blogs/menasource/working-group-on-egypt-writes-to-president-obama-on-the-ngo-trial.

"Working Group on Egypt Writes Secretary Clinton to Express Concern about Assault against Civil Society Groups in Egypt." Letter to Hillary Clinton. January 3, 2012. MS. Washington, DC. www.atlanticcouncil.org/news/in-the-news/8499-working-group-letter-to-secretary-clinton-calls-for-suspending-military-assistance-to-egypt.

Tlili, Mustapha. "The Mirage of Political Islam." *New York Times*, June 3, 2014. www.nytimes.com/2014/06/04/opinion/the-mirage-of-political-islam.html.

"Towards the End of Poverty." *The Economist,* June 1, 2013. www. economist.com/news/leaders/21578665-nearly-1-billion-people-have-been-taken-out-extreme-poverty-20-years-world-should-aim.

Trager, Eric. *Arab Fall: How the Muslim Brotherhood Won and Lost Egypt in 891 Days.* Washington, DC: Georgetown University Press, 2016.

Trager, Eric, Haroon Ullah, and Vish Sakthivel. "Islamists in Government: Do They Moderate once in Power?" *Policywatch* 2246 (2014). www.washingtoninstitute.org/policy-analysis/view/islamists-in-government-do-they-moderate-once-in-power.

Traub, James. *The Freedom Agenda: Why America Must Spread Democracy (Just Not the Way George Bush Did).* New York: Farrar, Straus, and Giroux, 2008.

United Nations Development Programme. *Arab Human Development Report 2002: Creating Opportunities for Future Generations.* New York: United Nations Publications, 2002. www.arab-hdr.org/publications/other/ahdr/ahdr2002e. pdf.

United Nations General Assembly (GA. Sixtieth Session, 2005 World Summit Outcome, ¶138–139. September 15, 2005. www.globalr2p.org/media/files/wsod_2005.pdf.

U.S. Department of State. "Action Memorandum from the Director of Policy Planning to the Secretary of State." *The Human Rights Policy: An Interim Assessment.* January 20, 1978. https://history.state.gov/historicaldocuments/frus1977–80v02/d105.

"Congressional Budget Justification Fiscal Year 2016." www.usaid.gov/sites/default/files/documents/9276/FY16CBJStateFORP.pdf.

Country Reports on Human Rights Practices, 1981. https://babel.hathitrust.org/cgi/pt?id=ien.35556011424686;view=1up;seq=22.

Country Reports on Human Rights Practices for 1982. February 1983. https://babel.hathitrust.org/cgi/pt?id=mdp.39015014164753;view=1up;seq=1.

"Themes." June 29, 1989. Document 33 in *Tiananmen Square, 1989: The Declassified History.* National Security Archive Electronic Briefing Book No. 16. National Security Archive, The George Washington University. http://nsarchive.gwu.edu/NSAEBB/NSAEBB16/docs/doc34.pdf.

"The National Security Strategy of the United States of America." September 2002. www.state.gov/documents/organization/63562.pdf.

"U.S. President Bush's Speech to United Nations." *CNN,* November 10, 2001. http://edition.cnn.com/2001/US/11/10/ret.bush.un.transcript/index .html.

Vaïsse, Justin. *Neoconservatism: The Biography of a Movement.* Cambridge, MA: Harvard University Press, 2011.

Vance, Cyrus. "Human Rights and Foreign Policy," April 30, 1977. Transcript. U.S. Department of State. https://history.state.gov/historicaldocuments/frus1977–80v01/d37.

Vogelsgang, Sandra. "What Price Principle? U.S. Policy on Human Rights." *Foreign Affairs* 56, (January 1978): 818–841. www.foreignaffairs.com/articles/1978–07–01/what-price-principle-us-policy-human-rights.

Warnke, Paul C. "Apes on a Treadmill." *Foreign Policy* 18 (Spring 1975): 12–29. www.jstor.org/stable/1147960.

Way, Lucan. "The Lessons of 1989." In *Democratization and Authoritarianism in the Arab World (A Journal of Democracy Book)*, edited by Larry Diamond and Marc Plattner, 151–161. Baltimore: Johns Hopkins University Press, 2014.

Wehrey, Fredric. "Saudi Arabia's Anxious Autocrats." In *Authoritarianism Goes Global*, edited by Larry Diamond, Marc Plattner, and Christopher Walker 105. Baltimore: Johns Hopkins University Press, 2016.

Weissenbach, Kristina. "Promoting Internal Party Democracy: Party Assistance of the German Political Foundations in Sub-Saharan Africa." NRW School of Governance, Universitat Duisburg Essen. https://ecpr.eu/Filestore/PaperProposal/0f72a5c2–8fc4–43b3–92ad-cff5fcf8226f.pdf.

Whitehead, Laurence. "Democratisation with the Benefit of Hindsight." In *The UN Role in Promoting Democracy: Between Ideals and Reality*, edited by Edward Newman and Roland Rich, 135–165. Tokyo: United Nations University Press, 2004.

Wicker, Tom. *George Herbert Walker Bush*. New York: Penguin, 2004.

Wiktorowicz, Quintan. "Civil Society as Social Control: State Power in Jordan." *Comparative Politics* 33, no. 1 (2000): 43–61. www.jstor.org/stable/422423.

Wilson, Woodrow. "Address to a Joint Session of Congress on the Conditions of Peace." January 8, 1918. Transcript. American Presidency Project, University of California-Santa Barbara. www.presidency.ucsb.edu/ws/?pid=65405.2.

Wollack, Kenneth. "Retaining the Human Dimension." In *Critical Mission: Essays on Democracy Promotion Curve*, edited by Thomas Carothers, 198–203. Washington, DC: Carnegie Endowment for International Peace, 2004. http://carnegieendowment.org/files/CrticalMissionTOC.pdf.

Woodward, Susan L., "Upside-Down Policy: The U.S. Debate on the Use of Force and the Case of Bosnia." In *The Use of Force after the Cold War*, edited by H. W. Brands, 111–136. College Station: Texas A&M University Press, 2000.

al-Youssoufi, Hala. "Tunisia Labor Union Serves as Political Mediator." *al-Monitor*, March 14, 2014. www.al-monitor.com/pulse/politics/2014/03/tunisia-labor-union-political-balance.html.

Zakaria, Fareed. "A New Middle East." *Time*, May 1, 2011. http://content.time.com/time/magazine/article/0,9171,2069033,00.html.

"The Rise of Illiberal Democracy." *Foreign Affairs* 76 (1997): 22–43. www.foreignaffairs.com/articles/1997-11-01/rise-illiberal-democracy.

Index